Susan B. Anthony

Rebel, Crusader, Humanitarian

By Alma Lutz

Published by Pantianos Classics

ISBN-13: 978-1540389848

First published in 1959

Contents

About the Author

Alma Lutz was born in 1890 and brought up in North Dakota, graduated from the Emma Willard School and Vassar College, and attended the Boston University School of Business Administration. She has written numerous articles and pamphlets and for many years has been a contributor to The Christian Science Monitor. Active in organizations working for the political, civil, and economic rights of women, she has also been interested in preserving the records of women's role in history and serves on the Advisory Board of the Radcliffe Women's Archives. Miss Lutz is the author of Emma Willard, Daughter of Democracy (1929), Created Equal, A Biography of Elizabeth Cady Stanton (1940), Challenging Years, The Memoirs of Harriot Stanton Blatch, with Harriot Stanton Blatch (1940), and the editor of With Love Jane, Letters from American Women on the War Fronts (1945).

To the young women of today

Preface

To strive for liberty and for a democratic way of life has always been a noble tradition of our country. Susan B. Anthony followed this tradition. Convinced that the principle of equal rights for all, as stated in the Declaration of Independence, must be expressed in the laws of a true republic, she devoted her life to the establishment of this ideal. Because she recognized in Negro slavery and in the legal bondage of women flagrant violations of this principle, she became an active, courageous, effective antislavery crusader and a champion of civil and political rights for women. She saw women's struggle for freedom from legal restrictions as an important phase in the development of American democracy. To her this struggle was never a battle of the sexes, but a battle such as any freedom-loving people would wage for civil and political rights.

While her goals for women were only partially realized in her lifetime, she prepared the soil for the acceptance not only of her long-hoped-for federal woman suffrage amendment but for a worldwide recognition of human rights, now expressed in the United Nations Charter and the Declaration of Human Rights. She looked forward to the time when throughout the world there would be no discrimination because of race, color, religion, or sex.

Acknowledgments

"The letters of a person ...," said Thomas Jefferson, "form the only full and genuine journal of his life."

Susan B. Anthony's letters, hundreds of them, preserved in libraries and private collections, and her diaries have been the basis of this biography, and I acknowledge my indebtedness to the following libraries and their helpful librarians: the American Antiquarian Society; the Bancroft Library of the University of California; the Boston Public Library; the Henry E. Huntington Library and Art Gallery; the Indiana State Library; the Kansas Historical Society; the Library of Congress; the Susan B. Anthony Memorial Collection of the Los Angeles Public Library, which has been transferred to the Henry E. Huntington Library; the New York Public Library; the New York State Library; the Ohio State Library; the Radcliffe Women's Archives; the Seneca Falls Historical Society; the Smith College Library; the Susan B. Anthony Memorial Inc., Rochester, New York; the University of Rochester Library; the University of Kentucky Library; and the Vassar College Library.

I am particularly indebted to Lucy E. Anthony, who asked me to write a biography of her aunt, lent me her aunt's diaries, and was most generous with her records and personal recollections. To her and to her sister, Mrs. Ann Anthony Bacon, I am very grateful for photographs and for permission to quote from Susan B. Anthony's diaries and from her letters and manuscripts.

Ida Husted Harper's Life and Work of Susan B. Anthony, written in collaboration with Susan B. Anthony, and the History of Woman Suffrage, compiled by Elizabeth Cady Stanton, Susan B. Anthony, Matilda Joslyn Gage, and Ida Husted Harper, have been invaluable. As many of the letters and documents used in the preparation of these books were destroyed, they have preserved an important record of the work of Susan B. Anthony and of the woman's rights movement.

I am especially grateful to Martha Taylor Howard for her unfailing interest and for the use of the valuable Susan B. Anthony Memorial Collection which she initiated and developed in Rochester, New York; and to Una R. Winter for her interest and for the use of her Susan B. Anthony Collection, most of which is now in the Henry E. Huntington Library.

I thank Edna M. Stantial for permission to examine and quote from the Blackwell Papers; Anna Dann Mason for permission to read her reminiscences and the many letters written to her by Susan B. Anthony; Ellen Garrison for permission to quote from letters of Lucretia Mott and Martha C. Wright; Eleanor W. Thompson for copies of Susan B. Anthony's letters to Amelia Bloomer; Henry R. Selden II whose grandfather was Susan B. Anthony's lawyer during her trial for voting; Judge John Van Voorhis whose grandfather was associated with Judge Selden in Miss Anthony's defense; William B. Brown for information about the early history of Adams, Massachusetts, the Susan B. Anthony birthplace, and the Friends Meeting House in Adams; Dr. James Harvey Young for information about Anna E. Dickinson; Margaret Lutz Fogg for help in connection with the trial of Susan B. Anthony; Dr. Blake McKelvey, City Historian of Rochester; Clara Sayre Selden and Wheeler Chapin Case of the Rochester Historical Society; the grand-nieces of Susan B. Anthony, Marion and Florence Mosher; Matilda Joslyn Gage II; Florence L. C. Kitchelt; and Rose Arnold Powell.

I thank The Christian Science Monitor for permission to use portions of an article published on October 24, 1958.

I am especially grateful to A. Marguerite Smith for her constructive criticism of the manuscript and her unfailing encouragement.

Alma Lutz
Highmeadow
Berlin, New York

Susan B. Anthony at the age of thirty-five

Quaker Heritage

"If Sally Ann knows more about weaving than Elijah," reasoned eleven-year-old Susan with her father, "then why don't you make her overseer?"

"It would never do," replied Daniel Anthony as a matter of course. "It would never do to have a woman overseer in the mill."

This answer did not satisfy Susan and she often thought about it. To enter the mill, to stand quietly and look about, was the best kind of entertainment, for she was fascinated by the whir of the looms, by the nimble fingers of the weavers, and by the general air of efficiency. Admiringly she watched Sally Ann Hyatt, the tall capable weaver from Vermont. When the yarn on the beam was tangled or there was something wrong with the machinery, Elijah, the overseer, always called out to Sally Ann, "I'll tend your loom, if you'll look after this." Sally Ann never failed to locate the trouble or to untangle the yarn. Yet she was never made overseer, and this continued to puzzle Susan.[1]

The manufacture of cotton was a new industry, developing with great promise in the United States, when Susan B. Anthony was born on February 15, 1820, in the wide valley at the foot of Mt. Greylock, near Adams, Massachusetts. Enterprising young men like her father, Daniel Anthony, saw a potential cotton mill by the side of every rushing brook, and young women, eager to earn the first money they could call their own, were leaving the farms, for a few months at least, to work in the mills. Cotton cloth was the new sensation and the demand for it was steadily growing. Brides were proud to display a few cotton sheets instead of commonplace homespun linen.

When Susan was two years old, her father built a cotton factory of twenty-six looms beside the brook which ran through Grandfather Read's meadow, hauling the cotton forty miles by wagon from Troy, New York. The millworkers, most of them young girls from Vermont, boarded, as was the custom, in the home of the millowner; Susan's mother, Lucy Read Anthony, although she had three small daughters to care for, Guelma, Susan, and Hannah, boarded eleven of the millworkers with only the help of a thirteen-year-old girl who worked for her after school hours. Lucy Anthony cooked their meals on the hearth of the big kitchen fireplace, and in the large brick oven beside it baked crisp brown loaves of bread. In addition, washing, ironing, mending, and spinning filled her days. But she was capable and strong and was doing only what all women in this new country were expected to do. She taught her young daughters to help her, and Susan, even before she was six, was very useful; by the time she was ten she could cook a good meal and pack a dinner pail.

Daniel Anthony, father of Susan B. Anthony Daniel Anthony, father of Susan B. Anthony

Hard work and skill were respected as Susan grew up in the rapidly expanding young republic which less than fifty years before had been founded and fought for. Settlers, steadily pushing westward, had built new states out of the wilderness, adding ten to the original thirteen. Everywhere the leaven of democracy was working and men were putting into practice many of the principles so boldly stated in the Declaration of Independence, claiming for themselves equal rights and opportunities. The new states entered the Union with none of the traditional property and religious limitations on the franchise, but with manhood suffrage and all voters eligible for office. The older states soon fell into line, Massachusetts in 1820 removing property qualifications for voters. Before long, throughout the United States, all free white men were enfranchised, leaving only women, Negroes, and Indians without the full rights of citizenship.

Lucy Read Anthony, mother of Susan B. Anthony Lucy Read Anthony, mother of Susan B. Anthony

Although women freeholders had voted in some of the colonies and in New Jersey as late as 1807,[2] just as in England in the fifteenth franchise had gradually found its way into the statutes, and women's rights as citizens were ignored, in spite of the contribution they had made to the defense and development of the new nation. However, European travelers, among them De Tocqueville, recognized that the survival of the New World experiment in government and the prosperity and strength of the people were due in large measure to the superiority of American women. A few women had urged their claims: Abigail Adams asked her husband, a member of the Continental Congress, "to remember the ladies" in the "new code of laws"; and Hannah Lee Corbin of Virginia pleaded with her brother, Richard Henry Lee, to make good the principle of "no taxation without representation" by enfranchising widows with property.[3]

Yet the legal bondage of women continued to be overlooked. It seemed a less obvious threat to free institutions and democratic government than the Negro in slavery. In fact, Negro slavery presented a problem which demanded attention again and again, flaring up alarmingly in 1820, the year Susan B. Anthony was born, when Missouri was admitted to the Union as a slave state.[4]

These were some of the forces at work in the minds of Americans during Susan's childhood. Her father, a liberal Quaker, was concerned over the extension of slavery, and she often heard him say that he tried to avoid purchasing cotton raised by slave labor. This early impression of the evil of slavery was never erased.

The Quakers' respect for women's equality with men before God also left its mark on young Susan. As soon as she was old enough she went regularly to Meeting with her father, for all of the Anthonys were Quakers. They had migrated to western Massachusetts from Rhode Island, and there on the frontier had built prosperous farms, comfortable homes, and a meeting house where they could worship God in their own way. Susan, sitting with the women and children on the hand-hewn benches near the big fireplace in the meeting house[5] which her ancestors had built, found peace and consecration in the simple unordered service, in the long reverent silence broken by both the men and the women in the congregation as they were led to say a prayer or give out a helpful message. Forty families now worshiped here, the women sitting on one side and the men on the other; but women took their places with men in positions of honor, Susan's own grandmother, Hannah Latham Anthony, an elder, sitting in the "high seat," and her aunt, Hannah Anthony Hoxie, preaching as the spirit moved her. With this valuation of women accepted as a matter of course in her church and family circle, Susan took it for granted that it existed everywhere.

Although her father was a devout Friend, she discovered that he had the reputation of thinking for himself, following the "inner light" even when its leading differed from the considered judgment of his fellow Quakers. For this he became a hero to her, especially after she heard the romantic story of his marriage to Lucy Read who was not a Quaker. The Anthonys and the Reads had been neighbors for years, and Lucy was one of the pupils at the "home school" which Grandfather Humphrey Anthony had built for his children on the farm, under the weeping willow at the front gate. Daniel and Lucy were schoolmates until Daniel at nineteen was sent to Richard Mott's Friends' boarding school at Nine Partners on the Hudson. When he returned as a teacher, he found his old playmate still one of the pupils, but now a beautiful tall young woman with deep blue eyes and glossy brown hair. Full of fun, a good dancer, and always dressed in the prettiest clothes, she was the most popular girl in the neighborhood. Promptly Daniel Anthony fell in love with her, but an almost insurmountable obstacle stood in the way: Quakers were not permitted to "marry out of Meeting." This, however, did not deter Daniel.

Susan B. Anthony Homestead, Adams, Massachusetts Susan B. Anthony Homestead, Adams, Massachusetts

It was harder for Lucy to make up her mind. She enjoyed parties, dances, and music. She had a full rich voice, and as she sat at her spinning wheel, singing and spinning, she often wished that she could "go into a ten acre lot with the bars down"[6] and let her voice out. If she married Daniel, she would have to give all this up, but she decided in favor of Daniel. A few nights before the wedding, she went to her last party and danced until four in the morning while Daniel looked on and patiently waited until she was ready to leave.

For his transgression of marrying out of Meeting, Daniel had to face the elders as soon as he returned from his wedding trip. They weighed the matter carefully, found him otherwise sincere and earnest, and decided not to turn him out. Lucy gave up her dancing and her singing. She gave up her pretty bright-colored dresses for plain somber clothes, but she did not adopt the Quaker dress or use the "plain speech." She went to meeting with Daniel but never became a Quaker, feeling always that she could not live up to their strict standard of righteousness.[7]

This was Susan's heritage—Quaker discipline and austerity lightened by her father's independent spirit and by the kindly understanding of her mother who had not forgotten her own fun-loving girlhood; an environment where men and women were partners in church and at home, where hard physical work was respected, where help for the needy and unfortunate was spontaneous, and where education was regarded as so important that Grandfather Anthony built a school for his children and the neighbors' in his front yard. Her childhood was close enough to the Revolution to make Grandfather Read's part in it very real and a source of great pride. Eagerly and often she listened to the story of how he enlisted in the Continental army as soon as the news of the Battle of Lexington reached Cheshire and served with outstanding bravery under Arnold at Quebec, Ethan Allen at Ticonderoga, and Colonel Stafford at Bennington while his young wife waited anxiously for him throughout the long years of the war.

The wide valley in the Berkshire Hills where Susan grew up made a lasting impression on her. There was beauty all about her—the fruit trees blooming in the spring, the meadows white with daisies, the brook splashing over the rocks and sparkling in the summer sun, the flaming colors of autumn, the strength and companionship of the hills when the countryside was white with snow. She seldom failed to watch the sun set behind Greylock.

Her father's cotton mill flourished. Regarded as one of the most promising, successful young men of the district, he soon attracted the attention of Judge John McLean, a cotton manufacturer of Battenville, New York, who, eager to enlarge his mills, saw in Daniel Anthony an able manager. Daniel, always ready to take the next step ahead, accepted McLean's offer, and on a sunny July day in 1826, Susan drove with her family through the hills forty-four miles to the new world of Battenville.

Here in the home of Judge McLean, she saw Negroes for the first time, Negroes working to earn their freedom. Startled by their black faces, she was a little afraid, but when her father explained that in the South they could be sold like cattle and torn from their families, her fear turned to pity.

At the district school, taught by a woman in summer and by a man in the winter, she learned to sew, spell, read, and write, and she wanted to study long division but the schoolmaster, unable to teach it, saw no reason why a woman should care for such knowledge. Her father, then realizing the need of better education for his five children, Guelma, Susan, Hannah, Daniel, and Mary, established a school for them in the new brick building where he had opened a store. Later on when their new brick house was finished, he set aside a large room for the school, and here for the first time in that district the pupils had separate seats, stools without backs, instead of the usual benches around the schoolroom walls. He engaged as teachers young women who had studied a year or two in a female seminary; and because female seminaries were rare in those days, women teachers with up-to-date training were hard to find. Only a few visionaries believed in the education of women. Nearby Emma Willard's recently established Troy Female Seminary was being watched with interest and suspicion. Mary Lyon, who had not yet founded her own seminary at Mt. Holyoke, was teaching at Zilpha Grant's school in Ipswich, Massachusetts, and one of her pupils, Mary Perkins, came to Battenville to teach the Anthony children. Mary Perkins brought new methods and new studies to the little school. She introduced a primer with small black illustrations which fascinated Susan. She taught the children to recite poetry, drilled them regularly in calisthenics, and longed to add music as well, but Daniel Anthony forbade this, for Quakers believed that music might seduce the thoughts of the young. So Susan, although she often had a song in her heart, had to repress it and never knew the joy of singing the songs of childhood.

Her father, looking upon the millworkers as part of his family, started an evening school for them, often teaching it himself or calling in the family teacher. He organized a temperance society among the workers, and all signed a pledge never to drink distilled liquor. When he opened a store in the new brick building, he refused to sell liquor, although Judge McLean warned him it would ruin his trade. Daniel Anthony went even further. He resolved not to serve liquor when the millworkers' houses were built and the neighbors came to the "raising." Again Judge McLean protested, feeling certain that the men and boys would demand their gin and their rum, but Susan and her sisters helped their mother serve lemonade, tea, coffee, doughnuts, and gingerbread in abundance. The men joked a bit about the lack of strong drink which they expected with every meal, but they did not turn away from the good substitutes which were offered and they were on hand for the next "raising." Hearing all of this discussed at home, Susan, again proud of her father, ardently advocated the cause of temperance.

The mill was still of great interest to her and she watched every operation closely in her spare time, longing to try her hand at the work. One day when a "spooler" was ill, Susan and her sister Hannah eagerly volunteered to take her place. Their father was ready to let them try, pleased by their interest and curious to see what they could do, but their mother protested that the mill was no place for children. Finally Susan's earnest pleading won her mother's reluctant consent, and the two girls drew lots for the job. It went to twelve-year-old Susan on the condition that she divide her earnings with Hannah. Every day for two weeks she went early to the mill in her plain homespun dress, her straight hair neatly parted and smoothed over her ears. Proudly she tended the spools. She was skillful and quick, and received the regular wage of $1.50 a week, which she divided with Hannah, buying with her share six pale blue coffee cups for her mother who had allowed her this satisfying adventure.

A few weeks before her thirteenth birthday, Susan became a member of the Society of Friends which met in nearby Easton, New York, and learned to search her heart and ask herself, "Art thou faithful?" Parties, dancing, and entertainments were generally ruled out of her life as sinful, and rarely were a temptation, but occasionally her mother, remembering her own good times, let her and her sisters go to parties at the homes of their Presbyterian neighbors, and for this her father was criticized at Friends' Meeting. Condemning bright colors, frills, and jewelry as vain and worldly, Susan accepted plain somber clothing as a mark of righteousness, and when she deviated to the extent of wearing the Scotch-plaid coat which her mother had bought her, she wondered if the big rent torn in it by a dog might not be deserved punishment for her pride in wearing it.

That same year, the family moved into their new brick house of fifteen rooms, with hard-finish plaster walls and light green woodwork, the finest house in that part of the country. Here Susan's brother Merritt was born the next April, and her two-year-old sister, Eliza, died.

Susan, Guelma, and Hannah continued their studies longer than most girls in the neighborhood, for Quakers not only encouraged but demanded education for both boys and girls. As soon as Susan and her sister Guelma were old enough, they taught the "home" school in the summer when the younger children attended, and then went further afield to teach in nearby villages. At fifteen Susan was teaching a district school for $1.50 a week and board, and although it was hard for her to be away from home, she accepted it as a Friend's duty to provide good education for children. Now Presbyterian neighbors criticized her father, protesting that well-to-do young ladies should not venture into paid work. Daniel Anthony was now a wealthy man, his factory the largest and most prosperous in that part of the country, and he could afford more and better education for his daughters. He sent Guelma, the eldest, to Deborah Moulson's Friends' Seminary near Philadelphia, where for $125 a year "the inculcation of the principles of Humility, Morality, and Virtue" received particular attention; and when Guelma was asked to stay on a second year as a teacher, he suggested that Susan join her there as a pupil.

It was a long journey from Battenville to Philadelphia in 1837, and when Susan left her home on a snowy afternoon with her father, she felt as if the parting would be forever. Her first glimpse of the world beyond Battenville interested her immensely until her father left her at the seminary, and then she confessed to her diary, "Oh what pangs were felt. It seemed impossible for me to part with him. I could not speak to bid him farewell."[8] She tried to comfort herself by writing letters, and wrote so many and so much that Guelma often exclaimed, "Susan, thee writes too much; thee should learn to be concise." As it was a rule of the seminary that each letter must first be written out carefully on a slate, inspected by Deborah Moulson, then copied with care, inspected again, and finally sent out after four or five days of preparation, all spontaneity was stifled and her letters were stilted and overvirtuous. This censorship left its mark, and years later she confessed, "Whenever I take my pen in hand, I always seem to be mounted on stilts."[9]

To her diary she could confide her real feelings—her discouragement over her lack of improvement and her inability to understand her many "sins," such as not dotting an i, too much laughter, or smiling at her friends instead of reproving them for frivolous conduct. She wrote, "Thought so much of my resolutions to do better in the future that even my dreams were filled with these desires.... Although I have been guilty of much levity and nonsensical conversation, and have also admitted thoughts to occupy my mind which should have been far distant from it, I do not consider myself as having committed any wilful offense but perhaps the reason I cannot see my own defects is because my heart is hardened."[10]

The girls studied a variety of subjects, arithmetic, algebra, literature, chemistry, philosophy, physiology, astronomy, and bookkeeping. Men came to the school to conduct some of the classes, and Deborah Moulson was also assisted by several student teachers, one of whom, Lydia Mott, became Susan's lifelong friend. Susan worked hard, for she was a conscientious child, but none of her efforts seemed to satisfy Deborah Moulson, who was a hard taskmaster. Her reproofs cut deep, and once when Susan protested that she was always censured while Guelma was praised, Deborah Moulson sternly replied, "Thy sister Guelma does the best she is capable of, but thou dost not. Thou hast greater abilities and I demand of thee the best of thy capacity."[11]

Mail from home was a bright spot, bringing into those busy austere days news of her friends, and when she read that one of them had married an old widower with six children, she reflected sagely, "I should think any female would rather live and die an old maid."[12]

Then came word that her father's business had been so affected by the financial depression that the family would have to give up their home in Battenville. Sorrowfully she wrote in her diary, "O can I ever forget that loved residence in Battenville, and no more to call it home seems impossible."[13] It helped little to realize that countless other families throughout the country were facing the future penniless because banks had failed, mills were shut down, and work on canals and railroads had ceased. In April 1838, Daniel Anthony came to the seminary to take his daughters home. Susan felt keenly her father's sorrow over the failure of his business and the loss of the home he had built for his family, and she resolved at once to help out by teaching in Union Village, New York. In May 1838, she wrote in her diary, "On last evening ... I again left my home to mingle with strangers which seems to be my sad lot. Separation was rendered more trying on account of the embarrassing condition of our business affairs, an inventory was expected to be taken today of our furniture by assignees.... Spent this day in school, found it small and quite disorderly. O, may my patience hold out to persevere without intermission."[14]

Her patience did hold out, and also her courage, as the news came from home telling her how everything had to be sold to satisfy the creditors, the furniture, her mother's silver spoons, their clothing and books, the flour, tea, coffee, and sugar in the pantries. She rejoiced to hear that Uncle Joshua Read from Palatine Bridge, New York, had come to the rescue, had bought their most treasured and needed possessions and turned them over to her mother.

On a cold blustery March day in 1839, when she was nineteen, Susan moved with her family two miles down the Battenkill to the little settlement of Hardscrabble, later called Center Falls, where her father owned a satinet factory and grist mill, built in more prosperous times. These were now heavily mortgaged but he hoped to save them. They moved into a large house which had been a tavern in the days when lumber had been cut around Hardscrabble. It was disappointing after their fine brick house in Battenville, but they made it comfortable, and their love for and loyalty to each other made them a happy family anywhere. As it had been a halfway house on the road to Troy and travelers continued to stop there asking for a meal or a night's lodging, they took them in, and young Daniel served them food and nonintoxicating drinks at the old tavern bar.

Susan, when her school term was over, put her energies into housework, recording in her diary, "Did a large washing today.... Spent today at the spinning wheel.... Baked 21 loaves of bread.... Wove three yards of carpet yesterday."[15] The attic of the tavern had been finished off for a ballroom with bottles laid under the floor to give a nice tone to the music of the fiddles, and now the young people of the village wanted to hold their dancing school there. Susan's father, true to his Quaker training, felt obliged to refuse, but when they came the second time to tell him that the only other place available was a disreputable tavern where liquor was sold, he relented a little, and talked the matter over with his wife and daughters. Lucy Anthony, recalling her love of dancing, urged him to let the young people come. Finally he consented on the condition that Guelma, Hannah, and Susan would not dance. They agreed. Every two weeks all through the winter, the fiddles played in the attic room and the boys and girls of the neighborhood danced the Virginia reel and their rounds and squares, while the three Quaker girls sat around the wall, watching and longing to join in the fun.

Such frivolous entertainment in the home of a Quaker could not be condoned, and Daniel Anthony was not only severely censured by the Friends but read out of Meeting, "because he kept a place of amusement in his house." But he did not regret his so-called sin any more than he regretted marrying out of Meeting. He continued to attend Friends' Meeting, but grew more and more liberal as the years went by. At this time, like all Quakers, he refused to vote, not wishing in any way to support a government that believed in war, and this influenced Susan who for some years regarded voting as unimportant. He refused to pay taxes for the same reason, and she often saw him put his pocketbook on the table and then remark drily to the tax collector, "I shall not voluntarily pay these taxes. If thee wants to rifle my pocketbook, thee can do so."[16]

To help her father with his burden of debt was now Susan's purpose in life, and in the spring she again left the family circle to teach at Eunice Kenyon's Friends' Seminary in New Rochelle, New York. There were twenty-eight day pupils and a few boarders at the seminary, and for long periods while Eunice Kenyon was ill, Susan took full charge.

She wrote her family all the little details of her life, but their letters never came often enough to satisfy her. Occasionally she received a paper or a letter from Aaron McLean, Judge McLean's grandson, who had been her good friend and Guelma's ever since they had moved to Battenville. His letters almost always started an argument which both of them continued with zest. After hearing the Quaker preacher, Rachel Barker, she wrote him, "I guess if you would hear her you would believe in a woman's preaching. What an absurd notion that women have not intellectual and moral faculties sufficient for anything but domestic concerns."[17]

When New Rochelle welcomed President Van Buren with a parade, bands playing, and crowds in the streets, this prim self-righteous young woman took no part in this hero worship, but gave vent to her disapproval in a letter to Aaron. Disturbed over the treatment Negroes received at Friends' Meeting in New Rochelle, she impulsively wrote him, "The people about here are anti-abolitionist and anti everything else that's good. The Friends raised quite a fuss about a colored man sitting in the meeting house, and some left on account of it.... What a lack of Christianity is this!"[18]

Her school term of fifteen weeks, for which she was paid $30, was over early in September, just in time for her to be at home for Guelma's wedding to Aaron McLean, and afterward she stayed on to teach the village school in Center Falls. This made it possible for her to join in the social life of the neighborhood. Often the young people drove to nearby villages, twenty buggies in procession. On a drive to Saratoga, her escort asked her to give up teaching to marry him. She refused, as she did again a few years later when a Quaker elder tried to entice her with his fine house, his many acres, and his sixty cows. Although she had reached the age of twenty, when most girls felt they should be married, she was still particular, and when a friend married a man far inferior mentally, she wrote in her diary, "'Tis strange, 'tis passing strange that a girl possessed of common sense should be willing to marry a lunatic—but so it is."[19]

During the next few years, both she and Hannah taught school almost continuously, for $2 to $2.50 a week. Time and time again Susan replaced a man who had been discharged for inefficiency. Although she made a success of the school, she discovered that she was paid only a fourth the salary he had received, and this rankled.

Almost everywhere except among Quakers, she encountered a false estimate of women which she instinctively opposed. After spending several months with relatives in Vermont, where she had the unexpected opportunity of studying algebra, she stopped over for a visit with Guelma and Aaron in Battenville, where Aaron was a successful merchant. Eagerly she told them of her latest accomplishment. Aaron was not impressed. Later at dinner when she offered him the delicious cream biscuits which she had baked, he remarked with his most tantalizing air of male superiority, "I'd rather see a woman make biscuits like these than solve the knottiest problem in algebra."
"There is no reason," she retorted, "why she should not be able to do both."[20]

Widening Horizons

Unable to recoup his business losses in Center Falls and losing even the satinet factory, Susan's father had looked about in Virginia and Michigan as well as western New York for an opportunity to make a fresh start. A farm on the outskirts of Rochester looked promising, and with the money which Lucy Anthony had inherited from Grandfather Read and which had been held for her by Uncle Joshua Read, the first payment had been made on the farm by Uncle Joshua, who held it in his name and leased it to Daniel.[21] Had it been turned over to Susan's mother, it would have become Daniel Anthony's property under the law and could have been claimed by his creditors.

Only Susan, Merritt, and Mary climbed into the stage with their parents, early in November 1845, on the first lap of their journey to their new home, near Rochester, New York. Guelma and Hannah[22] were both married and settled in homes of their own, and young Daniel, clerking in Lenox, had decided to stay behind.

After a visit with Uncle Joshua at Palatine Bridge, they boarded a line boat on the Erie Canal, taking with them their gray horse and wagon; and surrounded by their household goods, they moved slowly westward. Standing beside her father in the warm November sunshine, Susan watched the strong horses on the towpath, plodding patiently ahead, and heard the wash of the water against the prow and the noisy greeting of boat horns. As they passed the snug friendly villages along the canal and the wide fertile fields, now brown and bleak after the harvest, she wondered what the new farm would be like and what the future would bring; and at night when the lights twinkled in the settlements along the shore, she thought longingly of her old home and the sisters she had left behind.

After a journey of several days, they reached Rochester late in the afternoon. Her father took the horse and wagon off the boat, and in the chill gray dusk drove them three miles over muddy roads to the farm. It was dark when they arrived, and the house was cold, empty, and dismal, but after the fires were lighted and her mother had cooked a big kettle of cornmeal mush, their spirits revived. Within the next few days they transformed it into a cheerful comfortable home.

The house on a little hill overlooked their thirty-two acres. Back of it was the barn, a carriage house, and a little blacksmith shop.[23] Looking out over the flat snowy fields toward the curving Genesee River and the church steeples in Rochester, Susan often thought wistfully of the blue hills around Center Falls and Battenville and of the good times she had had there.

The winter was lonely for her in spite of the friendliness of their Quaker neighbors, the De Garmos, and the Quaker families in Rochester who called at once to welcome them. Her father found these neighbors very congenial and they readily interested him in the antislavery movement, now active in western New York. Within the next few months, several antislavery meetings were held in the Anthony home and opened a new world to Susan. For the first time she heard of the Underground Railroad which secretly guided fugitive slaves to Canada and of the Liberty party which was making a political issue of slavery. She listened to serious, troubled discussion of the annexation of Texas, bringing more power to the proslavery block, which even the acquisition of free Oregon could not offset. She read antislavery tracts and copies of William Lloyd Garrison's Liberator, borrowed from Quaker friends; and on long winter evenings, as she sat by the fire sewing, she talked over with her father the issues they raised.

When spring came and the trees and bushes leafed out, she took more interest in the farm, discovering its good points one by one—the flowering quince along the driveway, the pinks bordering the walk to the front door, the rosebushes in the yard, and cherry trees, currant and gooseberry bushes in abundance. Her father planted peach and apple orchards and worked the "sixpenny farm,"[24] as he called it, to the best of his ability, but the thirty-two acres seemed very small compared with the large Anthony and Read farms in the Berkshires, and he soon began to look about for more satisfying work. This he found a few years later with the New York Life Insurance Company, then developing its business in western New York. Very successful in this new field, he continued in it the rest of his life, but he always kept the farm for the family home.

The first member of the family to leave the Rochester farm was Susan. The cherry trees were in bloom when she received an offer from Canajoharie Academy to teach the female department. As Canajoharie was across the river from Uncle Joshua Read's home in Palatine Bridge and he was a trustee of the academy, she read between the lines his kindly interest in her. He was an influential citizen of that community, a bank director and part owner of the Albany-Utica turnpike and the stage line to Schenectady. Accepting the offer at once, she made the long journey by canal boat to Canajoharie, and early in May 1846 was comfortably settled in the home of Uncle Joshua's daughter, Margaret Read Caldwell.

She soon loved Margaret as a sister and was devoted to her children. None of her new friends were Quakers and she enjoyed their social life thoroughly, leaving behind her forever the somber clothing which she had heretofore regarded as a mark of righteousness. She began her school with twenty-five pupils and a yearly salary of approximately $110. This was more than she had ever earned before, and for the first time in her life she spent her money freely on herself. Her first quarterly examination, held before the principal, the trustees, and parents, established her reputation as a teacher, and in addition everyone said, "The schoolmarm looks beautiful."[25] She had dressed up for the occasion, wearing a new plaid muslin, purple, white, blue, and brown, with white collar and cuffs, and had hung a gold watch and chain about her neck. She wound the four braids of her smooth brown hair around her big shell comb and put on her new prunella gaiters with patent-leather heels and tips. She looked so pretty, so neat, and so capable that many of the parents feared some young man would fall desperately in love with her and rob the academy of a teacher. She did have more than her share of admirers. She soon saw her first circus and went to her first ball, a real novelty for the young woman who had sat demurely along the wall in the attic room of her Center Falls home while her more worldly friends danced.

In spite of all her good times, she missed her family, but because of the long trip to Rochester, she did not return to the farm for two years. She spent her vacations with Guelma and Hannah, who lived only a few hours away, or in Albany with her former teacher at Deborah Moulson's seminary, Lydia Mott, a cousin by marriage of Lucretia Mott. In anticipation of a vacation at home, she wrote her parents, "Sometimes I can hardly wait for the day to come. They have talked of building a new academy this summer, but I do not believe they will. My room is not fit to stay in and I have promised myself that I would not pass another winter in it. If I must forever teach, I will seek at least a comfortable house to do penance in. I have a pleasant school of twenty scholars, but I have to manufacture the interest duty compels me to exhibit.... Energy and something to stimulate is wanting! But I expect the busy summer vacation spent with my dearest and truest friends will give me new life and fresh courage to persevere in the arduous path of duty. Do not think me unhappy with my fate, no not so. I am only a little tired and a good deal lazy. That is all. Do write very soon. Tell about the strawberries and peaches, cherries and plums.... Tell me how the yard looks, what flowers are in bloom and all about the farming business."[26]

During her visits in Albany with Lydia Mott, who was now an active abolitionist, Susan heard a great deal about antislavery work. At this time, however, Canajoharie took little interest in this reform movement, but temperance was gaining a foothold. Throughout the country, Sons of Temperance were organizing and women wanted to help, but the men refused to admit them to their organizations, protesting that public reform was outside women's sphere.

Unwilling to be put off when the need was so great, women formed their own secret temperance societies, and then, growing bolder, announced themselves as Daughters of Temperance.

Canajoharie had its Daughters of Temperance, and Susan, long an advocate of temperance, gladly joined the crusade, and made her first speech when the Daughters of Temperance held a supper meeting to interest the people of the village. Few women at this time could have been persuaded to address an audience of both men and women, believing this to be bold, unladylike, and contrary to the will of God; but the young Quaker, whose grandmother and aunts had always spoken in Meeting when the spirit moved them, was ready to say her word for temperance, taking it for granted that it was not only woman's right but her responsibility to speak and work for social reform.

About two hundred people assembled for the supper, and entering the hall, Susan found it festooned with cedar and red flannel and to her amazement saw letters in evergreen on one of the walls, spelling out Susan B. Anthony.

"I hardly knew how to conduct myself amidst so much kindly regard,"[27] she confided to her family.

She had carefully written out her speech and had sewn the pages together in a blue cover. Now in a clear serious voice, she read its formal flowery sentences telling of the weekly meetings of "this now despised little band" which had awakened women to the great need of reform.

"It is generally conceded," she declared, "that our sex fashions the social and moral state of society. We do not assume that females possess unbounded power in abolishing the evil customs of the day; but we do believe that were they en masse to discontinue the use of wine and brandy as beverages at both their public and private parties, not one of the opposite sex, who has any claim to the title of gentleman, would so insult them as to come into their presence after having quaffed of that foul destroyer of all true delicacy and refinement.... Ladies! There is no neutral position for us to assume...."[28]

The next day the village buzzed with talk of the meeting; only a few criticized Susan for speaking in public, and almost all agreed that she was the smartest woman in Canajoharie.

While she was busy with her temperance work, there were stirrings among women in other parts of New York State in the spring and early summer of 1848. Through the efforts of a few women who circulated petitions and the influence of wealthy men who saw irresponsible sons-in-law taking over the property they wanted their daughters to own, a Married Women's Property Law passed the legislature; this made it possible for a married woman to hold real estate in her own name. Heretofore all property owned by a woman at marriage and all received by gift or inheritance had at once become her husband's and he had had the right to sell it or will it away without her consent and to collect the rents or the income. The new law was welcomed in the Anthony household, for now Lucy Anthony's inheritance, which had bought the Rochester farm, could at last be put in her own name and need no longer be held for her by her brother.

In the newspapers in July, Susan read scornful, humorous, and indignant reports of a woman's rights convention in Seneca Falls, New York, at which women had issued a Declaration of Sentiments, announcing themselves men's equals. They had protested against legal, economic, social, and educational discriminations and asked for the franchise. A woman's rights convention in the 1840s was a startling event. Women, if they were "ladies" did not attend public gatherings where politics or social reforms were discussed, because such subjects were regarded as definitely out of their sphere. Much less did they venture to call meetings of their own and issue bold resolutions.

Susan was not shocked by this break with tradition, but she did not instinctively come to the defense of these rebellious women, nor champion their cause. She was amused rather than impressed. Yet Lucretia Mott's presence at the convention aroused her curiosity. Among her father's Quaker friends in Rochester, she had heard only praise of Mrs. Mott, and she herself, when a pupil at Deborah Moulson's seminary, had been inspired by Mrs. Mott's remarks at Friends' Meeting in Philadelphia.

So far Susan had encountered few barriers because she was a woman. She had had little personal contact with the hardships other women suffered because of their inferior legal status. To be sure, it had been puzzling to her as child that Sally Hyatt, the most skillful weaver in her father's mill, had never been made overseer, but the fact that her mother had not the legal right to hold property in her own name did not at the time make an impression upon her. Brought up as a Quaker, she had no obstacles put in the way of her education. She had an exceptional father who was proud of his daughters' intelligence and ability and respected their opinions and decisions. Her only real complaint was the low salary she had been obliged to accept as a teacher because she was a woman. She sensed a feeling of male superiority, which she resented, in her brother-in-law, Aaron McLean, who did not approve of women preachers and who thought it more important for a woman to bake biscuits than to study algebra. She met the same arrogance of sex in her Cousin Margaret's husband, but she had not analyzed the cause, or seen the need of concerted action by women.

Returning home for her vacation in August, she found to her surprise that a second woman's rights convention had been held in Rochester in the Unitarian church, that her mother, her father, and her sister Mary, and many of their Quaker friends had not only attended, but had signed the Declaration of Sentiments and the resolutions, and that her cousin, Sarah Burtis Anthony, had acted as secretary. Her father showed so much interest, as he told her about the meetings, that she laughingly remarked, "I think you are getting a good deal ahead of the times."[29] She countered Mary's ardent defense of the convention with good-natured ridicule. The whole family, however, continued to be so enthusiastic over the meetings and this new movement for woman's rights, they talked so much about Elizabeth Cady Stanton "with her black curls and ruddy cheeks"[30] and about Lucretia Mott "with her Quaker cap and her crossed handkerchief of the finest muslin," both "speaking so grandly and looking magnificent," that Susan's interest was finally aroused and she decided she would like to meet these women and talk with them. There was no opportunity for this, however, before she returned to Canajoharie for another year of teaching.

It proved to be a year of great sadness because of the illness of her cousin Margaret whom she loved dearly. In addition to her teaching, she nursed Margaret and looked after the house and children. She saw much to discredit the belief that men were the stronger and women the weaker sex, and impatient with Margaret's husband, she wrote her mother that there were some drawbacks to marriage that made a woman quite content to remain single. In explanation she added,

"Joseph had a headache the other day and Margaret remarked that she had had one for weeks. 'Oh,' said the husband, 'mine is the real headache, genuine pain, yours is sort of a natural consequence.'"[31]

Within a few weeks Margaret died. This was heart-breaking for Susan, and without her cousin, Canajoharie offered little attraction. Teaching had become irksome. The new principal was uncongenial, a severe young man from the South whose father was a slaveholder. Susan longed for a change, and as she read of the young men leaving for the West, lured by gold in California, she envied them their adventure and their opportunity to explore and conquer a whole new world.

Frederick Douglass

The peaches were ripe when Susan returned to the farm. The orchard which her father had planted, now bore abundantly. Restless and eager for hard physical work, she discarded the stylish hoops which impeded action, put on an old calico dress, and spent days in the warm September sunshine picking peaches. Then while she preserved, canned, and pickled them, there was little time to long for pioneering in the West.

She enjoyed the active life on the farm for she was essentially a doer, most happy when her hands and her mind were busy. As she helped with the housework, wove rag carpet, or made shirts by hand for her father and brothers, she dreamed of the future, of the work she might do to make her life count for something. Teaching, she decided, was definitely behind her. She would not allow her sister Mary's interest in that career to persuade her otherwise, even if teaching were the only promising and well-thought-of occupation for women. Reading the poems of Elizabeth Barrett Browning, she was deeply stirred and looked forward romantically to some great and useful life work.

The Liberator, with its fearless denunciation of Negro slavery, now came regularly to the Anthony home, and as she pored over its pages, its message fired her soul. Eagerly she called with her father at the home of Frederick Douglass, who had recently settled in Rochester and was publishing his paper, the North Star. Not only did she want to show friendliness to this free Negro of whose intelligence and eloquence she had heard so much, but she wanted to hear first-hand from him and his wife of the needs of his people.

Almost every Sunday the antislavery Quakers met at the Anthony farm. The Posts, the Hallowells, the De Garmos, and the Willises were sure to be there. Sometimes they sent a wagon into the city for Frederick Douglass and his family. Now and then famous abolitionists joined the circle when their work brought them to western New York—William Lloyd Garrison, looking with fatherly kindness at his friends through his small steel-rimmed spectacles; Wendell Phillips, handsome, learned, and impressive; black-bearded, fiery Parker Pillsbury; and the friendly Unitarian pastor from Syracuse, the Reverend Samuel J. May. Susan, helping her mother with dinner for fifteen or twenty, was torn between establishing her reputation as a good cook and listening to the interesting conversation. She heard them discuss woman's rights, which had divided the antislavery ranks. They talked of their antislavery campaigns and the infamous compromises made by Congress to pacify the powerful slaveholding interests. Like William Lloyd Garrison, all of them refused to vote, not wishing to take any part in a government which countenanced slavery. They called the

Constitution a proslavery document, advocated "No Union with Slaveholders," and demanded immediate and unconditional emancipation. All about them and with their help the Underground Railroad was operating, circumventing the Fugitive Slave Law and guiding Negro refugees to Canada and freedom. Amy and Isaac Post's barn, Susan knew, was a station on the Underground, and the De Garmos and Frederick Douglass almost always had a Negro hidden away. She heard of riots and mobs in Boston and Ohio; but in Rochester not a fugitive was retaken and there were no street battles, although the New York Herald advised the city to throw its "nigger printing press"[32] into Lake Ontario and banish Douglass to Canada.

As the Society of Friends in Rochester was unfriendly to the antislavery movement, Susan with her father and other liberal Hicksite Quakers left it for the Unitarian church. Here for the first time they listened to "hireling ministry" and to a formal church service with music. This was a complete break with what they had always known as worship, but the friendly Christian spirit expressed by both minister and congregation made them soon feel at home. This new religious fellowship put Susan in touch with the most advanced thought of the day, broke down some of the rigid precepts drilled into her at Deborah Moulson's seminary, and encouraged liberalism and tolerance. Although there had been austerity in the outward forms of her Quaker training, it had developed in her a very personal religion, a strong sense of duty, and a high standard of ethics, which always remained with her. It had fostered a love of mankind that reached out spontaneously to help the needy, the unfortunate, and the oppressed, and this now became the driving force of her life. It led her naturally to seek ways and means to free the Negro from slavery and to turn to the temperance movement to wipe out the evil of drunkenness.

These were the days when the reformed drunkard, John B. Gough, was lecturing throughout the country with the zeal of an evangelist, getting thousands to sign the total-abstinence pledge. Inspired by his example, the Daughters of Temperance were active in Rochester. They elected Susan their president, and not only did she plan suppers and festivals to raise money for their work but she organized new societies in neighboring towns. Her more ambitious plans for them were somewhat delayed by home responsibilities which developed when her father became an agent of the New York Life Insurance Company. This took him away from home a great deal, and as both her brothers were busy with work of their own and Mary was teaching, it fell to Susan to take charge of the farm. She superintended the planting, the harvesting, and the marketing, and enjoyed it, but she did not let it crowd out her interest in the causes which now seemed so vital.

Horace Greeley's New York Tribune came regularly to the farm, for the Anthonys, like many others throughout the country, had come to depend upon it for what they felt was a truthful report of the news. In this day of few magazines, it met a real need, and Susan, poring over its pages, not only kept in touch with current events, but found inspiration in its earnest editorials which so often upheld the ideals which she felt were important. She found thought-provoking news in the full and favorable report of the national woman's rights convention held in Worcester, Massachusetts, in October 1850. Better informed now through her antislavery friends about this new movement for woman's rights, she was ready to consider it seriously and she read all the stirring speeches, noting the caliber of the men and women taking part. Garrison, Phillips, Pillsbury, and Lucretia Mott were there, as well as Lucy Stone, that appealing young woman of whose eloquence on the antislavery platform Susan had heard so much, and Abby Kelley Foster, whose appointment to office in the American Antislavery Society had precipitated a split in the ranks on the "woman question."

A year later, when Abby Kelley Foster and her husband Stephen spoke at antislavery meetings in Rochester, Susan had her first opportunity to meet this fearless woman. Listening to Abby's speeches and watching the play of emotion on her eager Irish face under the Quaker bonnet, Susan wondered if she would ever have the courage to follow her example. Like herself, Abby had started as a schoolteacher, but after hearing Theodore Weld speak, had devoted herself to the antislavery cause, traveling alone through the country to say her word against slavery and facing not only the antagonism which abolition always provoked, but the unreasoning prejudice against public speaking by women, which was fanned into flame by the clergy. For listening to Abby Kelley, men and women had been excommunicated. Mobs had jeered at her and often pelted her with rotten eggs. She had married a fellow-abolitionist, Stephen Foster, even more unrelenting than she.

Sensing Susan's interest in the antislavery cause and hoping to make an active worker of her, Abby and Stephen suggested that she join them on a week's tour, during which she marveled at Abby's ability to hold the attention and meet the arguments of her unfriendly audiences and wondered if she could ever be moved to such eloquence.

Not yet ready to join the ranks as a lecturer, she continued her apprenticeship by attending antislavery meetings whenever possible and traveled to Syracuse for the convention which the mob had driven out of New York. Eager for more, she stopped over in Seneca Falls to hear William Lloyd Garrison and the English abolitionist, George Thompson, and was the guest of a temperance colleague, Amelia Bloomer, an enterprising young woman who was editing a temperance paper for women, The Lily.

To her surprise Susan found Amelia in the bloomer costume about which she had read in The Lily. Introduced in Seneca Falls by Elizabeth Smith Miller, the costume, because of its comfort, had so intrigued Amelia that she had advocated it in her paper and it had been dubbed with her name. Looking at Amelia's long full trousers, showing beneath her short skirt but modestly covering every inch of her leg, Susan was a bit startled. Yet she could understand the usefulness of the costume even if she had no desire to wear it herself. In fact she was more than ever pleased with her new gray delaine dress with its long full skirt.

Seneca Falls, however, had an attraction for Susan far greater than either William Lloyd Garrison or Amelia Bloomer, for it was the home of Elizabeth Cady Stanton whom she had longed to meet ever since 1848 when her parents had reported so enthusiastically about her and the Rochester woman's rights convention. Walking home from the antislavery meeting with Mrs. Bloomer, Susan met Mrs. Stanton. She liked her at once and later called at her home. They discussed abolition, temperance, and woman's rights, and with every word Susan's interest grew. Mrs. Stanton's interest in woman's rights and her forthright, clear thinking made an instant appeal. Never before had Susan had such a satisfactory conversation with another woman, and she thought her beautiful. Mrs. Stanton's deep blue eyes with their mischievous twinkle, her rosy cheeks and short dark hair gave her a very youthful appearance, and it was hard for Susan to realize she was the mother of three lively boys.

Susan listened enthralled while Mrs. Stanton told how deeply she had been moved as a child by the pitiful stories of the women who came to her father's law office, begging for relief from the unjust property laws which turned over their inheritance and their earnings to their husbands. For the first time, Susan heard the story of the exclusion of women delegates from the World's antislavery convention in London, in 1840, which Mrs. Stanton had attended with her husband and where she became the devoted friend of Lucretia Mott. She now better understood why these two women had called the first woman's rights convention in 1848 at which Mrs. Stanton had made the first public demand for woman suffrage.

They talked about the bloomer costume which Mrs. Stanton now wore and about dress reform which at the moment seemed to Mrs. Stanton an important phase of the woman's rights movement, and she pointed out to Susan the advantages of the bloomer in the life of a busy housekeeper who ran up and down stairs carrying babies, lamps, and buckets of water. She praised the freedom it gave from uncomfortable stays and tight lacing, confident it would be a big factor in improving the health of women.

Thoroughly interested, Susan left Seneca Falls with much to think about, but not yet converted to the bloomer costume, or even to woman suffrage. Of one thing, however, she was certain. She wanted this woman of vision and courage for her friend.

Freedom To Speak

Susan was soon rejoicing at the prospect of meeting Lucy Stone and Horace Greeley, the editor of the New York Tribune. Mrs. Stanton had invited her to Seneca Falls to discuss with them and other influential men and women the founding of a people's college. Unhesitatingly she joined forces with Mrs. Stanton and Lucy Stone to insist that the people's college be opened to women on the same terms as men. Lucy had proved the practicability of this as a student at Oberlin, the first college to admit women, and was one of the first women to receive a college degree. However, to suggest coeducation in those days was enough to jeopardize the founding of a college, and Horace Greeley stood out against them, his babylike face, fringed with throat whiskers, getting redder by the moment as he begged them not to agitate the question.

The people's college did not materialize, but out of this meeting grew a friendship between Susan, Elizabeth Stanton, and Lucy Stone, which developed the woman's rights movement in the United States. Susan discovered at once that Lucy, like Mrs. Stanton, was an ardent advocate of woman's rights. Brought up in a large family on a farm in western Massachusetts where a woman's lot was an unending round of hard work with no rights over her children or property, Lucy had seen much to make her rebellious. Resolving to free herself from this bondage, she had worked hard for an education, finally reaching Oberlin College. Here she held out for equal rights in education, and now as she went through the country, pleading for the abolition of slavery, she was not only putting into practice woman's right to express herself on public affairs, but was scattering woman's rights doctrine wherever she went. Listening to this rosy-cheeked, enthusiastic young woman with her little snub nose and soulful gray eyes, Susan began to realize how little opposition in comparison she herself had met because she was a woman. Not only had her father encouraged her to become a teacher, but he had actually aroused her interest in such causes as abolition, temperance, and woman's rights, while both Lucy and Mrs. Stanton had met disapproval and resistance all the way.

Lucy Stone

She found Lucy, as well as Mrs. Stanton, in the bloomer dress, praising its convenience. As Lucy traveled about lecturing, in all kinds of weather, climbing on trains, into carriages, and walking on muddy streets, she found it much more practical and comfortable than the fashionable long full skirts. Nevertheless, there was discomfort in being stared at on the streets and in the chagrin of her friends. This reform was much on their minds and they discussed it pro and con, for Mrs. Stanton was facing real persecution in Seneca Falls, with boys screaming "breeches" at her when she appeared in the street and with her husband's political opponents ridiculing her costume in their campaign speeches. Both women, however, felt it their duty to bear this cross to free women from the bondage of cumbersome clothing, hoping always that the bloomer, because of its utility, would win converts and finally become the fashion. Susan admired their courage, but still could not be persuaded to put on the bloomer.

Fired with their zeal, she began planning what she herself might do to rouse women. The idea of a separate woman's rights movement did not as yet enter her mind. Her thoughts turned rather to the two national reform movements already well under way, temperance and antislavery. While a career as an antislavery worker appealed strongly to her, she felt unqualified when she measured herself with the courageous Grimké sisters from South Carolina, or with Abby Kelley Foster, Lucy Stone, and the eloquent men in the movement. She had made a place for herself locally in temperance societies, and she decided that her work was there—to make women an active, important part of this reform.

That winter, as a delegate of the Rochester Daughters of Temperance, she went with high hopes to the state convention of the Sons of Temperance in Albany, where she visited Lydia Mott and her sister Abigail, who lived in a small house on Maiden Lane. Both Lydia and Abigail, because of their independence, interested Susan greatly. They supported themselves by "taking in" boarders from among the leading politicians in Albany. They also kept a men's furnishings store on Broadway and made hand-ruffled shirt bosoms and fine linen accessories for Thurlow Weed, Horatio Seymour, and other influential citizens. Their political contacts were many and important, and yet they were also among the very few in that conservative city who stood for temperance, abolition of slavery, and woman's rights. Their home was a rallying point for reformers and a refuge for fugitive slaves. It was to be a second home to Susan in the years to come.

When Susan and the other women delegates entered the convention of the Sons of Temperance, they looked forward proudly, if a bit timidly, to taking part in the meetings, but when Susan spoke to a motion, the chairman, astonished that a woman would be so immodest as to speak in a public meeting, scathingly announced, "The sisters were not invited here to speak, but to listen and to learn."[33]

21

This was the first time that Susan had been publicly rebuked because she was a woman, and she did not take it lightly. Leaving the hall with several other indignant women delegates, amid the critical whisperings of those who remained "to listen and to learn," she hurried over to Lydia's shop to ask her advice on the next step to be taken. Lydia, delighted that they had had the spirit to leave the meeting, suggested they engage the lecture room of the Hudson Street Presbyterian Church and hold a meeting of their own that very night. She went with them to the office of her friend Thurlow Weed, the editor of the Evening Journal, who published the whole story in his paper.

Susan B. Anthony engraving, c. 1855

Well in advance of the meeting, Susan was at the church, feeling very responsible, and when she saw Samuel J. May enter, she was greatly relieved. He had read the notice in the Evening Journal and persuaded a friend to come with him. To see his genial face in the audience gave her confidence, for he would speak easily and well if others should fail her. Only a few people drifted into the meeting, for the night was snowy and cold. The room was poorly lighted, the stove smoked, and in the middle of the speeches, the stovepipe fell down. Yet in spite of all this, a spirit of independence and accomplishment was born in that gathering and plans were made to call a woman's state temperance convention in Rochester with Susan in charge.

All this Susan reported to her new friend, Elizabeth Stanton, who promised to help all she could, urging that the new organization lead the way and not follow the advice of cautious, conservative women. Susan agreed, and as a first step in carrying out this policy, she asked Mrs. Stanton to make the keynote speech of the convention. Soon the Woman's State Temperance Society was a going concern with Mrs. Stanton as president and Susan as secretary. There was no doubt about its leading the way far ahead of the rank and file of the temperance movement when Mrs. Stanton, with Susan's full approval, recommended divorce on the grounds of drunkenness, declaring, "Let us petition our State government so to modify the laws affecting marriage and the custody of children that the drunkard shall have no claims on wife and child."[34]

Such independence on the part of women could not be tolerated, and both the press and the clergy ruthlessly denounced the Woman's State Temperance Society. Susan, however, did not take this too seriously, familiar as she was with the persecution antislavery workers endured when they frankly expressed their convictions.

Now recognized as the leader of women's temperance groups in New York, Susan traveled throughout the state, organizing temperance societies, getting subscriptions for Amelia Bloomer's temperance paper, The Lily, and attending temperance conventions in spite of the fact that she met determined opposition to the participation of women.

Impressed by the success of political action in Maine, where in 1851 the first prohibition law in the country had been passed, she now signed her letters, "Yours for Temperance Politics."[35] She appealed to women to petition for a Maine law for New York and brought a group of women before the legislature for the first time for a hearing on this prohibition bill. Realizing then that women's indirect influence could be of little help in political action, she saw clearly that women needed the vote.

However, it was the woman's rights convention in Syracuse, New York, in September 1852, which turned her thoughts definitely in the direction of votes for women. It was the first woman's rights gathering she had ever attended and she was enthusiastic over the people she met. She talked eagerly with the courageous Jewish lecturer, Ernestine Rose; with Dr. Harriot K. Hunt of Boston, one of the first women physicians, who was waging a battle against taxation without representation; with Clarina Nichols of Vermont, editor of the Windham County Democrat, and with Matilda Joslyn Gage, the youngest member of the convention. All of these became valuable, loyal friends in the years ahead. Susan renewed her acquaintance with Lucy Stone, and met Antoinette Brown who had also studied at Oberlin College and was now the first woman ordained as a minister. With real pleasure she greeted Mrs. Stanton's cousin, Gerrit Smith, now Congressman from New York, and his daughter, Elizabeth Smith Miller, the originator of the much-discussed bloomer. Best of all was her long-hoped-for meeting with James and Lucretia Mott and Lucretia's sister, Martha C. Wright. Only Paulina Wright Davis of Providence and Elizabeth Oakes Smith of Boston were disappointing, for they appeared at the meetings in short-sleeved, low-necked dresses with loose-fitting jackets of pink and blue wool, shocking her deeply intrenched Quaker instincts. Although she realized that they wore ultrafashionable clothes to show the world that not all woman's rights advocates were frumps wearing the hideous bloomer, she could not forgive them for what to her seemed bad taste. How could such women, she asked herself, hope to represent the earnest, hard-working women who must be the backbone of the equal rights movement? Always forthright, when a principle was at stake, she expressed her feelings frankly when James Mott, serving with her on the nominating committee, proposed Elizabeth Oakes Smith for president. His reply, that they must not expect all women to dress as plainly as the Friends, in no way quieted her opposition. To her delight, Lucretia Mott was elected, and her dignity and poise as president of this large convention of 2,000 won the respect even of the critical press. Susan was elected secretary and so clearly could her voice be heard as she read the minutes and the resolutions that the Syracuse Standard commented, "Miss Anthony has a capital voice and deserves to be clerk of the Assembly."[36]

James and Lucretia Mott

Not all of the newspapers were so friendly. Some labeled the gathering "a Tomfoolery convention" of "Aunt Nancy men and brawling women"; others called it "the farce at Syracuse,"[37] but for Susan it marked a milestone. Never before had she heard so many earnest, intelligent women plead so convincingly for property rights, civil rights, and the ballot. Never before had she seen so clearly that in a republic women as well as men should enjoy these rights. The ballot assumed a new importance for her. Her conversion to woman suffrage was complete.

This new interest in the vote was steadily nurtured by Elizabeth Stanton, whom Susan now saw more frequently. Whenever she could, Susan stopped over in Seneca Falls for a visit. Here she found inspiration, new ideas, and good advice, and always left the comfortable Stanton home ready to battle for the rights of women. While Susan traveled about, organizing temperance societies and attending conventions, Mrs. Stanton, tied down at home by a family of young children, wrote letters and resolutions for her and helped her with her speeches. Susan was very reluctant about writing speeches or making them. The moment she sat down to write, her thoughts refused to come and her phrases grew stilted. She needed encouragement, and Mrs. Stanton gave it unstintingly, for she had grown very fond of this young woman whose mental companionship she found so stimulating.

During one of these visits, Susan finally put on the bloomer and cut her long thick brown hair as part of the stern task of winning freedom for women. It was not an easy decision and she came to it only because she was unwilling to do less for the cause than Mrs. Stanton or Lucy Stone. Comfortable as the new dress was, it always attracted unfavorable attention and added fuel to the fire of an unfriendly press. This fire soon scorched her at the World's Temperance convention in New York, where women delegates faced the determined animosity of the clergy, who held the balance of power and quoted the Bible to prove that women were defying the will of God when they took part in public meetings. Obliged to withdraw, the women held meetings of their own in the Broadway Tabernacle, over which Susan presided with a poise and confidence undreamed of a few months before. A success in every way, they were nevertheless described by the press as a battle of the sexes, a free-for-all struggle in which shrill-voiced women in the bloomer costume were supported by a few "male Betties." The New York Sun spoke of Susan's "ungainly form rigged out in the bloomer costume and provoking the thoughtless to laughter and ridicule by her very motions on the platform."[38] Untruth was piled upon untruth until dignified ladylike Susan with her earnest pleasing appearance was caricatured into everything a woman should not be. Less courageous temperance women now began to wonder whether they ought to associate with such a strong-minded woman as Susan B. Anthony.

There were rumblings of discontent when the Woman's State Temperance Society met in Rochester for its next annual convention in June 1853, and Susan and Mrs. Stanton were roundly criticized because they did not confine themselves to the subject of temperance and talked too much about woman's rights. Not only was Mrs. Stanton defeated for the presidency but the by-laws were amended to make men eligible as officers. Men had been barred when the first by-laws were drafted by Susan and Mrs. Stanton because they wished to make the society a proving ground for women and were convinced that men holding office would take over the management, and women, less experienced, would yield to their wishes.

This now proved to be the case, as the men began to do all the talking, calling for a new name for the society and insisting that all discussion of woman's rights be ruled out. In the face of this clear indication of a determined new policy which few of the women wished to resist, Susan refused re-election as secretary and both she and Mrs. Stanton resigned.

This was Susan's first experience with intrigue and her first rebuff by women whom she had sincerely tried to serve. Defeated, hurt, and uncertain, she poured out her disappointment in troubled letters to Elizabeth Stanton, who, with the steadying touch of an older sister, roused her with the challenge, "We have other and bigger fish to fry."[39]

A few months later, Susan was off on a new crusade as she attended the state teachers' convention in Rochester. Of the five hundred teachers present, two-thirds were women, but there was not the slightest recognition of their presence. They filled the back seats of Corinthian Hall, forming an inert background for the vocal minority, the men. After sitting through two days' sessions and growing more and more impatient as not one woman raised her voice, Susan listened, as long as she could endure it, to a lengthy debate on the question, "Why the profession of teacher is not as much respected as that of lawyer, doctor, or minister."[40] Then she rose to her feet and in a low-pitched, clear voice addressed the chairman.

At the sound of a woman's voice, an astonished rustle of excitement swept through the audience, and when the chairman, Charles Davies, Professor of Mathematics at West Point, had recovered from his surprise, he patronizingly asked, "What will the lady have?"

"I wish, sir, to speak to the subject under discussion," she bravely replied.

Turning to the men in the front row, Professor Davies then asked, "What is the pleasure of the convention?"

"I move that she be heard," shouted an unexpected champion. Another seconded the motion. After a lengthy debate during which Susan stood patiently waiting, the men finally voted their approval by a small majority, and Professor Davies, a bit taken aback, announced, "The lady may speak."

"It seems to me, gentlemen," Susan began, "that none of you quite comprehend the cause of the disrespect of which you complain. Do you not see that so long as society says woman is incompetent to be a lawyer, minister, or doctor, but has ample ability to be a teacher, every man of you who chooses this profession tacitly acknowledges that he has no more brains than a woman? And this, too, is the reason that teaching is a less lucrative profession; as here men must compete with the cheap labor of woman. Would you exalt your profession, exalt those who labor with you. Would you make it more lucrative, increase the salaries of the women engaged in the noble work of educating our future Presidents, Senators, and Congressmen."

For a moment after this bombshell, there was complete silence. Then three men rushed down the aisle to congratulate her, telling her she had pluck, that she had hit the nail on the head, but the women near by glanced scornfully at her, murmuring, "Who can that creature be?"

Susan, however, had started a few women thinking and questioning, and the next morning, Professor Davies, resplendent in his buff vest and blue coat with brass buttons, opened the convention with an explanation. "I have been asked," he said, "why no provisions have been made for female lecturers before this association and why ladies are not appointed on committees. I will answer." Then, in flowery metaphor, he assured them that he would not think of dragging women from their pedestals into the dust.

"Beautiful, beautiful," murmured the women in the back rows, but Mrs. Northrup of Rochester offered resolutions recognizing the right of women teachers to share in all the privileges and deliberations of the organization and calling attention to the inadequate salaries women teachers received. These resolutions were kept before the meeting by a determined group and finally adopted. Susan also offered the name of Emma Willard as a candidate for vice-president, thinking the successful retired principal of the Troy Female Seminary, now interested in improving the public schools, might also be willing to lend a hand in improving the status of women in this educational organization. Mrs. Willard, however, declined the nomination, refusing to be drawn into Susan's rebellion.[41] Susan, nevertheless, left the convention satisfied that she had driven an entering wedge into Professor Davies' male stronghold, and she continued battering at this stronghold whenever she had an opportunity. She meant to put women in office and to win approval for coeducation and equal pay.

Teachers' conventions, however, were only a minor part of her new crusade, plans for which were still simmering in her mind and developing from day to day. Going back to many of the towns where she had held temperance meetings, she found that most of the societies she had organized had disbanded because women lacked the money to engage speakers or to subscribe to temperance papers. If they were married, they had no money of their own and no right to any interest outside their homes, unless their husbands consented.

Discouraged, she wrote in her diary, "As I passed from town to town I was made to feel the great evil of woman's entire dependency upon man for the necessary means to aid on any and every reform movement. Though I had long admitted the wrong, I never until this time so fully took in the grand idea of pecuniary and personal independence. It matters not how overflowing with benevolence toward suffering humanity may be the heart of woman, it avails nothing so long as she possesses not the power to act in accordance with these promptings. Woman must have a purse of her own, and how can this be, so long as the Wife is denied the right to her individual and joint earnings. Reflections like these, caused me to see and really feel that there was no true freedom for Woman without the possession of all her property rights, and that these rights could be obtained through legislation only, and so, the sooner the demand was made of the Legislature, the sooner would we be likely to obtain them."[42]

A Purse Of Her Own

The next important step in winning further property rights for women, it seemed to Susan, was to hold a woman's rights convention in the conservative capital city of Albany. This was definitely a challenge and she at once turned to Elizabeth Stanton for counsel. Somehow she must persuade Mrs. Stanton to find time in spite of her many household cares to prepare a speech for the convention and for presentation to the legislature. As eager as Susan to free women from unjust property laws, Mrs. Stanton asked only that Susan get a good lawyer, and one sympathetic to the cause, to look up New York State's very worst laws affecting women.[43] She could think and philosophize while she was baking and sewing, she assured Susan, but she had no time for research. Susan produced the facts for Mrs. Stanton, and while she worked on the speech, Susan went from door to door during the cold blustery days of December and January 1854 to get signatures on her petitions for married women's property rights and woman suffrage. Some of the women signed, but more of them slammed the door in her face, declaring indignantly that they had all the rights they wanted. Yet at this time a father had the legal authority to apprentice or will away a child without the mother's consent and an employer was obliged by law to pay a wife's wages to her husband.

In spite of the fact that the bloomer costume made it easier for her to get about in the snowy streets, she now found it a real burden because it always attracted unfavorable attention. Boys jeered at her and she was continually conscious of the amused, critical glances of the men and women she met. She longed to take it off and wear an inconspicuous trailing skirt, but if she had been right to put it on, it would be weakness to take it off. By this time Elizabeth Stanton had given it up except in her own home, convinced that it harmed the cause and that the physical freedom it gave was not worth the price. "I hope you have let down a dress and a petticoat," she now wrote Susan. "The cup of ridicule is greater than you can bear. It is not wise, Susan, to use up so much energy and feeling in that way. You can put them to better use. I speak from experience."[44]

Elizabeth Cady Stanton and her sons

Lucy Stone too was wavering and was thinking of having her next dress made long. The three women corresponded about it, and Lucy as well as Mrs. Stanton urged Susan to give up the bloomer. With these entreaties ringing in her ears, Susan set out for Albany in February 1854 to make final arrangements for the convention. On the streets in Albany, in the printing offices, and at the capitol, men stared boldly at her, some calling out hilariously, "Here comes my bloomer." She endured it bravely until her work was done, but at night alone in her room at Lydia Mott's she poured out her anguish in letters to Lucy. "Here I am known only," she wrote, "as one of the women who ape men—coarse, brutal men! Oh, I can not, can not bear it any longer."[45]

Even so she did not let down the hem of her skirt, but wore her bloomer costume heroically during the entire convention, determined that she would not be stampeded into a long skirt by the jeers of Albany men or the ridicule of the women. However, she made up her mind that immediately after the convention she would take off the bloomer forever. She had worn it a little over a year. Never again could she be lured into the path of dress reform.

The Albany Register scoffed at the "feminine propagandists of woman's rights" exhibiting themselves in "short petticoats and long-legged boots."[46] Nevertheless, the convention aroused such genuine interest that evening meetings were continued for two weeks, featuring as speakers Ernestine Rose, Antoinette Brown, Samuel J. May, and William Henry Channing, the young Unitarian minister from Rochester; and when the men appeared on the platform, the audience called for the women.

Susan could not have asked for anything better than Elizabeth Stanton's moving plea for property rights for married women and the attention it received from the large audience in the Senate Chamber. Her heart swelled with pride as she listened to her friend, and so important did she think the speech that she had 50,000 copies printed for distribution.

To back up Mrs. Stanton's words with concrete evidence of a demand for a change in the law, Susan presented petitions with 10,000 signatures, 6,000 asking that married women be granted the right to their wages and 4,000 venturing to be recorded for woman suffrage.

Enthusiastic over her Albany success, she impetuously wrote Lucy Stone, "Is this not a wonderful time, an era long to be remembered?"[47]

Although the legislature failed to act on the petitions, she knew that her cause had made progress, for never before had women been listened to with such respect and never had newspapers been so friendly. She cherished these words of praise from Lucy, "God bless you, Susan dear, for the brave heart that will work on even in the midst of discouragement and lack of helpers. Everywhere I am telling people what your state is doing, and it is worth a great deal to the cause. The example of positive action is what we need."[48]

Susan continued her "example of positive action," this time against the Kansas-Nebraska bill, pending in Congress, which threatened repeal of the Missouri Compromise by admitting Kansas and Nebraska as territories with the right to choose for themselves whether they would be slave or free. "I feel that woman should in the very capitol of the nation lift her voice against that abominable measure," she wrote Lucy Stone, with whom she was corresponding more and more frequently. "It is not enough that H. B. Stowe should write."[49] Harriet Beecher Stowe's Uncle Tom's Cabin had been published in 1852 and during that year 300,000 copies were sold.

Ernestine Rose

With Ernestine Rose, Susan now headed for Washington. These two women had been drawn together by common interests ever since they had met in Syracuse in 1852. Susan was not frightened, as many were, by Ernestine's reputed atheism. She appreciated Ernestine's intelligence, her devotion to woman's rights, and her easy eloquence. Conscious of her own limitations as an orator, she recognized her need of Ernestine for the many meetings she planned for the future.

As they traveled to Washington together, she learned more about this beautiful, impressive, black-haired Jewess from Poland, who was ten years her senior. The daughter of a rabbi, Ernestine had found the limitations of orthodox religion unbearable for a woman and had left her home to see and learn more of the world in Prussia, Holland, France, Scotland, and England. She had married an Englishman sympathetic to her liberal views, and together they had come to New York where she began her career as a lecturer in 1836 when speaking in public branded women immoral. She spoke easily and well on education, woman's rights, and the evils of slavery. Her slight foreign accent added charm to her rich musical voice, and before long she was in demand as far west as Ohio and Michigan. With a colleague as experienced as Ernestine, Susan dared arrange for meetings even in the capital of the nation.

Washington was tense over the slavery issue when they arrived, and Ernestine's friends warned her not to mention the subject in her lectures. Unheeding she commented on the Kansas-Nebraska bill, but the press took no notice and her audiences showed no signs of dissatisfaction. In fact, two comparatively unknown women, billed to lecture on the "Educational and Social Rights of Women" and the "Political and Legal Rights of Women," attracted little attention in a city accustomed to a blaze of Congressional oratory. Hoping to draw larger audiences and to lend dignity to their meetings, Susan asked for the use of the Capitol on Sunday, but was refused because Ernestine was not a member of a religious society. Making an attempt for Smithsonian Hall, Ernestine was told it could not risk its reputation by presenting a woman speaker.[50]

A failure financially, their Washington venture was rich in experience. Susan took time out for sightseeing, visiting the "President's house" and Mt. Vernon, which to her surprise she found in a state of "delapidation and decay." "The mark of slavery o'ershadows the whole," she wrote in her diary. "Oh the thought that it was here that he whose name is the pride of this Nation, was the Slave Master."[51]

Again and again in the Capitol, she listened to heated debates on the Kansas-Nebraska bill, astonished at the eloquence and fervor with which the "institution of slavery" could be defended. Seeing slavery first-hand, she abhorred it more than ever and observed with dismay its degenerating influence on master as well as slave. She began to feel that even she herself might be undermined by it almost unwittingly and confessed to her diary, "This noon, I ate my dinner without once asking myself are these human beings who minister to my wants, Slaves to be bought and sold and hired out at the will of a master?... Even I am getting accustomed to Slavery ... so much so that I have ceased continually to be made to feel its blighting, cursing influence."[52]

A few months later, Susan and Ernestine were in Philadelphia at a national woman's rights convention, and when Ernestine was proposed for president, Susan had her first opportunity to champion her new friend. A foreigner and a free-thinker, Ernestine encountered a great deal of prejudice even among liberal reformers, and Susan was surprised at the strength of feeling against her. Impressed during their trip to Washington by Ernestine's essentially fine qualities and her value to the cause, Susan fought for her behind the scenes, insisting that freedom of religion or the freedom to have no religion be observed in woman's rights conventions, and she had the satisfaction of seeing Ernestine elected to the office she so richly deserved.

Freedom of religion or freedom to have no religion had become for Susan a principle to hold on to, as she listened at these early woman's rights meetings to the lengthy fruitless discussions regarding the lack of Scriptural sanction for women's new freedom. Usually a clergyman appeared on the scene, volubly quoting the Bible to prove that any widening of woman's sphere was contrary to the will of God. But always ready to refute him were Antoinette Brown, now an ordained minister, William Lloyd Garrison, and occasionally Susan herself. To the young Quaker broadened by her Unitarian contacts and unhampered by creed or theological dogma, such debates were worse than useless; they deepened theological differences, stirred up needless antagonisms, solved no problems, and wasted valuable time. During this convention, she was one of the twenty-four guests in Lucretia Mott's comfortable home at 238 Arch Street. Every meal, with its stimulating discussions, was a convention in itself. Susan's great hero, William Lloyd Garrison, sat at Lucretia's right at the long table in the dining room, Susan on her left, and at the end of each meal, when the little cedar tub filled with hot soapy water was brought in and set before Lucretia so that she could wash the silver, glass, and fine china at the table, Susan dried them on a snowy-white towel while the interesting conversation continued. There was talk of woman's rights, of temperance, and of spiritualism, which was attracting many new converts. There were thrilling stories of the opening of the West and the building of transcontinental railways; but most often and most earnestly the discussion turned to the progress of the antislavery movement, to the infamous Kansas-Nebraska bill, to the New England Emigrant Aid Company,[53] which was sending free-state settlers to Kansas, to the weakness of the government in playing again and again into the hands of the proslavery faction. Most of them saw the country headed toward a vast slave empire which would embrace Cuba, Mexico, and finally Brazil; and William Lloyd Garrison fervently reiterated his doctrine, "No Union with Slaveholders."

Before leaving home Susan had heard first-hand reports of the bitter bloody antislavery contest in Kansas from her brother Daniel, who had just returned from a trip to that frontier territory with settlers sent out by the New England Emigrant Aid Company. Now talking with William Lloyd Garrison, she found herself torn between these two great causes for human freedom, abolition and woman's rights, and it was hard for her to decide which cause needed her more.

She had not, however, forgotten her unfinished business in New York State. The refusal of the legislature to amend the property laws had doubled her determination to continue circulating petitions until married women's civil rights were finally recognized. It took courage to go alone to towns where she was unknown to arrange for meetings on the unpopular subject of woman's rights. Not knowing how she would be received, she found it almost as difficult to return to such towns as Canajoharie where she had been highly respected as a teacher six years before. In Canajoharie, however, she was greeted affectionately by her uncle Joshua Read. He and his friends let her use the Methodist church for her lecture, and when the trustees of the academy urged her to return there to teach, Uncle Joshua interrupted with a vehement "No!" protesting that others could teach but it was Susan's work "to go around and set people thinking about the laws."[54]

Returning to the scene of her girlhood in Battenville and Easton, visiting her sisters Guelma and Hannah, and meeting many of her old friends, Susan realized as never before how completely she had outgrown her old environment. In her enthusiasm for her new work, she exposed "many of her heresies," and when her friends labeled William Lloyd Garrison an agnostic and rabble rouser, she protested that he was the most Christlike man she had ever known. "Thus it is belief, not Christian benevolence," she confided to her diary in 1854, "that is made the modern test of Christianity."[55]

After eight strenuous months away from home, she was welcomed warmly by a family who believed in her work. She found abolition uppermost in everyone's mind. Her brother Merritt, fired by Daniel's tales of the West and the antislavery struggle in Kansas, was impatient to join the settlers there and could talk of nothing else. While he poured out the latest news about Kansas, he and a cousin Mary Luther helped Susan fold handbills for future woman's rights meetings. Susan listened eagerly and approvingly as he told of the 750 free-state settlers who during the past summer had gone out to Kansas, traveling up the Missouri on steamboats and over lonely trails in wagons marked "Kansas." Most of them were not abolitionists but men who wanted Kansas a free-labor state which they could develop with their own hard work. She heard of the ruthless treatment these "Yankee" settlers faced from the proslavery Missourians who wanted Kansas in the slavery bloc. There was bloodshed and there would be more. John Brown's sons had written from Kansas, "Send us guns. We need them more than bread."[56] Merritt was ready and eager to join John Brown.

The Anthony farm was virtually a hotbed of insurrection with Merritt planning resistance in Kansas and Susan reform in New York. Susan mapped out an ambitious itinerary, hoping to canvass with her petitions every county in the state. With her father as security, she borrowed money to print her handbills and notices, and then wrote Wendell Phillips asking if any money for a woman's rights campaign had been raised by the last national convention. He replied with his own personal check for fifty dollars. His generosity and confidence touched her deeply, for already he had become a hero to her second only to William Lloyd Garrison. This tall handsome intellectual, a graduate of Harvard and an unsurpassed orator, had forfeited friends, social position, and a promising career as a lawyer to plead for the slave. He was also one of the very few men who sympathized with and aided the woman's rights cause.

Horace Greeley too proved at this time to be a good friend, writing, "I have your letter and your programme, friend Susan. I will publish the latter in all our editions, but return your dollars."[57]

Her earnestness and ability made a great appeal to these men. They marveled at her industry. Thirty-four years old now, not handsome but wholesome, simply and neatly dressed, her brown hair smoothly parted and brought down over her ears, she had nothing of the scatterbrained impulsive reformer about her, and no coquetry. She was practical and intelligent, and men liked to discuss their work with her. William Henry Channing, admiring her executive ability and her plucky reaction to defeat, dubbed her the Napoleon of the woman's rights movement. Parker Pillsbury, the fiery abolitionist from New Hampshire, broad-shouldered, dark-bearded, with blazing eyes and almost fanatical zeal, had become her devoted friend. He liked nothing better than to tease her about her idleness and pretend to be in search of more work for her to do.

So impatient was Susan to begin her New York State campaign that she left home on Christmas Day to hold her first meeting on December 26, 1854, at Mayville in Chatauqua County. The weather was cold and damp, but the four pounds of candles which she had bought to light the court house flickered cheerily while the small curious audience, gathered from several nearby towns, listened to the first woman most of them had ever heard speak in public. She would be, they reckoned, worth hearing at least once.

Traveling from town to town, she held meetings every other night. Usually the postmasters or sheriffs posted her notices in the town square and gave them to the newspapers and to the ministers to announce in their churches. Even in a hostile community she almost always found a gallant fair-minded man to come to her aid, such as the hotel proprietor who offered his dining room for her meetings when the court house, schoolhouse, and churches were closed to her, or the group of men who, when the ministers refused to announce her meetings, struck off handbills which they distributed at the church doors at the close of the services. The newspapers too were generally friendly.

As men were the voters with power to change the laws, she aimed to attract them to her evening meetings, and usually they came, seeking diversion, and listened respectfully. Some of them scoffed, others condemned her for undermining the home, but many found her reasoning logical and by their questions put life into the meetings. A few even encouraged their wives to enlist in the cause.

The women, on the other hand, were timid or indifferent, although she pointed out to them the way to win the legal right to their earnings and their children. It was difficult to find among them a rebellious spirit brave enough to head a woman's rights society.

"Susan B. Anthony is in town," wrote young Caroline Cowles, a Canandaigua school girl, in her diary at this time. "She made a special request that all seminary girls should come to hear her as well as all the women and girls in town. She had a large audience and she talked very plainly about our rights and how we ought to stand up for them and said the world would never go right until the women had just as much right to vote and rule as the men.... When I told Grandmother about it, she said she guessed Susan B. Anthony had forgotten that St. Paul said women should keep silence. I told her, no, she didn't, for she spoke particularly about St. Paul and said if he had lived in these times ... he would have been as anxious to have women at the head of the government as she was. I could not make Grandmother agree with her at all."[58]

Many of the towns Susan visited were not on a railroad. Often after a long cold sleigh ride she slept in a hotel room without a fire; in the morning she might have to break the ice in the pitcher to take the cold sponge bath which nothing could induce her to omit since she had begun to follow the water cure, a new therapeutic method then in vogue.

For a time Ernestine Rose came to her aid and it was a relief to turn over the meetings to such an accomplished speaker. But for the most part Susan braved it alone. Steadily adding names to her petitions and leaving behind the leaflets which Elizabeth Stanton had written, she aroused a glimmer of interest in a new valuation of women.

Parker Pillsbury

On the stagecoach leaving Lake George on a particularly cold day, she found to her surprise a wealthy Quaker, whom she had met at the Albany convention, so solicitous of her comfort that he placed heated planks under her feet, making the long ride much more bearable. He turned up again, this time with his own sleigh, at the close of one of her meetings in northern New York, and wrapped in fur robes, she drove with him behind spirited gray horses to his sisters' home to stay over Sunday, and then to all her meetings in the neighborhood. It was pleasant to be looked after and to travel in comfort and she enjoyed his company, but when he urged her to give up the hard life of a reformer to become his wife, there was no hesitation on her part. She had dedicated her life to freeing women and Negroes and there could be no turning aside. If she ever married, it must be to a man who would encourage her work for humanity, a great man like Wendell Phillips, or a reformer like Parker Pillsbury.

Returning home in May 1855, she took stock of her accomplishments. She had canvassed fifty-four counties and sold 20,000 tracts. Her expenses had been $2,291 and she had paid her way by selling tracts and by a small admission charge for her meetings. She even had seventy dollars over and above all expenses. She promptly repaid the fifty dollars which Wendell Phillips had advanced, but he returned it for her next campaign.

However, her heart quailed at the prospect of another such winter, as she recalled the long, bitter-cold days of travel and the indifference of the women she was trying to help. Even the unfailing praise of her family and of Elizabeth Stanton, even the kindness and interest of the new friends she made paled into insignificance before the thought of another lone crusade. She was exhausted and suffering with rheumatic pains, and yet she would not rest, but prepared for an ambitious convention at Saratoga Springs, then the fashionable summer resort of the East.

She had braved this center of fashion and frivolity the year before with her message of woman's rights, and to her great surprise, crowds seeking entertainment had come to her meetings, their admission fees and their purchase of tracts making the venture a financial success. Here was fertile ground. Susan was counting on Lucy Stone and Antoinette Brown to help her, for Elizabeth Stanton, then expecting her sixth baby, was out of the picture. Now, to her dismay, Lucy and Antoinette married the Blackwell brothers, Henry and Samuel.

Fearing that they too like Elizabeth Stanton would be tied down with babies and household cares, Susan saw a bleak lonely road ahead for the woman's rights movement. She did so want her best speakers and most valuable workers to remain single until the spade work for woman's rights was done. Almost in a panic at the prospect of being left to carry on the Saratoga convention alone, Susan wrote Lucy irritable letters instead of praising her for drawing up a marriage contract and keeping her own name. Later, however, she realized what it had meant for Lucy to keep her own name, and then she wrote her, "I am more and more rejoiced that you have declared by actual doing that a woman has a name and may retain it all through her life."[59]

So persistently did she now pursue Lucy and Antoinette that they both kept their promise to speak at the Saratoga convention, Lucy traveling all the way from Cincinnati where she was visiting in the Blackwell home. Lucy was loudly cheered by a large audience, eager to see this young woman whose marriage had attracted so much notice in the press. In fact Lucy Stone, who had kept her own name and who with her husband had signed a marriage protest against the legal disabilities of a married woman, was as much of a novelty in this fashionable circle as one of Barnum's high-priced curiosities.

Pleased at Lucy's reception, Susan surveyed the audience hopefully—handsome men in nankeen trousers, red waistcoats, white neckcloths, and gray swallowtail coats, sitting beside beautiful young women wearing gowns of bombazine and watered silk with wide hoop skirts and elaborately trimmed bonnets which set off their curls. To her delight, they also applauded Antoinette Brown Blackwell, the first woman minister they had ever seen, and Ernestine Rose with her appealing foreign accent. They clapped loudly when she herself asked them to buy tracts and contribute to the work.

Complimentary as this was, she did not flatter herself that they had endorsed woman's rights. That they had come to her meetings in large numbers while vacationing in Saratoga Springs, this was important. In some a spark of understanding glowed, and this spark would light others. They came from the South, from the West, and from the large cities of the East. There were railroad magnates among them, rich merchants, manufacturers, and politicians. Charles F. Hovey, the wealthy Boston dry-goods merchant, listened attentively to every word, and in the years that followed became a generous contributor to the cause.

Realizing how very tired she was and that she must feel more physically fit before continuing her work, Susan decided to take the water cure at her cousin Seth Rogers' Hydropathic Institute in Worcester, Massachusetts. This well-known sanitorium prescribed water internally and externally as a remedy for all kinds of ailments, and in an age when meals were overhearty, baths infrequent, and clothing tight and confining, the drinking of water, tub baths, showers, and wet packs had enthusiastic advocates. The soothing baths relaxed Susan and the leisure to read refreshed and strengthened her. She read, one after another, Carlyle's Sartor Resartus, George Sand's Consuelo, Madame de Stael's Corinne, then Frances Wright's A Few Days in Athens and Mrs. Gaskell's Life of Charlotte Brontë, making notes in her diary (1855) of passages she particularly liked. She discussed current events with her cousin Seth on long drives in the country, finding him a delightful companion, well-read, understanding, and interested in people and causes. He took her to her first political meeting, where she was the only woman present and had a seat on the platform. It was one of the first rallies of the new Republican party which had developed among rebellious northern Whigs, Free-Soilers, and anti-Nebraska Democrats who opposed the extension of slavery. After listening to the speakers, among them Charles Sumner, she drew these conclusions: "Had the accident of birth given me place among the aristocracy of sex, I doubt not I should be an active, zealous advocate of Republicanism; unless perchance, I had received that higher, holier light which would have lifted me to the sublime height where now stand Garrison, Phillips, and all that small band whose motto is 'No Union with Slaveholders.'"[60]

After listening to the satisfying sermons of Thomas Wentworth Higginson at his Free Church in Worcester, she wrote in her diary, "It is plain to me now that it is not sitting under preaching I dislike, but the fact that most of it is not of a stamp that my soul can respond to."[61]

In September she interrupted "the cure" to attend a woman's rights meeting in Boston, and with Lucy Stone, Antoinette and Ellen Blackwell visited in the home of the wealthy merchant, Francis Jackson, making many new friends, among them his daughter, Eliza J. Eddy, whose unhappy marriage was to prove a blessing to the woman's rights cause.[62]

At tea at the Garrisons', she met many of the "distinguished" men and women she had "worshiped" from afar. She heard Theodore Parker preach a sermon which filled her soul, and with Mr. Garrison called on him in his famous library. "It really seemed audacious in me to be ushered into such a presence and on such a commonplace errand as to ask him to come to Rochester to speak in a course of lectures I am planning," she wrote her family, "but he received me with such kindness and simplicity that the awe I felt on entering was soon dissipated. I then called on Wendell Phillips in his sanctum for the same purpose. I have invited Ralph Waldo Emerson by letter and all three have promised to come. In the evening with Mr. Jackson's son James, Ellen Blackwell and I went to see Hamlet. In spite of my Quaker training, I find I enjoy all these worldly amusements intensely."[63]

In January 1856, Susan set out again on a woman's rights tour of New York State to gather more signatures for her petitions. This time she persuaded Frances D. Gage of Ohio, a temperance worker and popular author of children's stories, to join her. An easy extemporaneous speaker, Mrs. Gage was an attraction to offer audiences, who drove eight or more miles to hear her; and in the cheerless hotels at night and on the long cold sleigh rides from town to town, she was a congenial companion.

The winter was even colder and snowier than that of the year before. "No trains running," Susan wrote her family, "and we had a 36-mile ride in a sleigh.... Just emerged from a long line of snow drifts and stopped at this little country tavern, supped, and am now roasting over the hot stove."[64]

Confronted almost daily with glaring examples of the injustices women suffered under the property laws, she was more than ever convinced that her work was worth-while. "We stopped at a little tavern where the landlady was not yet twenty and had a baby, fifteen months old," she reported. "Her supper dishes were not washed and her baby was crying.... She rocked the little thing to sleep, washed the dishes and got our supper; beautiful white bread, butter, cheese, pickles, apple and mince pie, and excellent peach preserves. She gave us her warm room to sleep in.... She prepared a six o'clock breakfast for us, fried pork, mashed potatoes, mince pie, and for me at my special request, a plate of sweet baked apples and a pitcher of rich milk.... When we came to pay our bill, the dolt of a husband took the money and put it in his pocket. He had not lifted a finger to lighten that woman's burdens.... Yet the law gives him the right to every dollar she earns, and when she needs two cents to buy a darning needle she has to ask him and explain what she wants it for."[65]

When after a few weeks Mrs. Gage was called home by illness in her family, Susan appealed hopefully to Lucretia Mott's sister, Martha C. Wright, in Auburn, New York, "You can speak so much better, so much more wisely, so much more everything than I can." Then she added, "I should like a particular effort made to call out the Teachers, the Sewing Women, the Working Women generally—Can't you write something for your papers that will make them feel that it is for them that we work more than [for] the wives and daughters of the rich?"[66] Mrs. Wright, however, could help only in Auburn, and Susan was obliged to continue her scheduled meetings alone. She interrupted them only to present her petitions to the legislature.

The response of the legislature to her two years of hard work was a sarcastic, wholly irrelevant report issued by the judiciary committee some weeks later to a Senate roaring with laughter. In the Albany Register Susan read with mounting indignation portions of this infuriating report: "The ladies always have the best places and the choicest tidbit at the table. They have the best seats in cars, carriages, and sleighs; the warmest place in winter, the coolest in summer. They have their choice on which side of the bed they will lie, front or back. A lady's dress costs three times as much as that of a gentleman; and at the present time, with the prevailing fashion, one lady occupies three times as much space in the world as a gentleman. It has thus appeared to the married gentlemen of your committee, being a majority ... that if there is any inequality or oppression in the case, the gentlemen are the sufferers. They, however, have presented no petitions for redress, having doubtless made up their minds to yield to an inevitable destiny."[67]

Why, Susan wondered sadly, were woman's rights only a joke to most men—something to be laughed at even in the face of glaring proofs of the law's injustice.

There was encouragement, however, in the letters which now came from Lucy Stone in Ohio: "Hurrah Susan! Last week this State Legislature passed a law giving wives equal property rights, and to mothers equal baby rights with fathers. So much is gained. The petitions which I set on foot in Wisconsin for suffrage have been presented, made a rousing discussion, and then were tabledwith three men to defend them!... In Nebraska too, the bill for suffrage passed the House.... The world moves!"[68]

The world was moving in Great Britain as well, for as Susan read in her newspaper, women there were petitioning Parliament for married women's property rights, and among the petitioners were her well-beloved Elizabeth Barrett Browning, Harriet Martineau, Mrs. Gaskell, and Charlotte Cushman. Better still, Harriet Taylor, inspired by the example of woman's rights conventions in America, had written for the Westminster Review an article advocating the enfranchisement of women.

All this reassured Susan, even if New York legislators laughed at her efforts.

No Union With Slaveholders

Susan's thoughts during the summer of 1856 often strayed from woman's rights meetings toward Kansas, where her brother Merritt had settled on a claim near Osawatomie. Well aware of his eagerness to help John Brown, she knew that he must be in the thick of the bloody antislavery struggle. In fact the whole Anthony family had been anxiously waiting for news from Merritt ever since the wires had flashed word in May 1856 of the burning of Lawrence by proslavery "border ruffians" from Missouri and of John Brown's raid in retaliation at Pottawatomie Creek.

Merritt had built a log cabin at Osawatomie. While Susan was at home in September, the newspapers reported an attack by proslavery men on Osawatomie in which thirty out of fifty settlers were killed. Was Merritt among them? Finally letters came through from him. Susan read and reread them, assuring herself of his safety. Although ill at the time, he had been in the thick of the fight, but was unharmed. Weak from the exertion he had crawled back to his cabin on his hands and knees and had lain there ill and alone for several weeks.

Parts of Merritt's letters were published in the Rochester Democrat, and the city took sides in the conflict, some papers claiming that his letters were fiction. Susan wrote Merritt, "How much rather would I have you at my side tonight than to think of your daring and enduring greater hardships even than our Revolutionary heroes. Words cannot tell how often we think of you or how sadly we feel that the terrible crime of this nation against humanity is being avenged on the heads of our sons and brothers.... Father brings the Democrat giving a list of killed, wounded, and missing and the name of our Merritt is not therein, but oh! the slain are sons, brothers, and husbands of others as dearly loved and sadly mourned."[69]

With difficulty, she prepared for the annual woman's rights convention, for the country was in a state of unrest not only over Kansas and the whole antislavery question, but also over the presidential campaign with three candidates in the field. Even her faithful friends Horace Greeley and Gerrit Smith now failed her, Horace Greeley writing that he could no longer publish her notices free in the news columns of his Tribune, because they cast upon him the stigma of ultraradicalism, and Gerrit Smith withholding his hitherto generous financial support because woman's rights conventions would not press for dress reform—comfortable clothing for women suitable for an active life, which he believed to be the foundation stone of women's emancipation.

Merritt Anthony

She watched the lively bitter presidential campaign with interest and concern. The new Republican party was in the contest, offering its first presidential candidate, the colorful hero and explorer of the far West, John C. Frémont. She had leanings toward this virile young party which stood firmly against the extension of slavery in the territories, and discussed its platform with Elizabeth and Henry B. Stanton, both enthusiastically for "Frémont and Freedom." Yet she was distrustful of political parties, for they eventually yielded to expediency, no matter how high their purpose at the start. Her ideal was the Garrisonian doctrine, "No Union with Slaveholders" and "Immediate Unconditional Emancipation," which courageously faced the "whole question" of slavery. There was no compromise among Garrisonians.

With the burning issue of slavery now uppermost in her mind, she began seriously to reconsider the offer she had received from the American Antislavery Society, shortly after her visit to Boston in 1855, to act as their agent in central and western New York. Unable to accept at that time because she was committed to her woman's rights program, she had nevertheless felt highly honored that she had been chosen. Still hesitating a little, she wrote Lucy Stone, wanting reassurance that no woman's rights work demanded immediate attention. "They talk of sending two companies of Lecturers into this state," she wrote Lucy, "wish me to lay out the route of each one and accompany one. They seem to think me possessed of a vast amount of executive ability. I shrink from going into Conventions where speaking is expected of me.... I know they want me to help about finance and that part I like and am good for nothing else."[70]

She also had the farm home on her mind. With her father in the insurance business, her brothers now both in Kansas, her sister Mary teaching in the Rochester schools and "looking matrimonially-wise," and her mother at home all alone, Susan often wondered if it might not be as much her duty to stay there to take care of her mother and father as it would be to make a home comfortable for a husband. Sometimes the quietness of such a life beckoned enticingly. But after the disappointing November elections which put into the presidency the conservative James Buchanan, from whom only a vacillating policy on the slavery issue could be expected, she wrote Samuel May, Jr., the secretary of the American Antislavery Society, "I shall be very glad if I am able to render even the most humble service to this cause. Heaven knows there is need of earnest, effective radical workers. The heart sickens over the delusions of the recent campaign and turns achingly to the unconsidered whole question."[71]

His reply came promptly, "We put all New York into your control and want your name to all letters and your hand in all arrangements."

For $10 a week and expenses, Susan now arranged antislavery meetings, displayed posters bearing the provocative words, "No Union with Slaveholders," planned tours for a corps of speakers, among them Stephen and Abby Kelley Foster, Parker Pillsbury, and two free Negroes, Charles Remond and his sister, Sarah.

In debt from her last woman's rights campaign, she could not afford a new dress for these tours, but she dyed a dark green the merino which she had worn so proudly in Canajoharie ten years before, bought cloth to match for a basque, and made a "handsome suit." "With my Siberian squirrel cape, I shall be very comfortable," she noted in her diary.[72]

She had met indifference and ridicule in her campaigns for woman's rights. Now she faced outright hostility, for northern businessmen had no use for abolition-mad fanatics, as they called anyone who spoke against slavery. Abolitionists, they believed, ruined business by stirring up trouble between the North and the South.

Usually antislavery meetings turned into debates between speakers and audience, often lasting until midnight, and were charged with animosity which might flame into violence. All of the speakers lived under a strain, and under emotional pressure. Consequently they were not always easy to handle. Some of them were temperamental, a bit jealous of each other, and not always satisfied with the tours Susan mapped out for them. She expected of her colleagues what she herself could endure, but they often complained and sometimes refused to fulfill their engagements.

When no one else was at hand, she took her turn at speaking, but she was seldom satisfied with her efforts. "I spoke for an hour," she confided to her diary, "but my heart fails me. Can it be that my stammering tongue ever will be loosed?" Lucy Stone, who spoke with such ease, gave her advice and encouragement. "You ought to cultivate your power of expression," she wrote. "The subject is clear to you and you ought to be able to make it so to others. It is only a few years ago that Mr. Higginson told me he could not speak, he was so much accustomed to writing, and now he is second only to Phillips. 'Go thou and do likewise.'"[73]

In March 1857, the Supreme Court startled the country with the Dred Scott decision, which not only substantiated the claim ofGarrisonians that the Constitution sanctioned slavery and protected the slaveholder, but practically swept away the Republican platform of no extention of slavery in the territories. The decision declared that the Constitution did not apply to Negroes, since they were citizens of no state when it was adopted and therefore had not the right of citizens to sue for freedom or to claim freedom in the territories; that the Missouri Compromise had always been void, since Congress did not have the right to enact a law which arbitrarily deprived citizens of their property.

Reading the decision word for word with dismay and pondering indignantly over the cold letter of the law, Susan found herself so aroused and so full of the subject that she occasionally made a spontaneous speech, and thus gradually began to free herself from reliance on written speeches. She spoke from these notes: "Consider the fact of 4,000,000 slaves in a Christian and republican government.... Antislavery prayers, resolutions, and speeches avail nothing without action.... Our mission is to deepen sympathy and convert into right action: to show that the men and women of the North are slaveholders, those of the South slave-owners. The guilt rests on the North equally with the South. Therefore our work is to rouse the sleeping consciousness of the North....[74]

"We ask you to feel as if you, yourselves, were the slaves. The politician talks of slavery as he does of United States banks, tariff, or any other commercial question. We demand the abolition of slavery because the slave is a human being and because man should not hold property in his fellowman.... We say disobey every unjust law; the politician says obey them and meanwhile labor constitutionally for repeal.... We preach revolution, the politicians, reform."

Instinctively she reaffirmed her allegiance to the doctrine, "No Union with Slaveholders," and she gloried in the courage of Garrison, Phillips, and Higginson, who had called a disunion convention, demanding that the free states secede. It was good to be one of this devoted band, for she sincerely believed that in the ages to come "the prophecies of these noble men and women will be read with the same wonder and veneration as those of Isaiah and Jeremiah inspire today."[75]

She gave herself to the work with religious fervor. Even so, she could not make her antislavery meetings self-supporting, and at the end of the first season, after paying her speakers, she faced a deficit of $1,000. This troubled her greatly but the Antislavery Society, recognizing her value, wrote her, "We cheerfully pay your expenses and want to keep you at the head of the work." They took note of her "business enterprise, practical sagacity, and platform ability," and looked upon the expenditure of $1,000 for the education and development of such an exceptional worker as a good investment.

This new experience was a good investment for Susan as well. She made many new friends. She won the further respect, confidence, and good will of men like William Lloyd Garrison, Wendell Phillips, and Francis Jackson. Her friendship with Parker Pillsbury deepened. "I can truly say," she wrote Abby Kelley Foster, "my spirit has grown in grace and that the experience of the past winter is worth more to me than all my Temperance and Woman's Rights labors—though the latter were the school necessary to bring me into the Antislavery work."[76]

Only the crusading spirit of the "antislavery apostles"[77] and what to them seemed the desperate state of the nation made the hard campaigning bearable. The animosity they faced, the cold, the poor transportation, the long hours, and wretched food taxed the physical endurance of all of them. "O the crimes that are committed in the kitchens of this land!"[78] wrote Susan in her diary, as she ate heavy bread and the cake ruined with soda and drank what passed for coffee. A good cook herself, she had little patience with those who through ignorance or carelessness neglected that art. Equally bad were the food fads they had to endure when they were entertained in homes of otherwise hospitable friends of the cause. Raw-food diets found many devotees in those days, and often after long cold rides in the stagecoach, these tired hungry antislavery workers were obliged to sit down to a supper of apples, nuts, and a baked mixture of coarse bran and water. Nor did breakfast or dinner offer anything more. Facing these diets seemed harder for the men than for Susan. Repeatedly in such situations, they hurried away, leaving her to complete two-or three-day engagements among the food cranks. How she welcomed a good beefsteak and a pot of hot coffee at home after these long days of fasting!

A night at home now was sheer bliss, and she wrote Lucy Stone, "Here I am once more in my own Farm Home, where my weary head rests upon my own home pillows.... I had been gone Four Months, scarcely sleeping the second night under the same roof."[79]

It was good to be with her mother again, to talk with her father when he came home from work and with Mary who had not married after all but continued teaching in the Rochester schools. Guelma and her husband, Aaron McLean, who had moved to Rochester, often came out to the farm with their children.

Turning for relaxation to work in the garden in the warm sun, Susan thought over the year's experience and planned for the future. "I can but acknowledge to myself that Antislavery has made me richer and braver in spirit," she wrote Samuel May, Jr., "and that it is the school of schools for the true and full development of the nobler elements of life. I find my raspberry field looking finely—also my strawberry bed. The prospect for peaches, cherries, plums, apples, and pears is very promising—Indeed all nature is clothed in her most hopeful dress. It really seems to me that the trees and the grass and the large fields of waving grain did never look so beautifully as now. It is more probable, however, that my soul has grown to appreciate Nature more fully...."[80]

Susan needed that growth of soul to face the events of the next few years and do the work which lay ahead. The whole country was tense over the slavery issue, which could no longer be pushed into the background. On public platforms and at every fireside, men and women were discussing the subject. Antislavery workers sensed the gravity of the situation and felt the onrush of the impending conflict between what they regarded as the forces of good and evil—freedom and slavery. When the Republican leader, William H. Seward, spoke in Rochester, of "an irrepressible conflict between opposing and enduring forces,"[81] he was expressing only what Garrisonian abolitionists, like Susan, always had recognized. In the West, a tall awkward country lawyer, Abraham Lincoln, debating with the suave Stephen A. Douglas, declared with prophetic wisdom, "'A house divided against itself cannot stand.' I believe this government cannot endure permanently half slave and half free.... It will become all one thing or all the other.'"[82]

So Susan believed, and she was doing her best to make it all free. Not only was she holding antislavery meetings, making speeches, and distributing leaflets whenever and wherever possible, but she was also lobbying in Albany for a personal liberty bill to protect the slaves who were escaping from the South. "Treason in the Capitol," the Democratic press labeled efforts for a personal liberty bill, and as Susan reported to William Lloyd Garrison,[83] even Republicans shied away from it, many of them regarding Seward's "irrepressible conflict" speech a sorry mistake. Such timidity and shilly-shallying were repugnant to her. She could better understand the fervor of John Brown although he fought with bullets.

Yet John Brown's fervor soon ended in tragedy, sowing seeds of fear, distrust, and bitter partisanship in all parts of the country. When, in October 1859, the startling news reached Susan of the raid on Harper's Ferry and the capture of John Brown, she sadly tried to piece together the story of his failure. She admired and respected John Brown, believing he had saved Kansas for freedom. That he had further ambitious plans was common knowledge among antislavery workers, for he had talked them over with Gerrit Smith, Frederick Douglass, and the three young militants, Thomas Wentworth Higginson, Frank Sanborn, and Samuel Gridley Howe. Somehow these plans had failed, but she was sure that his motives were good. He was imprisoned, accused of treason and murder, and in his carpetbag were papers which, it was said, implicated prominent antislavery workers. Now his friends were fleeing the country, Sanborn, Douglass, and Howe. Gerrit Smith broke down so completely that for a time his mind was affected. Thomas Wentworth

Higginson, defiant and unafraid, stuck by John Brown to the end, befriending his family, hoping to rescue him as he had rescued fugitive slaves.

Scanning the Liberator for its comment on John Brown, Susan found it colored, as she had expected, by Garrison's instinctive opposition to all war and bloodshed. He called the raid "a misguided, wild, apparently insane though disinterested and well-intentioned effort by insurrection to emancipate the slaves of Virginia," but even he added, "Let no one who glories in the Revolutionary struggle of 1776 deny the right of the slaves to imitate the example of our fathers."[84]

Behind closed doors and in public meetings, abolitionists pledged their allegiance to John Brown's noble purpose. He had wanted no bloodshed, they said, had no thought of stirring up slaves to brutal revenge. The raid was to be merely a signal for slaves to arise, to cast off slavery forever, to follow him to a mountain refuge, which other slave insurrections would reinforce until all slaves were free. To him the plan seemed logical and he was convinced it was God-inspired. To some of his friends it seemed possible—just a step beyond the Underground Railroad and hiding fugitive slaves. To Susan he was a hero and a martyr.

Southerners, increasingly fearful of slave insurrections, called John Brown a cold-blooded murderer and accused Republicans—"black Republicans," they classed them—of taking orders from abolitionists and planning evil against them. To law-abiding northerners, John Brown was a menace, stirring up lawlessness. Seward and Lincoln, speaking for the Republicans, declared that violence, bloodshed, and treason could not be excused even if slavery was wrong and Brown thought he was right. All saw before them the horrible threat of civil war.

During John Brown's trial, his friends did their utmost to save him. The noble old giant with flowing white beard, who had always been more or less of a legend, now to them assumed heroic proportions. His calmness, his steadfastness in what he believed to be right captured the imagination.

The jury declared him guilty—guilty of treason, of conspiring with slaves to rebel, guilty of murder in the first degree. The papers carried the story, and it spread by word of mouth—the story of those last tense moments in the courtroom when John Brown declared, "It is unjust that I should suffer such a penalty. Had I interferred ... in behalf of the rich, the powerful, the intelligent, the so-called great, or in behalf of any of their friends ... it would have been all right.... I say I am yet too young to understand that God is any respecter of persons. I believe that to have interferred as I have done, in behalf of His despised poor, I did no wrong but right. Now if it is deemed necessary that I should forfeit my life for the furtherance of the ends of justice and mingle my blood further with the blood of my children and with the blood of millions in this slave country whose rights are disregarded by wicked, cruel, and unjust enactments, I say, let it be done...."[85]

He was sentenced to die.

Susan, sick at heart, talked all this over with her abolitionist friends and began planning a meeting of protest and mourning in Rochester if John Brown were hanged. She engaged the city's most popular hall for this meeting, never thinking of the animosity she might arouse, and as she went from door to door selling tickets, she asked for contributions for John Brown's destitute family. She tried to get speakers from among respected Republicans to widen the popular appeal of the meeting, but her diary records, "Not one man of prominence in religion or politics will identify himself with the John Brown meeting."[86] Only a Free Church minister, the Rev. Abram Pryn, and the ever-faithful Parker Pillsbury were willing to speak.

There was still hope that John Brown might be saved and excitement ran high. Some like Higginson, unwilling to let him die, wanted to rescue him, but Brown forbade it. Others wanted to kidnap Governor Wise of Virginia and hold him on the high seas, a hostage for John Brown. Wendell Phillips was one of these. Parker Pillsbury, sending Susan the latest news from "the seat of war" and signing his letter, "Faithfully and fervently yours," wrote, "My voice is against any attempt at rescue. It would inevitably, I fear, lead to bloodshed which could not compensate nor be compensated. If the people dare murder their victim, as they are determined to do, and in the name of the law ... the moral effect of the execution will be without a parallel since the scenes on Calvary eighteen hundred years ago, and the halter that day sanctified shall be the cord to draw millions to salvation."[87]

On Friday, December 2, 1859, John Brown was hanged. Through the North, church bells tolled and prayers were said for him. Everywhere people gathered together to mourn and honor or to condemn. In New York City, at a big meeting which overflowed to the streets, it was resolved "that we regard the recent outrage at Harper's Ferry as a crime, not only against the State of Virginia, but against the Union itself...." In Boston, however, Ralph Waldo Emerson spoke to a tremendous audience of "the new saint, than whom none purer or more brave was ever led by love of man into conflict and death ... who will make the gallows glorious," and Henry Wadsworth Longfellow recorded in his diary, "This will be a great day in our history; the date of a new revolution." Far away in France, Victor Hugo declared, "The eyes of Europe are fixed on America. The hanging of John Brown will open a latent fissure that will finally split the union asunder.... You preserve your shame, but you kill your glory."[88]

In Rochester, three hundred people assembled. All were friends of the cause and there was no unfriendly disturbance to mar the proceedings. Susan presided and Parker Pillsbury, in her opinion, made "the grandest speech of his life," for it was the only occasion he ever found fully wicked enough to warrant "his terrific invective."[89]

Thus these two militant abolitionists, Susan B. Anthony and Parker Pillsbury, joined hundreds of others throughout the nation in honoring John Brown, sensing the portent of his martyrdom and prophesying that his soul would go marching on.

The True Woman

Susan's preoccupation with antislavery work did not lessen her interest in women's advancement. Her own expanding courage and ability showed her the possibilities for all women in widened horizons and activities. These possibilities were the chief topic of conversation when she and Elizabeth Stanton were together. With Mrs. Stanton's young daughters, Margaret and Harriot, in mind, they were continually planning ways and means of developing the new woman, or the "true woman" as they liked to call her; and one of these ways was physical exercise in the fresh air, which was almost unheard of for women except on the frontier.

Taking off her hoops and working in the garden in the freedom of her long calico dress, Susan was refreshed and exhilarated. "Uncovered the strawberry and raspberry beds ..." her diary records. "Worked with Simon building frames for the grapevines in the peach orchards.... Set out 18 English black currants, 22 English gooseberries and Muscatine grape vines.... Finished setting out the apple trees & 600 blackberry bushes...."[90]

She knew how little this strengthening work and healing influence touched the lives of most women. Hemmed in by the walls of their homes, weighed down by bulky confining clothing, fed on the tradition of weakness, women could never gain the breadth of view, courage, and stamina needed to demand and appreciate emancipation. She thought a great deal about this and how it could be remedied, and wrote her friend, Thomas Wentworth Higginson "The salvation of the race depends, in a great measure, upon rescuing women from their hot-house existence. Whether in kitchen, nursery or parlor, all alike are shut away from God's sunshine. Why did not your Caroline Plummer of Salem, why do not all of our wealthy women leave money for industrial and agricultural schools for girls, instead of ever and always providing for boys alone?"[91]

An exceptional opportunity was now offered Susan—to speak on the controversial subject of coeducation before the State Teachers' Association, which only a few years before had been shocked by the sound of a woman's voice. Deeply concerned over her ability to write the speech, she at once appealed to Elizabeth Stanton, "Do you please mark out a plan and give me as soon as you can...."[92]

Susan B. Anthony, 1856

Busy with preparations for woman's rights meetings in popular New York summer resorts, Saratoga Springs, Lake George, Clifton Springs, and Avon, she grew panicky at the prospect of her impending speech and dashed off another urgent letter to Mrs. Stanton, underlining it vigorously for emphasis: "Not a word written ... and mercy only knows when I can get a moment, and what is worse, as the Lord knows full well, is, that if I get all the time the world has—I can't get up a decent document.... It is of but small moment who writes the Address, but of vast moment that it be well done.... No woman but you can write from my standpoint for all would base their strongest argument on the unlikeness of the sexes....

"Those of you who have the talent to do honor to poor, oh how poor womanhood have all given yourselves over to baby-making and left poor brainless me to battle alone. It is a shame. Such a lady as I might be spared to rock cradles, but it is a crime for you and Lucy and Nette."[93]

On a separate page she outlined for Mrs. Stanton the points she wanted to make. Her title was affirmative, "Why the Sexes Should be Educated Together." "Because," she reasoned, "by such education they get true ideas of each other.... Because the endowment of both public and private funds is ever for those of the male sex, while all the Seminaries and Boarding Schools for Females are left to maintain themselves as best they may by means of their tuition fees— consequently cannot afford a faculty of first-class professors.... Not a school in the country gives to the girl equal privileges with the boy.... No school requires and but very few allow the girls to declaim and discuss side by side with the boys. Thus they are robbed of half of education. The grand thing that is needed is to give the sexes like motives for acquirement. Very rarely a person studies closely, without hope of making that knowledge useful, as a means of support...."[94]

Mrs. Stanton wrote her at once, "Come here and I will do what I can to help you with your address, if you will hold the baby and make the puddings."[95] Gratefully Susan hurried to Seneca Falls and together they "loaded her gun," not only for the teachers' convention but for all the summer meetings.

Addressing the large teachers' meeting in Troy, Susan declared that mental sex-differences did not exist. She called attention to the ever-increasing variety of occupations which women were carrying on with efficiency. There were women typesetters, editors, publishers, authors, clerks, engravers, watchmakers, bookkeepers, sculptors, painters, farmers, and machinists. Two hundred and fifty women were serving as postmasters. Girls, she insisted, must be educated to earn a living and more vocations must be opened to them as an incentive to study. "A woman," she added, "needs no particular kind of education to be a wife and mother anymore than a man does to be a husband and father. A man cannot make a living out of these relations. He must fill them with something more and so must women."[96]

Her advanced ideas did not cause as much consternation as she had expected and she was asked to repeat her speech at the Massachusetts teachers' convention; but the thoughts of many in that audience were echoed by the president when he said to her after the meeting, "Madam, that was a splendid production and well delivered. I could not have asked for a single thing different either in matter or manner; but I would rather have followed my wife or daughter to Greenwood cemetery than to have had her stand here before this promiscuous audience and deliver that address."[97]

It was one thing to talk about coeducation but quite another to offer a resolution putting the New York State Teachers' Association on record as asking all schools, colleges, and universities to open their doors to women. This Susan did at their next convention, and while there were enough women present to carry the resolution, most of them voted against it, listening instead to the emotional arguments of a group of conservative men who prophesied that coeducation would coarsen women and undermine marriage. Nor did she forget the Negro at these conventions, but brought much criticism upon herself by offering resolutions protesting the exclusion of Negroes from public schools, academies, colleges, and universities.

Such controversial activities were of course eagerly reported in the press, and Henry Stanton, reading his newspaper, pointed them out to his wife, remarking drily, "Well, my dear, another notice of Susan. You stir up Susan and she stirs up the world."[98]

The best method of arousing women and spreading new ideas, Susan decided, was holding woman's rights conventions, for the discussions at these conventions covered a wide field and were not limited merely to women's legal disabilities. The feminists of that day extolled freedom of speech, and their platform, like that of antislavery conventions, was open to anyone who wished to express an opinion. Always the limited educational opportunities offered to women were pointed out, and Oberlin College and Antioch, both coeducational, were held up as patterns for the future. Resolutions were passed, demanding that Harvard and Yale admit women. Women's low wages and the very few occupations open to them were considered, and whether it was fitting for women to be doctors and ministers. At one convention Lucy Stone made the suggestion that a prize be offered for a novel on women, like Uncle Tom's Cabin, to arouse the whole nation to the unjust situation of women whose slavery, she felt, was comparable to that of the Negro. At another, William Lloyd Garrison maintained that women had the right to sit in the Congress and in state legislatures and that there should be an equal number of men and women in all national councils. Inevitably Scriptural edicts regarding woman's sphere were thrashed out with Antoinette Brown, in her clerical capacity, setting at rest the minds of questioning women and quashing the protests of clergymen who thought they were speaking for God. Usually Ernestine Rose was on hand, ready to speak when needed, injecting into the discussions her liberal clear-cut feminist views. Nor was the international aspect of the woman's rights movement forgotten. The interest in Great Britain in the franchise for women of such men as Lord Brougham and John Stuart Mill was reported as were the efforts there among women to gain admission to the medical profession. Distributed widely as a tract was the "admirable" article in the Westminster Review, "The Enfranchisement of Women," by Harriet Taylor, now Mrs. John Stuart Mill.

In New York, Massachusetts, Pennsylvania, Ohio, and Indiana, where state conventions were held annually, women carried back to their homes and their friends new and stimulating ideas. National conventions, which actually represented merely the northeastern states and Ohio and occasionally attracted men and women from Indiana, Missouri, and Kansas, were scheduled by Susan to meet every year in New York, simultaneously with antislavery conventions. Thus she was assured of a brilliant array of speakers, for the Garrisonian abolitionists were sincere advocates of woman's rights.

Both Elizabeth Stanton and Lucy Stone were a great help to Susan in preparing for these national gatherings for which she raised the money. Elizabeth wrote the calls and resolutions, while Lucy could not only be counted upon for an eloquent speech, but through her wide contacts brought new speakers and new converts to the meetings. However, national woman's rights conventions would probably have lapsed completely during the troubled years prior to the Civil War, had it not been for Susan's persistence. She was obliged to omit the 1857 convention because all of her best speakers were either having babies or were kept at home by family duties. Lucy's baby, Alice Stone Blackwell, was born in September 1857, then Antoinette Brown's first child, and Mrs. Stanton's seventh.

Lucy Stone and her daughter, Alice Stone Blackwell

Impatient to get on with the work, Susan chafed at the delay and when Lucy wrote her, "I shall not assume the responsibility for another convention until I have had my ten daughters,"[99] Susan was beside herself with apprehension. When Lucy told her that it was harder to take care of a baby day and night than to campaign for woman's rights, she felt that Lucy regarded as unimportant her "common work" of hiring halls, engaging speakers, and raising money. This rankled, for although Susan realized it was work without glory, she did expect Lucy to understand its significance.

Mrs. Stanton sensed the makings of a rift between Susan and these young mothers, Lucy and Antoinette, and knowing from her own experience how torn a woman could be between rearing a family and work for the cause, she pleaded with Susan to be patient with them. "Let them rest a while in peace and quietness, and think great thoughts for the future," she wrote Susan. "It is not well to be in the excitement of public life all the time. Do not keep stirring them up or mourning over their repose. You need rest too. Let the world alone a while. We cannot bring about a moral revolution in a day or a year."[100]

But Susan could not let the world alone. There was too much to be done. In addition to her woman's rights and antislavery work, she gave a helping hand to any good cause in Rochester, such as a protest meeting against capital punishment, a series of Sunday evening lectures, or establishing a Free Church like that headed by Theodore Parker in Boston where no one doctrine would be preached and all would be welcome. There were days when weariness and discouragement hung heavily upon her. Then impatient that she alone seemed to be carrying the burden of the whole woman's rights movement, she complained to Lydia Mott, "There is not one woman left who may be relied on. All have first to please their husbands after which there is little time or energy left to spend in any other direction.... How soon the last standing monuments (yourself and myself, Lydia) will lay down the individual 'shovel and de hoe' and with proper zeal and spirit grasp those of some masculine hand, the mercies and the spirits only know. I declare to you that I distrust the powers of any woman, even of myself to withstand the mighty matrimonial maelstrom!"[101]

To Elizabeth Stanton she confessed, "I have very weak moments and long to lay my weary head somewhere and nestle my full soul to that of another in full sympathy. I sometimes fear that I too shall faint by the wayside and drop out of the ranks of the faithful few."[102]

Susan thought a great deal about marriage at this time, about how it interfered with the development of women's talents and their careers, how it usually dwarfed their individuality. Nor were these thoughts wholly impersonal, for she had attentive suitors during these years. Her diary mentions moonlight rides and adds, "Mr.—walked home with me; marvelously attentive. What a pity such powers of intellect should lack the moral spine."[103] Her standards of matrimony were high, and she carefully recorded in her diary Lucretia Mott's wise words, "In the true marriage relation, the independence of the husband and wife is equal, their dependence mutual, and their obligations reciprocal."[104]

Marriage and the differences of the sexes were often discussed at the many meetings she attended, and when remarks were made which to her seemed to limit in any way the free and full development of woman, she always registered her protest. She had no patience with any unrealistic glossing over of sex attraction and spurned the theory that woman expressed love and man wisdom, that these two qualities reached out for each other and blended in marriage. Because she spoke frankly for those days and did not soften the impact of her words with sentimental flowery phrases, her remarks were sometimes called "coarse" and "animal," but she justified them in a letter to Mrs. Stanton, who thought as she did, "To me it [sex] is not coarse or gross. If it is a fact, there it is."[105]

She was reading at this time Elizabeth Barrett Browning's Aurora Leigh, called by Ruskin the greatest poem in the English language, but criticized by others as an indecent romance revolting to the purity of many women. Susan had bought a copy of the first American edition and she carried it with her wherever she went. After a hard active day, she found inspiration and refreshment in its pages. No matter how dreary the hotel room or how unfriendly the town, she no longer felt lonely or discouraged, for Aurora Leigh was a companion ever at hand, giving her confidence in herself, strengthening her ambition, and helping her build a satisfying, constructive philosophy of life. On the flyleaf of her worn copy, which in later years she presented to the Library of Congress, she wrote, "This book was carried in my satchel for years and read and reread. The noble words of Elizabeth Barrett, as Wendell Phillips always called her, sunk deep into my heart. I have always cherished it above all other books. I now present it to the Congressional Library with the hope that women may more and more be like Aurora Leigh."

The beauty of its poetry enchanted her, and Elizabeth Barrett Browning's feminism found an echo in her own. She pencil-marked the passages she wanted to reread. When her "common work" of hiring halls and engaging speakers seemed unimportant and even futile, she found comfort in these lines:

"Be sure no earnest work
Of any honest creature, howbeit weak
Imperfect, ill-adapted, fails so much,
It is not gathered as a grain of sand
To enlarge the sum of human action used
For carrying out God's end....
... let us be content in work,
To do the thing we can, and not presume
To fret because it's little."[106]
Glorying in work, she read with satisfaction:
"The honest earnest man must stand and work:
The woman also, otherwise she drops
At once below the dignity of man,
Accepting serfdom. Free men freely work;
Who ever fears God, fears to sit at ease."

Could she have written poetry, these words, spoken by Aurora, might well have been her own:

"You misconceive the question like a man,
Who sees a woman as the complement
Of his sex merely. You forget too much
That every creature, female as the male,
Stands single in responsible act and thought,
As also in birth and death. Whoever says
To a loyal woman, 'Love and work with me,'
Will get fair answers, if the work and love
Being good of themselves, are good for her—the best
She was born for."

Inspired by Aurora Leigh, Susan planned a new lecture, "The True Woman," and as she wrote it out word for word, her thoughts and theories about women, which had been developing through the years, crystallized. In her opinion, the "true woman" could no more than Aurora Leigh follow the traditional course and sacrifice all for the love of one man, adjusting her life to his whims. She must, instead, develop her own personality and talents, advancing in learning, in the arts, in science, and in business, cherishing at the same time her noble womanly qualities. Susan hoped that some day the full development of woman's individuality would be compatible with marriage, and she held up as an ideal the words which Elizabeth Barrett Browning put into the mouth of Aurora Leigh:

"The world waits
For help. Beloved, let us work so well,
Our work shall still be better for our love
And still our love be sweeter for our work
And both, commended, for the sake of each,
By all true workers and true lovers born."

She expressed this hope in her own practical words to Lydia Mott: "Institutions, among them marriage, are justly chargeable with many social and individual ills, but after all, the whole man or woman will rise above them. I am sure my 'true woman' will never be crushed or dwarfed by them. Woman must take to her soul a purpose and then make circumstances conform to this purpose, instead of forever singing the refrain, 'if and if and if.'"[107]

Late in 1858, Susan received a letter from Wendell Phillips which put new life into all her efforts for women. He wrote her that an anonymous donor had given him $5,000 for the woman's rights cause and that he, Lucy Stone, and Susan had been named trustees to spend it wisely and effectively.

The man who felt that the woman's rights cause was important enough to rate a gift of that size proved to be wealthy Francis Jackson of Boston, in whose home Susan had visited a few years before with Lucy and Antoinette. Jubilant over the prospects, she at once began to make plans. She wanted to use all of the fund for lectures, conventions, tracts, and newspaper articles; Lucy thought part of the money should be spent to prove unconstitutional the law which taxed women without representation and Antoinette was eager for a share to establish a church in which she could preach woman's rights with the Gospel.

Both Wendell Phillips and Lucy Stone agreed that Susan should have $1,500 for the intensive campaign she had planned for New York, and for once in her life she started off without a financial worry, with money in hand to pay her speakers. She held meetings in all of the principal towns of the state, making them at least partially pay for themselves. Her lecturers each received $12 a week and she kept a like amount for herself, for planning the tour, organizing the meetings, and delivering her new lecture, "The True Woman."

"I am having fine audiences of thinking men and women," she wrote Mary Hallowell. "Oh, if we could but make our meetings ring like those of the antislavery people, wouldn't the world hear us? But to do that we must have souls baptized into the work and consecrated to it."[108]

Some souls were deeply stirred by the woman's rights gospel. One of these was the wealthy Boston merchant, Charles F. Hovey, who in his will left $50,000 in trust to Wendell Phillips, William Lloyd Garrison, Parker Pillsbury, Abby Kelley Foster, and others, to be spent for the "promotion of the antislavery cause and other reforms," among them woman's rights, and not less than $8,000 a year to be spent to promote these reforms. With all this financial help available, Susan expected great things to happen.

During the winter of 1860 while the legislature was in session, Susan spent six weeks in Albany with Lydia Mott, and day after day she climbed the long hill to the capitol to interview legislators on amendments to the married women's property laws. When these amendments were passed by the Senate, Assemblyman Anson Bingham urged her to bring their mutual friend, Elizabeth Cady Stanton, to Albany to speak before his committee to assure passage by the Assembly.

Once again Susan hurried to Seneca Falls, and unpacking her little portmanteau stuffed with papers and statistics, discussed the subject with Mrs. Stanton in front of the open fire late into the night. Then the next morning while Mrs. Stanton shut herself up in the quietest room in the house to write her speech, Susan gave the children their breakfast, sent the older ones off to school, watched over the babies, prepared the desserts, and made herself generally useful. By this time the children regarded her affectionately as "Aunt Thusan," and they knew they must obey her, for she was a stern disciplinarian whom even the mischievous Stanton boys dared not defy.

These visits of Susan's were happy, satisfying times for both these young women. A few days' respite from travel in a well-run home with a friend she admired did wonders for Susan, giving her perspective on the work she had already done and courage to tackle new problems, while for Mrs. Stanton this short period of stimulating companionship and freedom from household cares was a godsend. "Miss Anthony" had long ago become Susan to Elizabeth, but Susan all through her life called her very best friend "Mrs. Stanton," playfully to be sure, but with a remnant of that formality which it was hard for her to cast off.

The speech was soon finished. Mrs. Stanton's imagination, fired by her sympathetic understanding of women's problems, had turned Susan's cold hard facts into moving prose, while Susan, the best of critics, detected every weak argument or faltering phrase. They both felt they had achieved a masterpiece.

Mrs. Stanton delivered this address before a joint session of the New York legislature in March 1860. Susan beamed with pride as she watched the large audience crowd even the galleries and heard the long loud applause for the speech which she was convinced could not have been surpassed by any man in the United States.

The next day the Assembly passed the Married Women's Property Bill, and when shortly it was signed by the governor, Susan and Mrs. Stanton scored their first big victory, winning a legal revolution for the women of New York State. This new law was a challenge to women everywhere. Under it a married woman had the right to hold property, real and personal, without the interference of her husband, the right to carry on any trade or perform any service on her own account and to collect and use her own earnings; a married woman might now buy, sell, and make contracts, and if her husband had abandoned her or was insane, a convict, or a habitual drunkard, his consent was unnecessary; a married woman might sue and be sued, she was the joint guardian with her husband of her children, and on the decease of her husband the wife had the same rights that her husband would have at her death.

Susan did not then realize the full significance of what she had accomplished—that she had unleashed a new movement for freedom which would be the means of strengthening the democratic government of her country.

The Zealot

With a spirit of confidence inspired by her victory in New York State, Susan looked forward to the tenth national woman's rights convention in New York City in May 1860. At this convention she reported progress everywhere. Four thousand dollars from the Jackson and Hovey funds had been spent in the successful New York campaign, and similar work was scheduled for Ohio. In Kansas, women had won from the constitutional convention equal rights and privileges in state-controlled schools and in the management of the public schools, including the right to vote for members of school boards; mothers had been granted equal rights with fathers in the control and custody of their children, and married women had been given property rights. In Indiana, Maine, Missouri, and Ohio, married women could now control their own earnings.

"Each year we hail with pleasure," she continued, "new accessions to our faith. Brave men and true from the higher walks of literature and art, from the bar, the bench, the pulpit, and legislative halls are now ready to help woman wherever she claims to stand." She was thinking of the aid given her by Andrew J. Colvin and Anson Bingham of the New York legislature, of the young journalist, George William Curtis, just recently speaking for women, of Samuel Longfellow at his first woman's rights convention, and of the popular Henry Ward Beecher who, just a few months before, had delivered his great woman's rights speech, thereby identifying himself irrevocably with the cause. She announced with great satisfaction the news, which the papers had carried a few days before, that Matthew Vassar of Poughkeepsie had set aside $400,000 to found a college for women equal in all respects to Harvard and Yale.[109] Progress and good feeling were in the air, and the speakers were not heckled as in past years by the rowdies who had made it a practice to follow abolitionists into woman's rights meetings to bait them. Into this atmosphere of good will and rejoicing, Susan and Elizabeth Stanton now injected a more serious note, bringing before the convention the controversial question of marriage and divorce which heretofore had been handled with kid gloves at all woman's rights meetings, but which they sincerely believed demanded solution.

Divorce had been much in the news because several leading families in America and in England were involved in lawsuits complicated by stringent divorce laws. Invariably the wife bore the burden of censure and hardship, for no matter how unprincipled her husband might be, he was entitled to her children and her earnings under the property laws of most states.

In New York efforts were now being made to gain support for a liberal divorce bill, patterned after the Indiana law, and a variety of proposals were before the legislature, making drunkenness, insanity, desertion, and cruel and abusive treatment grounds for divorce. Horace Greeley in his Tribune had been vigorously opposing a more liberal law for New York, while Robert Dale Owen of Indiana wrote in its defense. Everywhere people were reading the Greeley-Owen debates in the Tribune. Through his widely circulated paper, Horace Greeley had in a sense become an oracle for the people who felt he was safe and good; while Robert Dale Owen, because of his youthful association with the New Harmony community and Frances Wright, was branded with radicalism which even his valuable service in the Indiana legislature and his two terms in Congress could not blot out.

Susan and Mrs. Stanton had no patience with Horace Greeley's smug old-fashioned opinions on marriage and divorce. In fact these Greeley-Owen debates in the Tribune were the direct cause of their decision to bring this subject before the convention, where they hoped for support from their liberal friends. They counted especially on Lucy Stone, who seemed to give her approval when she wrote, "I am glad you will speak on the divorce question, provided you yourself are clear on the subject. It is a great grave topic that one shudders to grapple, but its hour is coming.... God touch your lips if you speak on it."[110]

Neither Susan nor Mrs. Stanton shuddered to grapple with any subject which they believed needed attention. In fact, the discussion of marriage and divorce in woman's rights conventions had been on their minds for some time. Three years before Susan had written Lucy, "I have thought with you until of late that the Social Question must be kept separate from Woman's Rights, but we have always claimed that our movement was Human Rights, not Woman's specially.... It seems to me we have played on the surface of things quite long enough. Getting the right to hold property, to vote, to wear what dress we please, etc., are all to the good, but Social Freedom, after all, lies at the bottom of all, and unless woman gets that she must continue the slave of man in all other things."[111]

Consternation spread through the genial ranks of the convention as Mrs. Stanton now offered resolutions calling for more liberal divorce laws. Quick to sense the temper of an audience, Susan felt its resistance to being jolted out of the pleasant contemplation of past successes to the unpleasant recognition that there were still difficult ugly problems ahead. She was conscious at once of a stir of astonishment and disapproval when Mrs. Stanton in her clear compelling voice read, "Resolved, That an unfortunate or ill-assorted marriage is ever a calamity, but not ever, perhaps never a crime—and when society or government, by its laws or customs, compels its continuance, always to the grief of one of the parties, and the actual loss and damage of both, it usurps an authority never delegated to man, nor exercised by God, Himself...."[112]

Listening to Mrs. Stanton's speech in defense of her ten bold resolutions on marriage and divorce, Susan felt that her brave colleague was speaking for women everywhere, for wives of the present and the future. As the hearty applause rang out, she concluded that even the disapproving admired her courage; but before the applause ceased, she saw Antoinette Blackwell on her feet, waiting to be heard. She knew that Antoinette, like Horace Greeley, preferred to think of all marriages as made in heaven, and true to form Antoinette contended that the marriage relation "must be lifelong" and "as permanent and indissoluble as the relation of parent and child."[113] At once Ernestine Rose came to the rescue in support of Mrs. Stanton.

Then Wendell Phillips showed his displeasure by moving that Mrs. Stanton's resolutions be laid on the table and expunged from the record because they had no more to do with this convention than slavery in Kansas or temperance. "This convention," he asserted, "as I understand it, assembles to discuss the laws that rest unequally upon men and women, not those that rest equally on men and women."[114]

Aghast at this statement, Susan was totally unprepared to have his views supported by that other champion of liberty, William Lloyd Garrison, who, however, did not favor expunging the resolutions from the record.

It was incomprehensible to Susan that neither Garrison nor Phillips recognized woman's subservient status in marriage under prevailing laws and traditions, and she now stated her own views with firmness: "As to the point that this question does not belong to this platform—from that I totally dissent. Marriage has ever been a one-sided matter, resting most unequally upon the sexes. By it, man gains all—woman loses all; tyrant law and lust reign supreme with him—meek submission and ready obedience alone befit her."[115]

Warming to the subject, she continued, "By law, public sentiment, and religion from the time of Moses down to the present day, woman has never been thought of other than as a piece of property, to be disposed of at the will and pleasure of man. And this very hour, by our statute books, by our so-called enlightened Christian civilization, she has no voice in saying what shall be the basis of the relation. She must accept marriage as man proffers it or not at all...." When finally the vote was taken, Mrs. Stanton's resolutions were laid on the table, but not expunged from the record, and the convention adjourned with much to talk about and think about for some time to come.

The newspapers, of course, could not overlook such a piece of news as this heated argument on divorce in a woman's rights convention, and fanned the flames pro and con, most of them holding up Miss Anthony and Mrs. Stanton as dangerous examples of freedom for women. The Rev. A. D. Mayo, Unitarian clergyman of Albany, heretofore Susan's loyal champion, now made a point of reproving her. "You are not married," he declared with withering scorn. "You have no business to be discussing marriage." To this she retorted, "Well, Mr. Mayo, you are not a slave. Suppose you quit lecturing on slavery."[116]

Both Susan and Mrs. Stanton, amazed at the opposition and the disapproval they had aroused, were grateful for Samuel Longfellow's comforting words of commendation[117] and for the letters of approval which came from women from all parts of the state. Most satisfying of all was this reassurance from Lucretia Mott, whose judgment they so highly valued: "I was rejoiced to have such a defense of the resolutions as yours. I have the fullest confidence in the united judgment of Elizabeth Stanton and Susan Anthony and I am glad they are so vigorous in the work."[118]

Hardest to bear was the disapproval of Wendell Phillips whom they both admired so much. Difficult to understand and most disappointing was Lucy Stone's failure to attend the convention or come to their defense. Thinking over this first unfortunate difference of opinion among the faithful crusaders for freedom to whom she had always felt so close in spirit, Susan was sadly disillusioned, but she had no regrets that the matter had been brought up, and she defied her critics by speaking before a committee of the New York legislature in support of a liberal divorce bill. Nor was she surprised when a group of Boston women, headed by Caroline H. Dall, called a convention which they hoped would counteract this radical outbreak in the woman's rights movement by keeping to the safe subjects of education, vocation, and civil position.

Having learned by this time through the hard school of experience that the bona-fide reformer could not play safe and go forward, Susan thoughtfully commented, "Cautious, careful people, always casting about to preserve their reputation and social standing, never can bring about a reform. Those who are really in earnest must be willing to be anything or nothing in the world's estimation, and publicly and privately, in season and out, avow their sympathy with despised and persecuted ideas and their advocates, and bear the consequences."[119]

The repercussions of the divorce debates were soon drowned out by the noise and excitement of the presidential campaign of 1860. With four candidates in the field, Breckenridge, Bell, Douglas, and Lincoln, each offering his party's solution for the nation's critical problems, there was much to think about and discuss, and Susan found woman's rights pushed into the background. At the same time antagonism toward abolitionists was steadily mounting for they were being blamed for the tensions between the North and the South.

Dedicated to the immediate and unconditional emancipation of slavery, Susan saw no hope in the promises of any political party. Even the Republicans' opposition to the extension of slavery in the territories, which had won over many abolitionists, including Henry and Elizabeth Stanton, seemed to her a mild and ineffectual answer to the burning questions of the hour. For her to further the election of Abraham Lincoln was unthinkable, since he favored the enforcement of the Fugitive Slave Law and had stated he was not in favor of Negro citizenship.

At heart she was a nonvoting Garrisonian abolitionist and would not support a political party which in any way sanctioned slavery. Had she been eligible as a voter she undoubtedly would have refused to cast her ballot until a righteous antislavery government had been established. As she expressed it in a letter to Mrs. Stanton, she could not, if she were a man, vote for "the least of two evils, one of which the Nation must surely have in the presidential chair."[120]

She saw no possibility at this time of wiping out slavery by means of political abolition, because in spite of the fact that slavery had for years been one of the most pressing issues before the American people, no great political party had yet endorsed abolition, nor had a single prominent practical statesman[121] advocated immediate unconditional emancipation. As the Liberty party experiment had proved, an abolitionist running for office on an antislavery platform was doomed to defeat. Therefore the gesture made in this critical campaign by a small group of abolitionists in nominating Gerrit Smith for president appeared utterly futile to Susan. Abolitionists, she believed, followed the only course consistent with their principles when they eschewed politics, abstained from voting, and devoted their energies with the fervor of evangelists to a militant educational campaign.

So, whenever she could, she continued to hold antislavery meetings. "Crowded house at Port Byron," her diary records. "I tried to say a few words at opening, but soon curled up like a sensitive plant. It is a terrible martyrdom for me to speak."[122] Yet so great was the need to enlighten people on the evils of slavery that she endured this martyrdom, stepping into the breach when no other speaker was available. Taking as her subject, "What Is American Slavery?" she declared, "It is the legalized, systematic robbery of the bodies and souls of nearly four millions of men, women, and children. It is the legalized traffic in God's image."[123]

She asked for personal liberty laws to protect the human rights of fugitive slaves, adding that the Dred Scott decision had been possible only because it reflected the spirit and purpose of the American people in the North as well as the South. She heaped blame on the North for restricting the Negro's educational and economic opportunities, for barring him from libraries, lectures, and theaters, and from hotels and seats on trains and buses.

"Let the North," she urged, "prove to the South by her acts that she fully recognizes the humanity of the black man, that she respects his rights in all her educational, industrial, social, and political associations...."

This was asking far more than the North was ready to give, but to Susan it was justice which she must demand. No wonder free Negroes in the North honored and loved her and expressed their gratitude whenever they could. "A fine-looking colored man on the train presented me with a bouquet," she wrote in her diary. "Can't tell whether he knew me or only felt my sympathy."[124]

The threats of secession from the southern states, which followed Lincoln's election, brought little anxiety to Susan or her fellow-abolitionists, for they had long preached, "No Union with Slaveholders," believing that dissolution of the Union would prevent further expansion of slavery in the new western territories, and not only lessen the damaging influence of slavery on northern institutions, but relieve the North of complicity in maintaining slavery. Garrison in his Liberator had already asked, "Will the South be so obliging as to secede from the Union?" When, in December 1860, South Carolina seceded, Horace Greeley, who only a few months before had called the disunion abolitionists "a little coterie of common scolds," now wrote in the Tribune, "If the cotton states shall decide that they can do better out of the Union than in it, we insist in letting them go in peace. The right to secede may be a revolutionary one, but it exists nevertheless."[125]

William Lloyd Garrison

What abolitionists feared far more than secession was that to save the Union some compromise would be made which would fasten slavery on the nation. Susan agreed with Garrison when he declared in the Liberator, "All Union-saving efforts are simply idiotic. At last 'the covenant with death' is annulled, 'the agreement with Hell' broken—at least by the action of South Carolina and ere long by all the slave-holding states, for their doom is one."[126]

Compromise, however, was in the air. The people were appalled and confused by the breaking up of the Union and the possibility of civil war, and the government fumbled. Powerful Republicans, among them Thurlow Weed, speaking for eastern financial interests, favored the Crittenden Compromise which would re-establish the Mason-Dixon line, protect slavery in the states where it was now legal, sanction the domestic slave trade, guarantee payment by the United States for escaped slaves, and forbid Congress to abolish slavery in the District of Columbia without the consent of Virginia and Maryland. Even Seward suggested a constitutional amendment guaranteeing noninterference with slavery in the slave states for all time. In such an atmosphere as this, Susan gloried in Wendell Phillips's impetuous declarations against compromise.

While the whole country marked time, waiting for the inauguration of President Lincoln, abolitionists sent out their speakers, Susan heading a group in western New York which included Samuel J. May, Stephen S. Foster, and Elizabeth Cady Stanton. "All are united," she wrote William Lloyd Garrison, "that good faith and honor demand us to go forward and leave the responsibility of free speech or its suppression with the people of the places we visit." Then showing that she well understood the temper of the times, she added, "I trust ... no personal harm may come to you or Phillips or any of the little band of the true and faithful who shall defend the right...."[127]

Feeling was running high in Buffalo when Susan arrived with her antislavery contingent in January 1861, expecting disturbances but unprepared for the animosity of audiences which hissed, yelled, and stamped so that not a speaker could be heard. The police made no effort to keep order and finally the mob surged over the platform and the lights went out. Nevertheless, Susan who was presiding held her ground until lights were brought in and she could dimly see the milling crowd.

In small towns they were listened to with only occasional catcalls and boos of disapproval, but in every city from Buffalo to Albany the mobs broke up their meetings. Even in Rochester, which had never before shown open hostility to abolitionists, Susan's banner, "No Union with Slaveholders" was torn down and a restless audience hissed her as she opened her meeting and drowned out the speakers with their shouting and stamping until at last the police took over and escorted the speakers home through the jeering crowds.

All but Susan now began to question the wisdom of holding more meetings, but her determination to continue, and to assert the right of free speech, shamed her colleagues into acquiescence. Cayenne pepper, thrown on the stove, broke up their meeting at Port Byron. In Rome, rowdies bore down upon Susan, who was taking the admission fee of ten cents, brushed her aside, "big cloak, furs, and all,"[128] and rushed to the platform where they sang, hooted, and played cards until the speakers gave up in despair. Syracuse, well known for its tolerance and pride in free speech, now greeted them with a howling drunken mob armed with knives and pistols and rotten eggs. Susan on the platform courageously faced their gibes until she and her companions were forced out into the street. They then took refuge in the home of fellow-abolitionists while the mob dragged effigies of Susan and Samuel J. May through the streets and burned them in the square.

Not even this kept Susan from her last advertised meeting in Albany where Lucretia Mott, Martha C. Wright, Gerrit Smith, and Frederick Douglass joined her. Here the Democratic mayor, George H. Thatcher, was determined to uphold free speech in spite of almost overwhelming opposition, and calling at the Delavan House for the abolitionists, safely escorted them to their hall. Then, with a revolver across his knees, he sat on the platform with them while his policemen, scattered through the hall, put down every disturbance; but at the end of the day, he warned Susan that he could no longer hold the mob in check and begged her as a personal favor to him to call off the rest of the meetings. She consented, and under his protection the intrepid little group of abolitionists walked back to their hotel with the mob trailing behind them.

Looking back upon the tense days and nights of this "winter of mobs,"[129] Susan was proud of her group of abolitionists who so bravely had carried out their mission. In comparison, the Republicans had shown up badly, not a Republican mayor having the courage or interest to give them protection. In fact, she found little in the attitude of the Republicans to offer even a glimmer of hope that they were capable of governing in this crisis. Lincoln's inaugural address prejudiced her at once, for he said, "I have no purpose directly or indirectly to interfere with the institution of slavery in the states where it exists. I believe I have no lawful right to do so and I have no inclination to do so."[130] To her the future looked dark when statesmen would save the Union at such a price.

"No Compromise" was Susan's watchword these days, as a feminist as well as an abolitionist, even though this again set her at odds with Garrison and Phillips, the two men she respected above all others. They were now writing her stern letters urging her to reveal the hiding place of a fugitive wife and her daughter. Just before she had started on her antislavery crusade and while she was in Albany with Lydia Mott, a heavily veiled woman with a tragic story had come to them for help. She was the wife of Dr. Charles Abner Phelps, a highly respected member of the Massachusetts Senate, and the mother of three children. She had discovered, she told them, that her husband was unfaithful to her, and when she confronted him with the proof, he had insisted that she suffered from delusions and had her committed to an insane asylum. For a year and a half she had not been allowed to communicate with her children, but finally her brother, a prominent Albany attorney, obtained her release through a writ of habeas corpus, took her to his home, and persuaded Dr. Phelps to allow the children to visit her for a few weeks. Now she was desperate as she again faced the prospect of being separated from her children by Massachusetts law which gave even an unfaithful husband control of his wife's person and their children.

Well aware of how often her friends of the Underground Railroad had defied the Fugitive Slave Law and hidden and transported fugitive slaves, Susan decided she would do the same for this cultured intelligent woman, a slave to her husband under the law. Without a thought of the consequences, she took the train on Christmas Day for New York with Mrs. Phelps and her thirteen-year-old daughter, both in disguise, hoping that in the crowded city they could hide from Dr. Phelps and the law. Arriving late at night, they walked through the snow and slush to a hotel, only to be refused a room because they were not accompanied by a gentleman. They tried another hotel, with the same result, and then Susan, remembering a boarding house run by a divorced woman she knew, hopefully rang her doorbell. She too refused them, claiming all her boarders would leave if she harbored a runaway wife. By this time it was midnight. Cold and exhausted, they braved a Broadway hotel, where they were told there was no vacant room; but Susan, convinced this was only an excuse, said as much to the clerk, adding, "You can give us a place to sleep or we will sit in this office all night." When he threatened to call the police, she retorted, "Very well, we will sit here till they come to take us to the station."[131] Finally he relented and gave them a room without heat. Early the next morning, Susan began making the rounds of her friends in search of shelter for Mrs. Phelps and her daughter, and finally at the end of a discouraging day, Abby Hopper Gibbons, the Quaker who had so often hidden fugitive slaves, took this fugitive wife into her home.

Returning to Albany, Susan found herself under suspicion and threatened with arrest by Dr. Phelps and Mrs. Phelps's brothers, because she had broken the law by depriving a father of his child. Letters and telegrams, demanding that she reveal Mrs. Phelps's hiding place, followed her to Rochester and on her antislavery tour through western New York. Refusing to be intimidated, she ignored them all.

When Garrison wrote her long letters in his small neat hand, begging her not to involve the woman's rights and antislavery movements in any "hasty and ill-judged, no matter how well-meant" action, it was hard for her to reconcile this advice with his impetuous, undiplomatic, and dangerous actions on behalf of Negro slaves. "I feel the strongest assurance," she told him, "that what I have done is wholly right. Had I turned my back upon her I should have scorned myself.... That I should stop to ask if my act would injure the reputation of any movement never crossed my mind, nor will I allow such a fear to stifle my sympathies or tempt me to expose her to the cruel inhuman treatment of her own household. Trust me that as I ignore all law to help the slave, so will I ignore it all to protect an enslaved woman."[132]

When later they met at an antislavery convention, Garrison, renewing his efforts on behalf of Dr. Phelps, put this question to Susan, "Don't you know that the law of Massachusetts gives the father the entire guardianship and control of the children?"

"Yes, I know it," she answered. "Does not the law of the United States give the slaveholder the ownership of the slave? And don't you break it every time you help a slave to Canada? Well, the law which gives the father the sole ownership of the children is just as wicked and I'll break it just as quickly. You would die before you would deliver a slave to his master, and I will die before I will give up that child to its father."

Susan escaped arrest as she thought she would, for Dr. Phelps could not afford the unfavorable publicity involved. He managed to kidnap his child on her way to Sunday School, but his wife eventually won a divorce through the help of her friends.

The most trying part of this experience for Susan was the attitude of Garrison and Phillips, who, had now for the second time failed to recognize that the freedom they claimed for the Negro was also essential for women. They believed in woman's rights, to be sure, but when these rights touched the institution of marriage, their vision was clouded. Just a year before, they had fought Mrs. Stanton's divorce resolutions because they were unable to see that the existing laws of marriage did not apply equally to men and women. Now they sustained the father's absolute right over his child. What was it, Susan wondered, that kept them from understanding? Was it loyalty to sex, was it an unconscious clinging to dominance and superiority, or was it sheer inability to recognize women as human beings like themselves? "Very many abolitionists," she wrote in her diary, "have yet to learn the ABC of woman's rights."[133]

A War For Freedom

Six more southern states, Georgia, Alabama, Florida, Mississippi, Louisiana, and Texas, following the lead of South Carolina, seceded early in 1861 and formed the Confederate States of America. This breaking up of the Union disturbed Susan primarily because it took the minds of most of her colleagues off everything but saving the Union. Convinced that even in a time of national crisis, work for women must go on, she tried to prepare for the annual woman's rights convention in New York, but none of her hitherto dependable friends would help her. Nevertheless, she persisted, even after the fall of Fort Sumter and the President's call for troops. Only when the abolitionists called off their annual New York meetings did she reluctantly realize that woman's rights too must yield to the exigencies of the hour.

Influenced by her Quaker background, she could not see war as the solution of this or any other crisis. In fact, the majority of abolitionists were amazed and bewildered when war came because it was not being waged to free the slaves. Looking to their leaders for guidance, they heard Wendell Phillips declare for war before an audience of over four thousand in Boston. Garrison, known to all as a nonresistant, made it clear that his sympathies were with the government. He saw in "this grand uprising of the manhood of the North"[134] a growing appreciation of liberty and free institutions and a willingness to defend them. Calling upon abolitionists to stand by their principles, he at the same time warned them not to criticize Lincoln or the Republicans unnecessarily, not to divide the North, but to watch events and bide their time, and he opposed those abolitionists who wanted to withhold support of the government until it stood openly and unequivocally for the Negro's freedom. From the front page of the Liberator, he now removed his slogan, "No Union with Slaveholders." Kindly placid Samuel J. May, usually against all violence, now compared the sacrifices of the war to the crucifixion, and to Susan this was blasphemy. Even Parker Pillsbury wrote her, "I am rejoicing over Old Abe, but my voice is still for war."[135]

She was troubled, confused, and disillusioned by the attitude of these men and by that of most of her antislavery friends. Only very few, among them Lydia Mott, were uncompromising non-resistants. To one of them she wrote, "I have tried hard to persuade myself that I alone remained mad, while all the rest had become sane, because I have insisted that it is our duty to bear not only our usual testimony but one even louder and more earnest than ever before.... The Abolitionists, for once, seem to have come to an agreement with all the world that they are out of tune and place, hence should hold their peace and spare their rebukes and anathemas. Our position to me seems most humiliating, simply that of the politicians, one of expediency, not principle. I have not yet seen one good reason for the abandonment of all our meetings, and am more and more ashamed and sad that even the little Apostolic number have yielded to the world's motto—'the end justifies the means.'"[136]

Now the farm home was a refuge. Her father, leaving her in charge, traveled West for his long-dreamed-of visit with his sons in Kansas, with Daniel R., now postmaster at Leavenworth, and with Merritt and his young wife, Mary Luther, in their log cabin at Osawatomie. As a release from her pent-up energy, Susan turned to hard physical work. "Superintended the plowing of the orchard," she recorded in her diary. "The last load of hay is in the barn; and all in capital order.... Washed every window in the house today. Put a quilted petticoat in the frame.... Quilted all day, but sewing seems no longer to be my calling.... Fitted out a fugitive slave for Canada with the help of Harriet Tubman."[137] Although she filled her days, life on the farm in these stirring times seemed futile to her. She missed the stimulating exchange of ideas with fellow-abolitionists and confessed to her diary, "The all-alone feeling will creep over me. It is such a fast after the feast of great presences to which I have been so long accustomed."

The war was much on her mind. Eagerly she read Greeley's Tribune and the Rochester Democrat. The news was discouraging—the tragedy of Bull Run, the call for more troops, defeat after defeat for the Union armies. General Frémont in Missouri freeing the slaves of rebels only to have Lincoln cancel the order to avert antagonizing the border states.

"How not to do it seems the whole study of Washington," she wrote in her diary. "I wish the government would move quickly, proclaim freedom to every slave and call on every able-bodied Negro to enlist in the Union Army.... To forever blot out slavery is the only possible compensation for this merciless war."[138]

To satisfy her longing for a better understanding of people and events, she turned to books, first to Elizabeth Barrett Browning's Casa Guidi Windows, which she called "a grand poem, so fitting to our terrible struggle," then to her Sonnets from the Portuguese, and George Eliot's popular Adam Bede, recently published. More serious reading also absorbed her, for she wanted to keep abreast of the most advanced thought of the day. "Am reading Buckle's History of

Civilization and Darwin's Descent of Man," she wrote in her diary. "Have finished Origin of the Species. Pillsbury has just given me Emerson's poems."[139]

Eager to thrash out all her new ideas with Elizabeth Stanton, she went to Seneca Falls for a few days of good talk, hoping to get Mrs. Stanton's help in organizing a woman's rights convention in 1862; but not even Mrs. Stanton could see the importance of such work at this time, believing that if women put all their efforts into winning the war, they would, without question, be rewarded with full citizenship. Susan was skeptical about this and disappointed that even the best women were so willing to be swept aside by the onrush of events.

Although opposed to war, Susan was far from advocating peace at any price, and was greatly concerned over the confusion in Washington which was vividly described in the discouraging letters Mrs. Stanton received from her husband, now Washington correspondent for the New York Tribune. Both she and Mrs. Stanton chafed at inaction. They had loyalty, intelligence, an understanding of national affairs, and executive ability to offer their country, but such qualities were not sought after among women.

In the spring of 1862, Susan helped Mrs. Stanton move her family to a new home in Brooklyn, and spent a few weeks with her there, getting the feel of the city in wartime. She then had the satisfaction of discovering that at least one woman was of use to her country, young eloquent Anna E. Dickinson.[140] Susan listened with pride and joy while Anna spoke to an enthusiastic audience at Cooper Union on the issues of the war. She took Anna to her heart at once. Anna's youth, her fervor, and her remarkable ability drew out all of Susan's motherly instincts of affection and protectiveness. They became devoted friends, and for the next few years carried on a voluminous correspondence.

Harriet Hosmer and Rosa Bonheur also helped restore Susan's confidence in women during these difficult days when, forced to mark time, she herself seemed at loose ends. Visiting the Academy of Design, she studied "in silent reverential awe," the marble face of Harriet Hosmer's Beatrice Cenci, and declared, "Making that cold marble breathe and pulsate, Harriet Hosmer has done more to ennoble and elevate woman than she could possibly have done by mere words...." Of Rosa Bonheur, the first woman to venture into the field of animal painting, she said, "Her work not only surpasses anything ever done by a woman, but is a bold and successful step beyond all other artists."[141]

This confidence was soon dispelled, however, when a letter came from Lydia Mott containing the crushing news that the New York legislature had amended the newly won Married Woman's Property Law of 1860, while women's attention was focused on the war, and had taken away from mothers the right to equal guardianship of their children and from widows the control of the property left at the death of their husbands.

"We deserve to suffer for our confidence in 'man's sense of justice,'" she confessed to Lydia. " ... All of our reformers seem suddenly to have grown politic. All alike say, 'Have no conventions at this crisis!' Garrison, Phillips, Mrs. Mott, Mrs. Wright, Mrs. Stanton, etc. say, 'Wait until the war excitement abates....' I am sick at heart, but cannot carry the world against the wish and will of our best friends...."[142]

Unable to arouse even a glimmer of interest in woman's rights at this time, Susan started off on a lecture tour of her own, determined to make people understand that this war, so abhorrent to her, must be fought for the Negroes' freedom. "I cannot feel easy in my conscience to be dumb in an hour like this," she explained to Lydia, adding, "It is so easy to feel your power for public work slipping away if you allow yourself to remain too long snuggled in the Abrahamic bosom of home. It requires great will power to resurrect one's soul.[143]

"I am speaking now extempore," she continued, "and more to my satisfaction than ever before. I am amazed at myself, but I could not do it if any of our other speakers were listening to me. I am entirely off old antislavery grounds and on the new ones thrown up by the war."

Feeling particularly close to Lydia at this time, she gratefully added, "What a stay, counsel, and comfort you have been to me, dear Lydia, ever since that eventful little temperance meeting in that cold, smoky chapel in 1852. How you have compelled me to feel myself competent to go forward when trembling with doubt and distrust. I can never express the magnitude of my indebtedness to you."

In the small towns of western New York, people were willing to listen to Susan, for they were troubled by the defeats northern armies had suffered and by the appalling lack of unity and patriotism in the North. They were beginning to see that the problem of slavery had to be faced and were discussing among themselves whether Negroes were contraband, whether army officers should return fugitive slaves to their masters, whether slaves of the rebels should be freed, whether Negroes should be enlisted in the army.

Susan had an answer for them. "It is impossible longer to hold the African race in bondage," she declared, "or to reconstruct this Republic on the old slaveholding basis. We can neither go back nor stand still. With the nation as with the individual, every new experience forces us into a new and higher life and the old self is lost forever. Hundreds of men who never thought of emancipation a year ago, talk it freely and are ready to vote for it and fight for it now.[144]

"Can the thousands of Northern soldiers," she asked, "who in their march through Rebel States have found faithful friends and generous allies in the slaves ever consent to hurl them back into the hell of slavery, either by word, or vote, or sword? Slaves have sought shelter in the Northern Army and have tasted the forbidden fruit of the Tree of Liberty. Will they return quietly to the plantation and patiently endure the old life of bondage with all its degradation, its cruelties, and wrong? No, No, there can be no reconstruction on the old basis...." Far less degrading and ruinous, she earnestly added, would be the recognition of the independence of the southern Confederacy.

To the question of what to do with the emancipated slaves, her quick answer was, "Treat the Negroes just as you do the Irish, the Scotch, and the Germans. Educate them to all the blessings of our free institutions, to our schools and churches, to every department of industry, trade, and art.

"What arrogance in us," she continued, "to put the question, What shall we do with a race of men and women who have fed, clothed, and supported both themselves and their oppressors for centuries...."

Often she spoke against Lincoln's policy of gradual, compensated emancipation, which to an eager advocate of "immediate, unconditional emancipation" seemed like weakness and appeasement. She had to admit, however, that there had been some progress in the right direction, for Congress had recently forbidden the return of fugitive slaves to their masters, had decreed immediate emancipation in the District of Columbia, and prohibited slavery in the territories.

President Lincoln's promise of freedom on January 1, 1863, to slaves in all states in armed rebellion against the government, seemed wholly inadequate to her and to her fellow-abolitionists, because it left slavery untouched in the border states, but it did encourage them to hope that eventually Lincoln might see the light. Horace Greeley wrote Susan, "I still keep at work with the President in various ways and believe you will yet hear him proclaim universal freedom. Keep this letter and judge me by the event."[145]

It troubled her that public opinion in the North was still far from sympathetic to emancipation. Northern Democrats, charging Lincoln with incompetence and autocratic control, called for "The Constitution as it is, the Union as it was." They had the support of many northern businessmen who faced the loss of millions of credit given to southerners and the support of northern workmen who feared the competition of free Negroes. They had elected Horatio Seymour governor of New York, and had gained ground in many parts of the country. A militant group in Ohio, headed by Congressman Vallandigham, continued to oppose the war, asking for peace at once with no terms unfavorable to the South.

All these developments Susan discussed with her father, for she frequently came home between lectures. He was a tower of strength to her. When she was disillusioned or when criticism and opposition were hard to bear, his sympathy and wise counsel never failed her. There was a strong bond of understanding and affection between them.

His sudden illness and death, late in November 1862, were a shock from which she had to struggle desperately to recover. Her life was suddenly empty. The farm home was desolate. She could not think of leaving her mother and her sister Mary there all alone. Nor could she count on help from Daniel or Merritt, both of whom were serving in the army in the West, Daniel, as a lieutenant colonel, and Merritt as a captain in the 7th Kansas Cavalry. For many weeks she had no heart for anything but grief. "It seemed as if everything in the world must stop."[146]

Not even President Lincoln's Emancipation Proclamation, issued January 1, 1863, roused her. It took a letter from Henry Stanton from Washington to make her see that there was war work for her to do. He wrote her, "The country is rapidly going to destruction. The Army is almost in a state of mutiny for want of its pay and lack of a leader. Nothing can carry through but the southern Negroes, and nobody can marshal them into the struggle except the abolitionists.... Such men as Lovejoy, Hale, and the like have pretty much given up the struggle in despair. You have no idea how dark the cloud is which hangs over us.... We must not lay the flattering unction to our souls that the proclamation will be of any use if we are beaten and have a dissolution of the Union. Here then is work for you, Susan, put on your armor and go forth."[147]

A month later, Susan went to New York for a visit with Elizabeth Stanton, confident that if they counseled together, they could find a way to serve their country in its hour of need.

She was well aware that all through the country women were responding magnificently in this crisis, giving not only their husbands and sons to the war, but carrying on for them in the home, on the farm, and in business. Many were sewing and knitting for soldiers, scraping lint for hospitals, and organizing Ladies' Aid Societies, which, operating through the United States Sanitary Commission, the forerunner of the Red Cross, sent clothing and nourishing food to the inadequately equipped and poorly fed soldiers in the field. In the large cities women were holding highly successful "Sanitary Fairs" to raise funds for the Sanitary Commission. In fact, through the women, civilian relief was organized as never before in history. Individual women too, Susan knew, were making outstanding contributions to the war. Lucy

Stone's sister-in-law, Dr. Elizabeth Blackwell,[148] a friend and admirer of Florence Nightingale, was training much-needed nurses, while Dr. Mary Walker, putting on coat and trousers, ministered tirelessly to the wounded on the battlefield. Dorothea Dix, the one-time schoolteacher who had awakened the people to their barbarous treatment of the insane, had offered her services to the Surgeon-General and was eventually appointed Superintendent of Army Nurses, with authority to recruit nurses and oversee hospital housekeeping. Clara Barton, a government employee, and other women volunteers were finding their way to the front to nurse the wounded who so desperately needed their help; and Mother Bickerdyke, living with the armies in the field, nursed her boys and cooked for them, lifting their morale by her motherly, strengthening presence. Through the influence of Anna Ella Carroll, Maryland had been saved for the Union and she, it was said, was ably advising President Lincoln.

Susan herself had felt no call to nurse the wounded, although she had often skillfully nursed her own family; nor had she felt that her qualifications as an expert housekeeper and good executive demanded her services at the front to supervise army housekeeping. Instead she looked for some important task to which other women would not turn in these days when relief work absorbed all their attention. It was not enough, she felt, for women to be angels of mercy, valuable and well-organized as this phase of their work had become. A spirit of awareness was lacking among them, also a patriotic fervor, and this led her to believe that northern women needed someone to stimulate their thinking, to force them to come to grips with the basic issues of the war and in so doing claim their own freedom. Women, she reasoned, must be aroused to think not only in terms of socks, shirts, and food for soldiers or of bandages and nursing, but in terms of the traditions of freedom upon which this republic was founded. Women must have a part in molding public opinion and must help direct policy as Anna Ella Carroll was proving women could do. Here was the best possible training for prospective women voters. To all this Mrs. Stanton heartily agreed.

As they sat at the dining-room table with Mrs. Stanton's two daughters, Maggie and Hattie, all busily cutting linen into small squares and raveling them into lint for the wounded, they discussed the state of the nation. They were troubled by the low morale of the North and by the insidious propaganda of the Copperheads, an antiwar, pro-Southern group, which spread discontent and disrespect for the government. Profiteering was flagrant, and through speculation and war contracts, large fortunes were being built up among the few, while the majority of the people not only found their lives badly disrupted by the war but suffered from high prices and low wages. So far no decisive victory had encouraged confidence in ultimate triumph over the South. In newspapers and magazines, women of the North were being unfavorably compared with southern women and criticized because of their lack of interest in the war. Writing in the Atlantic Monthly, March, 1863, Gail Hamilton, a rising young journalist, accused northern women of failing to come up to the level of the day. "If you could have finished the war with your needles," she chided them, "it would have been finished long ago, but stitching does not crush rebellion, does not annihilate treason...."

Thinking along these same lines, Susan and Mrs. Stanton now decided to go a step further. They would act to bring women abreast of the issues of the day, Susan with her flare for organizing women, Mrs. Stanton with her pen and her eloquence. They would show women that they had an ideal to fight for. They would show them the uselessness of this bloody conflict unless it won freedom for all of the slaves. Freedom for all, as a basic demand of the republic, would be their watchword. Men were forming Union Leagues and Loyal Leagues to combat the influence of secret antiwar societies, such as the Knights of the Golden Circle. "Why not organize a Women's National Loyal League?" Susan and Mrs. Stanton asked each other.

They talked their ideas over first with the New York abolitionists, then with Horace Greeley, Henry Ward Beecher, and his dashing young friend, Theodore Tilton, and with Robert Dale Owen, now in the city as the recently appointed head of the Freedman's Inquiry Commission. These men were in touch with Charles Sumner and other antislavery members of Congress. All agreed that the Emancipation Proclamation must be implemented by an act of Congress, by an amendment to the Constitution, and that public opinion must be aroused to demand a Thirteenth Amendment. If women would help, so much the better.

Susan at once thought of petitions. If petitions had won the Woman's Property Law in New York, they could win the Thirteenth Amendment. The largest petition ever presented to Congress was her goal.

Carefully Susan and Mrs. Stanton worked over an Appeal to the Women of the Republic, sending it out in March 1863 with a notice of a meeting to be held in New York. It left no doubt in the minds of those who received it that women had a responsibility to their country beyond services of mercy to the wounded and disabled.

From all parts of the country, women responded to their call. The veteran antislavery and woman's rights worker, Angelina Grimké Weld, came out of her retirement for the meeting. Ernestine Rose, the ever faithful, was on hand. Lucy Stone and Antoinette Brown Blackwell were there, and the popular Hutchinson family, famous for their stirring abolition songs. They helped Susan and Mrs. Stanton steer the course of the meeting into the right channels, to show the women assembled that the war was being fought not merely to preserve the Union, but also to preserve the American way of life, based on the principle of equal rights and freedom for all, to save it from the encroachments of slavery and a slaveholding aristocracy. Susan proposed a resolution declaring that there can never be a true peace until the civil and political rights of all citizens are established, including those of Negroes and women. The introduction of the woman's rights issue into a war meeting with an antislavery program was vigorously opposed by women from Wisconsin, but the faithful feminists came to the rescue and the controversial resolution was adopted.

Although she always instinctively related all national issues to woman's rights and vice versa, Susan did not allow this subject to overshadow the main purpose of the meeting. Instead she analyzed the issue of the war and reproached Lincoln for suppressing the fact that slavery was the real cause of the war and for waiting two long years before calling the four million slaves to the side of the North. "Every hour's delay, every life sacrificed up to the proclamation that called the slave to freedom and to arms," she declared, "was nothing less than downright murder by the government.... I therefore hail the day when the government shall recognize that it is a war for freedom."[149]

A Women's National Loyal League was organized, electing Susan secretary and Mrs. Stanton president. They sent a long letter to President Lincoln thanking him for the Emancipation Proclamation, especially for the freedom it gave Negro women, and assuring him of their loyalty and support in this war for freedom. Their own immediate task, they decided, was to circulate petitions asking for an act of Congress to emancipate "all persons of African descent held in involuntary servitude." As Susan so tersely expressed it, they would "canvass the nation for freedom."

All the oratory over, Susan now undertook the hard work of making the Women's National Loyal League a success, assuming the initial financial burden of printing petitions and renting an office, Room 20, at Cooper Institute, where she was busy all day and where New York members met to help her. To each of the petitions sent out, she attached her battle cry, "There must be a law abolishing slavery.... Women, you cannot vote or fight for your country. Your only way to be a power in the government is through the exercise of this one, sacred, constitutional 'right of petition,' and we ask you to use it now to the utmost...." She also asked those signing the petitions to contribute a penny to help with expenses and in this way she slowly raised $3,000.[150]

At first the response was slow, although both Republican and antislavery papers were generous in their praise of this undertaking, but when the signed petitions began to come in, she felt repaid for all her efforts, and when the Hovey Fund trustees appropriated twelve dollars a week for her salary, the financial burden lifted a little. Yet it was ever present. For herself she needed little. She wrote her mother and Mary, "I go to a little restaurant nearby for lunch every noon. I always take strawberries with two tea rusks. Today I said, 'all this lacks is a glass of milk from my mother's cellar,' and the girl replied, 'We have very nice Westchester milk.' So tomorrow I shall add that to my bill of fare. My lunch costs, berries five cents, rusks five, and tomorrow the milk will be three."[151]

The cost of postage mounted as the petitions continued to go out to all parts of the country. In dire need of funds, Susan decided to appeal to Henry Ward Beecher; and wearily climbing Columbia Heights to his home, she suddenly felt a strong hand on her shoulder and a familiar voice asking, "Well, old girl, what do you want now?" He took up a collection for her in Plymouth Church, raising $200. Gerrit Smith sent her $100, when she had hoped for $1,000, and Jessie Benton Frémont, $50. Before long, her "war of ideas" won the support of Wendell Phillips, Frederick Douglass, Horace Greeley, George William Curtis, and other popular lecturers who spoke for her at Cooper Union to large audiences whose admission fees swelled her funds; and eventually Senator Sumner, realizing how important the petitions could be in arousing public opinion for the Thirteenth Amendment, saved her the postage by sending them out under his frank.[152]

She made her home with the Stantons, who had moved from Brooklyn to 75 West 45th Street, New York, and the comfortable evenings of good conversation and her busy days at the office helped mightily to heal her grief for her father. In the bustling life of the city she felt she was living more intensely, more usefully, as these critical days of war demanded. Henry Stanton, now an editorial writer for Greeley's Tribune, brought home to them the inside story of the news and of politics. All of them were highly critical of Lincoln, impatient with his slowness and skeptical of his plans for slaveholders and slaves in the border states. They questioned Garrison's wisdom in trusting Lincoln. Susan could not feel that Lincoln was honest when he protested that he did not have the power to do all that the abolitionists asked. "The pity is," she wrote Anna E. Dickinson, "that the vast mass of people really believe the man honest—that he believes he has not the power—I wish I could...."[153]

New York seethed with unrest as time for the enforcement of the draft drew near. Indignant that rich men could avoid the draft by buying a substitute, workingmen were easily incited to riot, and the city was soon overrun by mobs bent on destruction. The lives of all Negroes and abolitionists were in danger. The Stanton home was in the thick of the rioting, and when Susan and Henry Stanton came home during a lull, they all decided to take refuge for the night at the home of Mrs. Stanton's brother-in-law, Dr. Bayard. Here they also found Horace Greeley hiding from the mob, for hoodlums were marching through the streets shouting, "We'll hang old Horace Greeley to a sour apple tree."

The next morning Susan started for the office as usual, thinking the worst was over, but as not a single horsecar or stage was running, she took the ferry to Flushing to visit her cousins. Here too there was rioting, but she stayed on until order was restored by the army. She returned to the city to find casualties mounting to over a thousand and a million dollars' worth of property destroyed. Negroes had been shot and hung on lamp posts, Horace Greeley's Tribune office had been wrecked and the homes of abolitionist friends burned. "These are terrible times," she wrote her family, and then went back to work, staying devotedly at it through all the hot summer months.[154]

By the end of the year, she had enrolled the signatures of 100,000 men and women on her petitions, and assured by Senator Sumner that these petitions were invaluable in creating sentiment for the Thirteenth Amendment, she raised the number of signatures in the next few months to 400,000.

In April 1864, the Thirteenth Amendment passed the Senate and the prospects for it in the House were good. This phase of her work finished, Susan disbanded the Women's National Loyal League and returned to her family in Rochester.

In despair over the possible re-election of Abraham Lincoln, Susan had joined Henry and Elizabeth Stanton in stirring up sentiment for John C. Frémont. Abolitionists were sharply divided in this presidential campaign. Garrison and Phillips disagreed on the course of action, Garrison coming out definitely for Lincoln in the Liberator, while Phillips declared himself emphatically against four more years of Lincoln. Susan, the Stantons, and Parker Pillsbury were among those siding with Phillips because they feared premature reconstruction under Lincoln. They cited Lincoln's Amnesty Proclamation as an example of his leniency toward the rebels. They saw danger in leaving free Negroes under the control of southerners embittered by war, and called for Negro suffrage as the only protection against oppressive laws. They opposed the readmission of Louisiana without the enfranchisement of Negroes. Lincoln, they knew, favored the extension of suffrage only to literate Negroes and to those who had served in the military forces. In fact, Lincoln held back while they wanted to go ahead under full steam and they looked to Frémont to lead them.

Following the presidential campaign anxiously from Rochester, Susan wrote Mrs. Stanton, "I am starving for a full talk with somebody posted, not merely pitted for Lincoln...." The persistent cry of the Liberator and the Antislavery Standard to re-elect Lincoln and not to swap horses in midstream did not ring true to her. "We read no more of the good old doctrine 'of two evils choose neither,'" she wrote Anna E. Dickinson. She confessed to Anna, "It is only safe to seek and act the truth and to profess confidence in Lincoln would be a lie in me."[155]

As the war dragged on through the summer without decisive victories for the North, Lincoln's prospects looked bleak, and to her dismay, Susan saw the chances improving for McClellan, the candidate of the northern Democrats who wanted to end the war, leave slavery alone, and conciliate the South. The whole picture changed, however, with the capture of Atlanta by General Sherman in September. The people's confidence in Lincoln revived and Frémont withdrew from the contest. One by one the anti-Lincoln abolitionists were converted; and Susan, anxiously waiting for word from Mrs. Stanton, was relieved to learn that she was not one of them, nor was Wendell Phillips whose judgment and vision both of them valued above that of any other man. With approval she read these lines which Phillips had just written Mrs. Stanton, "I would cut off both hands before doing anything to aid Mac's [McClellan's] election. I would cut oft my right hand before doing anything to aid Abraham Lincoln's election. I wholly distrust his fitness to settle this thing and indeed his purpose."[156]

There is nothing to indicate any change of opinion on Susan's part regarding Lincoln's unfitness for a second term. That he was the lesser of two evils, she of course acknowledged. For her these pre-election days were discouraging and frustrating. She had very definite ideas on reconstruction which she felt in justice to the Negro must be carried out, and Lincoln did not meet her requirements.

After Lincoln's re-election, she again looked to Wendell Phillips for an adequate policy at this juncture, and she was not disappointed. "Phillips has just returned from Washington," Mrs. Stanton wrote her. "He says the radical men feel they are powerless and checkmated.... They turn to such men as Phillips to say what politicians dare not say.... We say now, as ever, 'Give us immediately unconditional emancipation, and let there be no reconstruction except on the broadest basis of justice and equality!...' Phillips and a few others must hold up the pillars of the temple.... I cannot tell you how happy I am to find Douglass on the same platform with us. Keep him on the right track. Tell him in this revolution, he, Phillips, and you and I must hold the highest ground and truly represent the best type of the white man, the black man, and the woman."[157]

Susan, holding "the highest ground," found it difficult to mark time until she could find her place in the reconstruction. "The work of the hour," she wrote Anna E. Dickinson, "is not alone to put down the Rebels in arms, but to educate

Thirty Millions of People into the idea of a True Republic. Hence every influence and power that both men and women can bring to bear will be needed in the reconstruction of the Nation on the broad basis of justice and equality."[158]

The Negro's Hour

Susan's thoughts now turned to Kansas, as they had many times since her brothers had settled there. Daniel and Annie, his young wife from the East, urged her to visit them.[159] Daniel was well established in Kansas, the publisher of his own newspaper and the mayor of Leavenworth. He had served a little over a year in the Union army in the First Kansas Cavalry. She longed to see him and the West that he loved.

Now for the first time she felt free to make the long journey, for her mother and Mary had sold the farm on the outskirts of Rochester and had moved into the city, buying a large red brick house shaded by maples and a beautiful horse chestnut. It had been a wrench for Susan to give up the farm with its memories of her father, but there were compensations in the new home on Madison Street, for Guelma, her husband, Aaron McLean, and their family lived with them there. Hannah and her family had also settled in Rochester, and when they bought the house next door, Susan had the satisfaction of living again in the midst of her family.[160]

She was particularly devoted to Guelma's twenty-three-year-old daughter, Ann Eliza, whose "merry laugh" and "bright, joyous presence" brought new life into the household. Ann Eliza was a stimulating intelligent companion, and Susan looked forward to seeing many of her own dreams fulfilled in her niece. Then suddenly in the fall of 1864, Ann Eliza was taken ill, and her death within a few days left a great void.[161]

In the midst of this sorrow, Daniel sent Susan a ticket and a check for a trip to Kansas. Hesitating no longer, she waited only until her "tip-top Rochester dressmaker" made up "the new, five-dollar silk" which she had bought in New York.[162]

Before leaving for Kansas, in January, 1865, she pasted on the first page of her diary a clipping of a poem by Henry Wadsworth Longfellow, "Something Left Undone," which seemed so perfectly to interpret her own feelings:

Labor with what zeal we will
Something still remains undone
Something uncompleted still
Waits the rising of the sun....
Till at length it is or seems
Greater than our strength can bear
As the burden of our dreams
Pressing on us everywhere....[163]

With "the burden of her dreams" pressing on her, Susan traveled westward. The future of the Negro was much on her mind, for the Thirteenth Amendment abolishing slavery had just been sent to the states for ratification. That it would be ratified she had no doubt, but she recognized the responsibility facing the North to provide for the education and rehabilitation of thousands of homeless bewildered Negroes trying to make their way in a still unfriendly world, and she looked forward to taking part in this work.

Beyond Chicago, where she stopped over to visit her uncle Albert Dickinson and his family, her journey was rugged, and when she reached Leavenworth she reveled in the comfort of Daniel's "neat, little, snow-white cottage with green blinds." She liked Daniel's wife, Annie, at once, admired her gaiety and the way she fearlessly drove her beautiful black horse across the prairie. "They have a real 'Aunt Chloe' in the kitchen," she wrote Mrs. Stanton, "and a little Darkie boy for errands and table waiter. I never saw a girl to match. The more I see of the race, the more wonderful they are to me."[164]

There was always good companionship in Daniel's home, for friends from both the East and the West found it a convenient stopping place, and there was much discussion of politics, the Negro question, and the future of the West. Business was booming in Leavenworth, then the most thriving town between St. Louis and San Francisco. Eight years before, when Daniel had first settled there, it boasted a population of 4,000. Now it had grown to 22,000, was lighted with gas, and was building its business blocks of brick. As Susan drove through the busy streets with Annie, she saw emigrants coming in by steamer and train to settle in Kansas and watched for the covered wagons that almost every day stopped in Leavenworth for supplies before moving on to the far West. Driving over the wide prairie, sometimes a warm brown, then again white with snow under a wider expanse of deep blue sky than she had ever seen before, she relaxed as she had not in many a year and began to feel the call of the West. She even thought she might like to settle in Kansas until she was caught up by the sharp realization of how she would miss the stimulating companionship of her friends in the East.

Daniel Anthony, brother of Susan B. Anthony

When Daniel was busy with his campaign for his second term as mayor, she helped him edit the Bulletin. He warned her not to fill his paper up with woman's rights, and in spite of his sympathy for the Negro, forbade her to advocate Negro suffrage in his paper.

"I wish I could talk through it the things I'd like to say to the young martyr state ..." she wrote Mrs. Stanton. "The Legislature gave but six votes for Negro suffrage the other day.... The idea of Kansas refusing her loyal Negroes."

Again and again she was shocked at the prejudice against Negroes in Kansas, as when Daniel employed a Negro typesetter and the printers, refusing to admit him to their union, went out on strike until he was discharged.

"In this city," she reported to Mrs. Stanton, "there are four thousand ex-Missouri slaves who have sought refuge here within the three past years." Making it her business to learn what was being done to help them and educate them, she visited their schools, their Sunday schools, and the Colored Home, and gave much of her time to them. To encourage them to demand their rights, she organized an Equal Rights League among them. This was one thing she could do, even if she could not plead for Negro suffrage in Daniel's newspaper.[165]

Then one breath-taking piece of news followed another—Lee's surrender, April 9, 1865, and in less than a week, Lincoln's assassination, his death, and Andrew Johnson's succession to the Presidency.

Susan looked upon Lincoln's assassination and death as an act of God. She wrote to Mrs. Stanton, "Was there ever a more terrific command to a Nation to 'stand still and know that I am God' since the world began? The Old Book's terrible exhibitions of God's wrath sink into nothingness. And this fell blow just at the very hour he was declaring his willingness to consign those five million faithful, brave, and loving loyal people of the South to the tender mercies of the ex-slave lords of the lash."[166]

She longed "to go out and do battle for the Lord once more," but when she could have expressed her opinions at the big mass meeting held in memory of Lincoln, she remained silent. "My soul was full," she confessed to Mrs. Stanton, "but the flesh not equal to stemming the awful current, to do what the people have called make an exhibition of myself. So quenched the spirit and came home ashamed of myself."

Then she added, "Dear-a-me—how overfull I am, and how I should like to be nestled into some corner away from every chick and child with you once more."

Disturbing news came from the East of dissension in the antislavery ranks, of Garrison's desire to dissolve the American Antislavery Society after the ratification of the Thirteenth Amendment, and of Phillips' insistence that it continue until freedom for the Negro was firmly established. While Garrison maintained that northern states, denying the ballot to the Negro, could not consistently make Negro suffrage a requirement for readmitting rebel states to the

Union, Phillips demanded Negro suffrage as a condition of readmission. Immediately abolitionists took sides. Parker Pillsbury, Lydia and Lucretia Mott, Frederick Douglass, Anna E. Dickinson, the Stantons, and others lined up with Phillips, whose vehement and scathing criticism of reconstruction policies seemed to them the need of the hour. Susan also took sides, praising "dear ever glorious Phillips" and writing in her diary, "The disbanding of the American Antislavery Society is fully as untimely as General Grant's and Sherman's granting parole and pardon to the whole Rebel armies."[167]

To her friends in the East, she wrote, "How can anyone hold that Congress has no right to demand Negro suffrage in the returning Rebel states because it is not already established in all the loyal ones? What would have been said of Abolitionists ten or twenty years ago, had they preached to the people that Congress had no right to vote against admitting a new state with slavery, because it was not already abolished in all the old States? It is perfectly astounding, this seeming eagerness of so many of our old friends to cover up and apologize for the glaring hate toward the equal recognition of the manhood of the black race."[168]

She rejoiced when word came that the American Antislavery Society would continue under the presidency of Phillips, with Parker Pillsbury as editor of the Antislavery Standard; but she was saddened by the withdrawal of Garrison, whom she had idolized for so many years and whose editorials in the Liberator had always been her inspiration.[169]

As she read the weekly New York Tribune, which came regularly to Daniel, she grew more and more concerned over President Johnson's reconstruction policy and more and more convinced of the need of a crusade for political and civil rights for the Negro. Asked to deliver the Fourth of July oration at Ottumwa, Kansas, she decided to put into it all her views on the controversial subject of reconstruction.

Traveling by stage the 125 miles to Ottumwa, she found good company en route and "great talk on politics, Negro equality, and temperance," and thought the "grand old prairies ... perfectly splendid and the timber-skirted creeks ... delightful."[170]

Before a large gathering of Kansas pioneers, many of whom had driven forty or fifty miles to hear her, she stood tall, straight, and earnest, as she reminded them of the noble heritage of Kansas, of the bloody years before the war when in the free-state fight, Kansas men and women "taught the nation anew" the principles of the Declaration of Independence. Lashing out with the vehemence of Phillips against President Johnson's reconstruction policy, she warned, "There has been no hour fraught with so much danger as the present.... To be foiled now in gathering up the fruits of our blood-bought victories and to re-enthrone slavery under the new guise of Negro disfranchisement ... would be a disaster, a cruelty and crime, which would surely bequeath to coming generations a legacy of wars and rumors of wars...."[171]

She then cited the results of the elections in Virginia, South Carolina, and Tennessee to prove her point that unless Negroes were given the vote, rebels would be put in office and a new code of laws apprenticing Negroes passed, establishing a new form of slavery.

She urged her audience to be awake to the politicians who were using the peoples' reverence and near idolatry of Lincoln to push through anti-Negro legislation under the guise of carrying out his policies. Then putting behind her the prejudice and impatience with Lincoln which she had felt during his lifetime, she added, "If the administration of Abraham Lincoln taught the American people one lesson above another, it was that they must think and speak and proclaim, and that he as their President was bound to execute their will, not his own. And if Lincoln were alive today, he would say as he did four years ago, 'I wait the voice of the people.'"

In her special pleading for the Negro, she did not forget women. Calling attention to the fact that our nation had never been a true republic because the ballot was exclusively in the hands of the "free white male," she asked for a government "of the people," men and women, white and black, with Negro suffrage and woman suffrage as basic requirements.

Wendell Phillips

So enthusiastic were the Republicans over her speech that they urged her to prepare it for publication, suggesting, however, that she delete the passage on woman suffrage. This was her first intimation that Republicans might balk at enfranchising women. So great had been women's contribution to the winning of the war and so indebted were the Republicans to women for creating sentiment for the Thirteenth Amendment, that she had come to expect, along with Mrs. Stanton, that the ballot would without question be given them as a reward.

It was soon obvious to Susan that politicians in the East as well as in Kansas were shying away from woman suffrage. Mrs. Stanton reported that even Wendell Phillips was backsliding, not wishing to campaign for Negro suffrage and woman suffrage at the same time. "While I could continue as heretofore, arguing for woman's rights, just as I do for temperance every day," he had written, "still I would not mix the movements.... I think such mixture would lose for the Negro far more than we should gain for the woman. I am now engaged in abolishing slavery in a land] where the abolition of slavery means conferring or recognizing citizenship, and where citizenship supposes the ballot for all men."[172]

Such reasoning filled Susan with despair, for she firmly believed that women who had been asking for full citizenship for seventeen years deserved precedence over the Negro. Mrs. Stanton agreed. To them, Negro suffrage without woman suffrage was unthinkable, an unbearable humiliation. Half of the Negroes were women, and manhood suffrage would fasten upon them a new form of slavery. How could Wendell Phillips, they asked each other, fail to recognize not only the timeliness of woman suffrage, but the fact that women were better qualified for the ballot than the majority of Negroes, who, because of their years in slavery, were illiterate and the easy prey of unscrupulous politicians? By all means enfranchise Negroes, they argued with him, but enfranchise women as well, and if there must be a limitation on suffrage, let it be on the basis of literacy, not on the basis of sex.

Among Republican members of Congress and abolitionists, there was serious discussion of a Fourteenth Amendment to extend to the Negro civil rights and the ballot. Susan, reading about this in Kansas, and Mrs. Stanton, discussing it in New York with her husband, Wendell Phillips, and Robert Dale Owen, saw in such a revision of the Constitution a just and logical opportunity to extend woman's rights at the same time. Previously committed to state action on woman suffrage but only because it had then seemed the necessary first step, both women welcomed the more direct road offered by an amendment to the Constitution. Only they of all the old woman's rights workers were awake to this opportunity.

Throughout the United States, people were thinking about the Constitution as Americans had not done since the Bill of Rights was ratified in 1791. Not only were amendments to the federal Constitution in the air, not only were rebel states being readmitted to the Union with new constitutions, but state constitutions in the North were being revised, and western territories sought statehood. In Susan's opinion the time was ripe to proclaim equal rights for all. This clearly was woman's hour.

"Come back and help," pleaded Elizabeth Stanton, who grew more and more alarmed as she saw all interest in woman suffrage crowded out of the minds of reformers by their zeal for the Negro. "I have argued constantly with Phillips and the whole fraternity, but I fear one and all will favor enfranchising the Negro without us. Woman's cause is in deep water.... There is pressing need of our woman's rights convention...."[173]

Susan's spirits revived at the prospect of holding a woman's rights convention, and plans for the future began to take shape as she read the closing lines of Mrs. Stanton's letter: "I hope in a short time to be comfortably located in a new house where we will have a room ready for you.... I long to put my arms about you once more and hear you scold me for all my sins and shortcomings.... Oh, Susan, you are very dear to me. I should miss you more than any other living being on this earth. You are entwined with much of my happy and eventful past, and all my future plans are based on you as coadjutor. Yes, our work is one, we are one in aim and sympathy and should be together. Come home."

Parker Pillsbury also added his plea, "Why have you deserted the field of action at a time like this, at an hour unparalleled in almost twenty centuries?... It is not for me to decide your field of labor. Kansas needed John Brown and may need you ... but New York is to revise her constitution next year and, if you are absent, who is to make the plea for woman?"

Reading her newspaper a few days later, she found that the politicians had made their first move, introducing in the House of Representatives a resolution writing the word "male" into the qualifications of voters in the second section of the proposed Fourteenth Amendment. She started at once for the East.

On the long journey back, in the heat of August, traveling by stage and railroad with many stops to make the necessary connections, Susan not only visited her many relatives who had moved to the West, but also called on antislavery and woman suffrage workers, and held meetings to plead for free schools for Negroes and for the ballot for Negroes and women. She found people relieved to have the war over and busy with their own affairs, but with prejudices smoldering. Public speaking was still an ordeal for her and she confessed to her diary, "Made a labored talk.... Had a struggle to get through with speech," and again, "Had a hard time. Thoughts nor words would come—Staggered through."[174] However, she was a determined woman. The message must be carried to the people and she would do it whether she suffered in the process or not.

Late in September, she reached her own comfortable home in Rochester, but she had too much on her mind to stay there long, and within a few weeks was in New York with Elizabeth Stanton, deep in a serious discussion of how to create an overwhelming demand for woman suffrage at this crucial time. Again they decided to petition Congress, this time for the vote for both women and Negroes. Five years had now passed since the last national woman's rights convention, and the workers were scattered; some had lost interest and others thought only of the need of the Negro. Lucretia Mott, Lydia Mott, and Parker Pillsbury responded at once. Susan sought out Lucy Stone in spite of the differences that had grown up between them, and after talking with Lucy, confessed to herself that she had been unjustly impatient with her.[175]

Hoping for aid from the Jackson or Hovey Fund, she went to New England to revive interest there and in Concord talked with the Emersons, Bronson Alcott, and Frank Sanborn. When she asked Emerson whether he thought it wise to demand woman suffrage at this time, he replied, "Ask my wife. I can philosophize, but I always look to her to decide for me in practical matters." Unhesitatingly Mrs. Emerson agreed with Susan that Congress must be petitioned immediately to enfranchise women either before Negroes were granted the vote or at the same time.[176]

Even Wendell Phillips, who did not want to mix Negro and woman suffrage, gave Susan $500 from the Hovey Fund to finance the petitions, but many of the friends upon whom she had counted needed a verbal lashing to rouse them out of their apathy. Very soon she had to face the unpleasant fact that by pressing for woman suffrage now, she was estranging many abolitionists. Nevertheless she and Mrs. Stanton went ahead undaunted, determined that a petition for woman suffrage would go to Congress even if it carried only their own two signatures.

However, petitions with many signatures were reaching Congress in January 1866—the very first demand ever made for Congressional action on woman suffrage. Senator Sumner, for whom women had rolled up 400,000 signatures for the Thirteenth Amendment, now presented under protest "as most inopportune" a petition headed by Lydia Maria Child, who for years had been his valiant aid in antislavery work; and Thaddeus Stevens, heretofore friendly to woman suffrage and ever zealous for the Negro, ignored a petition from New York headed by Elizabeth Cady Stanton.[177]

By this time it was clear to Susan that since the two powerful Republicans, Senator Sumner and Thaddeus Stevens, both basically friendly to woman suffrage, were determined to devote themselves wholly to Negro suffrage and to the extension of their party's influence, she could expect no help from lesser party members. Her only alternative was to appeal to the Democrats or to an occasional recalcitrant Republican, and she allowed nothing to stand in her way, not even the frenzied pleas of her abolitionist friends. She found James Brooks of New York, Democratic leader of the House, willing to present her petitions, and she made use of him, although he was regarded by abolitionists as a Copperhead and although he was now advocating conciliatory reconstruction for the South of which she herself disapproved. Other Democrats came to the rescue in the Senate as well as in the House—a few because they saw justice in the demands of the women, others because they believed white women should have political precedence over Negroes, and still others because they saw in their support of woman suffrage an opportunity to harass the Republicans. During 1866, petitions for woman suffrage with 10,000 signatures were presented by Democrats and irregular Republicans.

In the meantime, conferences in New York with Henry Ward Beecher and Theodore Tilton were encouraging, and for a time Susan thought she had found an enthusiastic ally in Tilton, the talented popular young editor of the Independent. Theodore Tilton, with his long hair and the soulful face of a poet, with his eloquence as a lecturer and his flare for journalism, was at the height of his popularity. He had winning ways and was full of ideas. After the ratification of the Thirteenth Amendment abolishing slavery, in December 1865, he had proposed that the American Antislavery Society and the woman's rights group merge to form an American Equal Rights Association which would fight for equal rights for all, for Negro and woman suffrage. Wendell Phillips he suggested for president, and the Antislavery Standard as the paper of the new organization.

This sounded reasonable and hopeful to Susan, and she hurried to Boston with a group from New York, including Lucy Stone, to consult Wendell Phillips and his New England colleagues. Wendell Phillips, however, was cool to the proposition, pointing out the necessity of amending the constitution of the American Antislavery Society before any such action could be taken. Never dreaming that he would actually oppose their plan, Susan expected this would be taken care of; but when she convened her woman's rights convention in New York in May 1866, simultaneously with that of the American Antislavery Society, she found to her dismay that no formal notice of the proposed union had been given to the members of the antislavery group and therefore there was no way for them to vote their organization into an Equal Rights Association. Not to be sidetracked, she then asked the woman's rights convention to broaden its platform to include rights for the Negro. To her this seemed a natural development as she had always thought of woman's rights as part of the larger struggle for human rights.

"For twenty years," she declared, "we have pressed the claims of women to the right of representation in the government.... Up to this hour we have looked only to State action for the recognition of our rights; but now by the results of the war, the whole question of suffrage reverts back to the United States Constitution. The duty of Congress at this moment is to declare what shall be the basis of representation in a republican form of government.

"There is, there can be, but one true basis," she continued. "Taxation and representation must be inseparable; hence our demand must now go beyond woman.... We therefore wish to broaden our woman's rights platform and make it in name what it has ever been in spirit, a human rights platform."[178]

The women, so often accused in later years of fighting only for their own rights, had the courage at this time to attempt a practical experiment in generosity. Susan and Mrs. Stanton with all their hearts wanted this experiment to succeed, and yet as they resolved their woman's rights organization into the American Equal Rights Association, they were apprehensive.

They did not have to wait long for disillusionment. Meeting Wendell Phillips and Theodore Tilton in the office of the Antislavery Standard to plan a campaign for the Equal Rights Association, they discussed with them what should be done in New York, preparatory to the revision of the state constitution. Emphatically Wendell Phillips declared that the time was ripe for striking the word "white" out of the constitution, but not the word "male." That could come, he added, when the constitution was next revised, some twenty or thirty years later. To their astonishment, Theodore Tilton heartily agreed. Then he added, "The question of striking out the word 'male,' we as an equal rights association shall of course present as an intellectual theory, but not as a practical thing to be accomplished at this convention." Completely unprepared for such an attitude on Tilton's part, Susan retorted with indignation, "I would sooner cut off my right hand than ask for the ballot for the black man and not for woman." Then telling the two men just what she thought of them for their betrayal of women, she swept out of the office to keep another appointment.[179]

Equally exasperated with these men, Mrs. Stanton stayed on, hoping to heal the breach, but when Susan returned to the Stanton home that evening, she found her highly indignant, declaring she was through boosting the Negro over her own head. Then and there they vowed that they would devote themselves with all their might and main to woman suffrage and to that alone.

By this time, Congress had passed a civil rights bill over President Johnson's veto, conferring the rights of citizenship upon freedmen, and a Fourteenth Amendment to make these rights permanent was now before Congress. The latest developments regarding the various drafts of the Fourteenth Amendment were passed along to Susan and Mrs. Stanton by Robert Dale Owen. Senator Sumner, he reported, had yielded to party pressure and now supported the Fourteenth Amendment, although in the past he had always maintained such an amendment wholly unnecessary since there was already enough justice, liberty, and equality in the Constitution to protect the humblest citizen. Senator Sumner opposed and defeated a clause in the amendment referring to "race" and "color," words which had never previously been mentioned in the Constitution, but he raised no serious objection to the introduction of the word "male" as a qualification for suffrage, which was also unprecedented. That he tried time and time again to avoid the word "male" when he was redrafting the amendment or that Thaddeus Stevens tried to substitute "legal voters" for "male citizens" was no comfort to Susan and Mrs. Stanton, as they saw the Fourteenth Amendment writing discrimination against women into the federal Constitution for the first time.[180]

As they carefully read over the first section of the Fourteenth Amendment, which conferred citizenship on every person born or naturalized in the United States, women's rights seemed assured:

"All persons born or naturalized in the United States, and subject to the jurisdiction thereof, are citizens of the United States and of the State wherein they reside. No State shall make or enforce any law which shall abridge the privileges or immunities of citizens of the United States; nor shall any State deprive any person of life, liberty, or property, without due process of law; nor deny to any person within its jurisdiction the equal protection of the laws."

Then in the controversial second section which provided the penalty of reduction of representation in Congress for states depriving Negroes of the ballot, they saw themselves written out of the Constitution by the words, "male inhabitants" and "male citizens," used to define legal voters. It was baffling to be kept from their goal by a single word in a provision which at best was the unsatisfactory compromise arrived at by radical and conservative Republicans and which sincere abolitionists felt was unfair to the Negro. That it was unfair to women, there was no doubt.

With determination, Susan and Mrs. Stanton fought this injustice. Were they not "persons born ... in the United States," they asked. Were they forever to be regarded as children or as lower than persons, along with criminals, idiots, and the insane? Were women not counted in the basis of representation and should they not have a voice in the election of those representatives whose office their numbers helped to establish?

As Susan studied the Constitution, she saw that the question of suffrage had up to this time been left to the states and that there were no provisions defining suffrage or citizenship or limiting the right of suffrage. Only now was the precedent being broken by the Fourteenth Amendment which conferred citizenship on Negroes and limited suffrage to males. How could this be constitutional, she reasoned, when the first lines of the Constitution read, "We, the people of the United States, in order to ... establish justice ... and secure the Blessings of Liberty to ourselves and our Posterity, do ordain and establish this Constitution for the United States of America." Of course "the people" must include women, if the English language meant what it said.

The Fourteenth Amendment with the limiting word "male" was passed by Congress and referred to the states for ratification in June 1866. As never before, Susan felt the curse of the tradition of the unimportance of women. Once more politicians and reformers had ignored women's inherent rights as human beings. In spite of women's intelligence and their wartime service to their country, no statesman of power or vision felt it at all necessary to include women under the Fourteenth Amendment's broad term of "persons." Yet according to statements made in later years by John A. Bingham and Roscoe Conkling, both sponsors of the amendment and concerned with its drafting, the possibility was considered of protecting corporations and the property of individuals from the interference of state and municipal legislation, through the federal control extended by this amendment. At any rate, they wrought well for the corporations which have received abundant protection under the Fourteenth Amendment, along with all male citizens, while women were left outside the pale.[181]

Tactfully the Republicans explained to women that even Negro suffrage could not be definitely spelled out in the Fourteenth Amendment, if it were to be accepted by the people; and added that Negro suffrage was all the strain that the Republican party could bear at this time; but neither Susan nor Mrs. Stanton were fooled by this sophistry. They knew that Republican politicians saw in the Negro vote in the South the means of keeping their party in power for a long time to come, and could entirely overlook justice to Negro women since they were assured of enough votes without them. The women of the North need not be considered, since they had nothing to offer politically. They would vote, it was thought, just as their husbands voted.

Completely deserted by all their former friends in the Republican party, Susan and Mrs. Stanton now made use of an irregular Republican, Senator Cowan of Pennsylvania, whom the abolitionists had labeled "the watchdog of slavery." When Benjamin Wade's bill "to enfranchise each and every male person" in the District of Columbia "without any distinction on account of color or race," was discussed on the Senate floor in December 1866, Senator Cowan offered an amendment striking out the word "male" and thus leaving the door open for women. He stated the case for woman suffrage well and with eloquence, and although he was accused of being insincere and wishing merely to cloud the issue, he forced the Republicans to show their hands. In the three-day debate which followed, Senator Wilson of Massachusetts declared emphatically that he was opposed to connecting the two issues, woman and Negro suffrage, but would at any time support a separate bill for woman's enfranchisement. Senator Pomeroy of Kansas objected to jeopardizing the chances of Negro suffrage by linking it with woman suffrage, but Senator Wade of Ohio boldly expressed his approval of woman suffrage, even casting a vote for Senator Cowan's amendment, as did B. Gratz Brown of Missouri. In the final vote, nine votes were counted for woman suffrage and thirty-seven against.[182]

Susan recorded even this defeat as progress, for woman suffrage had for the first time been debated in Congress and prominent Senators had treated it with respect. The Republican press, however, was showing definite signs of disapproval, even Horace Greeley's New York Tribune. Almost unbelieving, she read Greeley's editorial, "A Cry from the Females," in which he said, "Talk of a true woman needing the ballot as an accessory of power when she rules the world with the glance of an eye." With the Democratic press as always solidly against woman suffrage and the Antislavery Standard avoiding the subject as if it did not exist, no words favorable to votes for women now reached the public.[183]

It was hard for Susan to forgive the Antislavery Standard for what she regarded as a breach of trust. Financed by the Hovey Fund, it owed allegiance, she believed, to women as well as the Negro. In protest Parker Pillsbury resigned his post as editor, but among the leading men in the antislavery ranks, only he, Samuel J. May, James Mott, and Robert Purvis, the cultured, wealthy Philadelphia Negro, were willing to support Susan and Mrs. Stanton in their campaign for woman suffrage at this time. The rest aligned themselves unquestioningly with the Republicans, although in the past they had always been distrustful of political parties.

Discouraging as this was for Susan, their influence upon the antislavery women was far more alarming. These women one by one temporarily deserted the woman's rights cause, persuaded that this was the Negro's hour and that they must be generous, renounce their own claims, and work only for the Negroes' civil and political rights. Less than a dozen remained steadfast, among them Lucretia Mott, Martha C. Wright, Ernestine Rose, and for a time Lucy Stone, who wrote John Greenleaf Whittier in January 1867, "You know Mr. Phillips takes the ground that this is 'the Negro's hour,' and that the women, if not criminal, are at least, not wise to urge their own claim. Now, so sure am I that he is mistaken and that the only name given, by which the country can be saved, is that of woman, that I want to ask you ... to use your influence to induce him to reconsider the position he has taken. He is the only man in the nation to whom has been given the charm which compels all men, willing or unwilling, to listen when he speaks ... Mr. Phillips used to say, 'take your part with the perfect and abstract right, and trust God to see that it shall prove expedient.' Now he needs someone to help him see that point again."[184]

Times That Tried Women's Souls

Bitterly disillusioned, Susan as usual found comfort in action. She carried to the New York legislature early in 1867 her objections to the Fourteenth Amendment in a petition from the American Equal Rights Association, signed by Lucy Stone, Henry Blackwell, Elizabeth Cady Stanton, and herself. People generally were critical of the amendment, many fearing it would too readily reinstate rebels as voters, and she hoped to block ratification by capitalizing on this dissatisfaction. She saw no disloyalty to Negroes in this, for she regarded the amendment as "utterly inadequate."[185]

This protest made, she turned her attention to New York's constitutional convention, which provided an unusual opportunity for writing woman suffrage into the new constitution. First she sought an interview with Horace Greeley, hoping to regain his support which was more important than ever since he had been chosen a delegate to this convention. When she and Mrs. Stanton asked him for space in the Tribune to advocate woman suffrage as well as Negro suffrage, he emphatically replied, "No! You must not get up any agitation for that measure.... Help us get the word 'white' out of the constitution. This is the Negro's hour.... Your turn will come next."[186]

Convinced that this was also woman's hour, Susan disregarded his opinions and his threats and circulated woman suffrage petitions in all parts of the state. She won the support of the handsome, highly respected George William Curtis, now editor of Harper's Magazine and also a convention delegate, and of the popular Henry Ward Beecher and Gerrit Smith. The sponsorship of the cause by these men helped mightily. New York women sent in petitions with hundreds of signatures, but the Republican party was at work, cracking its whip, and Horace Greeley was appointed chairman of the committee on the right of suffrage.

Both Susan and Mrs. Stanton spoke at the constitutional convention's hearing on woman suffrage, Susan with her usual forthrightness answering the many questions asked by the delegates, spreading consternation among them by declaring that women would eventually serve as jurors and be drafted in time of war. Assuming women unable to bear arms for their country, the delegates smugly linked the ballot and the bullet together, and Horace Greeley gleefully asked the two women, "If you vote, are you ready to fight?" Instantly, Susan replied, "Yes, Mr. Greeley, just as you fought in the late war—at the point of a goose quill." Then turning to the other delegates, she reminded them that several hundred women, disguised as men, had fought in the Civil War, and instead of being honored for their services and paid, they had been discharged in disgrace.[187]

Confident that Horace Greeley would sooner or later fall back on his oft-repeated, trite remark, "The best women I know do not want to vote," Susan had asked Mrs. Greeley to roll up a big petition in Westchester County, and believing heartily in woman suffrage she had complied. This gave Susan and Mrs. Stanton a trump card to play, should Horace Greeley present an adverse report as they were informed he would do.[188]

In Albany to hear the report, these two conspirators gloated over their plan as they surveyed the packed galleries and noted the many reporters who would jump at a bit of spicy news to send their papers. Just before Horace Greeley was to give his report, George William Curtis announced with dignity and assurance, "Mr. President, I hold in my hand a petition from Mrs. Horace Greeley and 300 other women, citizens of Westchester, asking that the word 'male' be stricken from the Constitution."[189]

Ripples of amusement ran through the audience, and reporters hastily took notes, as Horace Greeley, the top of his head red as a beet, looked up with anger at the galleries, and then in a thin squeaky voice and with as much authority as he could muster declared, "Your committee does not recommend an extension of the elective franchise to women...." As a result, New York's new constitution enfranchised only male citizens.[190]

Horace Greeley justified his opposition to woman suffrage in a letter to Moncure D. Conway: "The keynote of my political creed is the axiom that 'Governments derive their just powers from the consent of the governed....' I sought information from different quarters ... and practically all agreed in the conclusion that the women of our state do not choose to vote. Individuals do, at least three fourths of the sex do not. I accepted their choice as decisive; just as I reported in favor of enfranchising the Blacks because they do wish to vote. The few may not; but the many do; and I think they should control the situation.... It seems but fair to add that female suffrage seems to me to involve the balance of the family relation as it has hitherto existed...."[191]

Horace Greeley never forgave Susan and Mrs. Stanton for humiliating him in the constitutional convention or for the headlines in the evening papers which coupled his adverse report with his wife's petition. When they met again in New York a few weeks later at one of Alice Cary's popular evening receptions, he ignored their friendly greeting and brusquely remarked, "You two ladies are the most maneuvering politicians in the State of New York."[192]

While Susan's work in New York State was at its height, appeals for help had reached her from Republicans in Kansas, where in November 1867 two amendments would be voted upon, enfranchising women and Negroes. Unable to go to Kansas herself at that time or to spare Elizabeth Stanton, she rejoiced when Lucy Stone consented to speak throughout Kansas and when she and Lucy, as trustees of the Jackson Fund, outvoting Wendell Phillips, were able to appropriate $1,500 for this campaign.

Lucy was soon sending enthusiastic reports to Susan from Kansas, where she and her husband, Henry Blackwell, were winning many friends for the cause. "I fully expect we shall carry the State," Lucy confidently wrote Susan. "The women here are grand, and it will be a shame past all expression if they don't get the right to vote.... But the Negroes are all against us.... These men ought not to be allowed to vote before we do, because they will be just so much dead weight to lift."[193]

One cloud now appeared on the horizon. Republicans in Kansas began to withdraw their support from the woman suffrage amendment they had sponsored. It troubled Lucy and Susan that the New York Tribune and the Independent, both widely read in Kansas, published not one word favorable to woman suffrage, for these two papers with their influence and prestige could readily, they believed, win the ballot for women not only in Kansas but throughout the nation. Soon the temper of the Republican press changed from indifference to outright animosity, striking at Lucy and Henry Blackwell by calling them "free lovers," because Lucy was traveling with her husband as Lucy Stone and not as Mrs. Henry B. Blackwell. Still Lucy was hopeful, believing the Democrats were ready to take them up, but she reminded Susan, "It will be necessary to have a good force here in the fall, and you will have to come."

Never for a moment did the importance of this election in Kansas escape Susan, and her estimate of it was also that of John Stuart Mill, who wrote from England to the sponsor of the Kansas woman suffrage amendment, Samuel N. Wood, "If your citizens next November give effect to the enlightened views of your Legislature, history will remember one of the youngest states in the civilized world has been the first to adopt a measure of liberation destined to extend all over the earth and to be looked back to ... as one of the most fertile in beneficial consequences of all improvements yet effected in human affairs."[194]

Susan fully expected Kansas to pioneer for woman suffrage just as it had taken its stand against slavery when the rest of the country held back. Her first problem, however, was to raise the money to get herself and Elizabeth Stanton there. The grant from the Jackson Fund had been spent by the Blackwells and Olympia Brown of Michigan, who most providentially volunteered to continue their work when they returned to the East. Olympia Brown, recently graduated from Antioch College and ordained as a minister in the Universalist church, was a new recruit to the cause. Young and indefatigable, she reached every part of Kansas during the summer, driving over the prairies with the Singing Hutchinsons.[195]

Olympia Brown's valiant help made waiting in New York easier for Susan as she tried in every way to raise money. Further grants from the Jackson Fund were cut off by an unfavorable court decision; and the trustees of the Hovey Fund, established to further the rights of both Negroes and women, refused to finance a woman suffrage campaign in Kansas.

"We are left without a dollar," she wrote State Senator Samuel N. Wood. "Every speaker who goes to Kansas must now pay her own expenses out of her own private purse, unless money should come from some unexpected source. I shall run the risk—as I told you—and draw upon almost my last hundred to go. I tell you this that you may not contract debts under the impression that our Association can pay for them—for it cannot."[196]

She did find a way to finance the printing of leaflets so urgently needed for distribution in Kansas. Soliciting advertisements up and down Broadway during the heat of July and August, she collected enough to pay the printer for 60,000 tracts, with the result that along with the dignified, eloquent speeches of Henry Ward Beecher, Theodore Parker, George William Curtis, and John Stuart Mill went advertisements of Howe sewing machines, Mme. Demorest's millinery and patterns, Browning's washing machines, and Decker pianofortes to attract the people of Kansas.

With both New York and Kansas on her mind, Susan had had little time to be with her family, although she had often longed to slip out to Rochester for a visit with her mother and Guelma who had been ill for several months. Finally she spent a few days with them on her way to Kansas.

On the long train journey from Rochester to Kansas with such a congenial companion as Elizabeth Stanton, she enjoyed every new experience, particularly the new Palace cars advertised as the finest, most luxurious in the world, costing $40,000 each. The comfortable daytime seats transformed into beds at night and the meals served by solicitous Negro waiters were of the greatest interest to these two good housekeepers and the last bit of comfort they were to enjoy for many a day.

As soon as they reached Kansas, they set out immediately on a two-week speaking tour of the principal towns, and as usual Susan starred Mrs. Stanton while she herself acted as general manager, advertising the meetings, finding a suitable hall, sweeping it out if necessary, distributing and selling tracts, and perhaps making a short speech herself. The meetings were highly successful, but traveling by stage and wagon was rugged; most of the food served them was green with soda or floating in grease and the hotels were infested with bedbugs. Susan wrote her family of sleepless nights and of picking the "tormentors" out of their bonnets and the ruffles of their dresses.[197]

Occasionally there was an oasis of cleanliness and good food, as when they stopped at the railroad hotel in Salina and found it run by Mother Bickerdyke, who, marching through Georgia with General Sherman, had nursed and fed his soldiers. At such times Kansas would take on a rosy glow and Susan could report, "We are getting along splendidly. Just the frame of a Methodist Church with sidings and roof, and rough cottonwood boards for seats, was our meeting place last night ...; and a perfect jam it was, with men crowded outside at all the windows.... Our tracts do more than half the battle; reading matter is so very scarce that everybody clutches at a book of any kind.... All that great trunk full were sold and given away at our first 14 meetings, and we in return received $110 which a little more than paid our railroad fare—eight cents per mile—and hotel bills. Our collections thus far fully equal those at the East. I have been delightfully disappointed for everybody said I couldn't raise money in Kansas meetings."[198]

The reputation of both women preceded them to Kansas. Susan had to win her way against prejudice built up by newspaper gibes of past years which had caricatured her as a meddlesome reformer and a sour old maid, but gradually her friendliness, hominess, and sincerity broke down these preconceptions. Kansas soon respected this tall slender energetic woman who, as she overrode obstacles, showed a spirit akin to that of the frontiersman.

Mrs. Stanton, on the other hand, was welcomed at once with enthusiasm. The fact that she was the mother of seven children as well as a brilliant orator opened the way for her. She was good to look at, a queenly woman at fifty-two, with a fresh rosy complexion and carefully curled soft white hair. Her motherliness and refreshing sense of humor built up a bond of understanding with her audiences. People were eager to see her, hear her, talk with her, and entertain her.

This preference was obvious to Susan, but it aroused no jealousy. She sent Mrs. Stanton out through the state by mule team to all the small towns and settlements far from the railroad, along with their popular and faithful Republican ally, Charles Robinson, first Free State Governor of Kansas, counting on these two to build up good will. In the meantime, making her headquarters in Lawrence, she reorganized the campaign to meet the increasing opposition of the Republican machine, against which the continued support of a few prominent Kansas Republicans availed little. As the state was predominantly Republican, the prospects were gloomy, for the Democrats had not yet taken them up as Lucy Stone had predicted, but still opposed both the Negro and woman suffrage amendments. A new liquor law, which it was thought women would support, further complicated the situation, aligning the liquor interests and the German and Irish settlers solidly against votes for women.

While Susan was searching desperately for some way of appealing to the Democrats, help came from an unexpected source. The St. Louis Suffrage Association urged George Francis Train to come to the aid of women in Kansas, and always ready to champion a new and unpopular cause, he telegraphed his willingness to win the Democratic vote and pay his own expenses. Knowing little about him except that he was wealthy, eccentric, and interested in developing the Union Pacific Railroad, Susan turned tactfully to her Kansas friends for advice, although she herself welcomed his help. They wired him, "The people want you, the women want you";[199] and he came into the state in a burst of glory, speaking first in Leavenworth and Lawrence to large curious audiences. A tall handsome man with curly brown hair and keen gray eyes, flashily dressed in a blue coat with brass buttons, white vest, black trousers, patent-leather boots, and lavender kid gloves, he was a sight worth driving miles to see, and he gave his audiences the best entertainment they had had in many a day, shouting jingles at them in the midst of his speeches and mercilessly ridiculing the Republicans. Here was none of the boredom of most political speeches, none of the long sonorous sentences with classical allusions which the big-name orators of the day poured out. His bold statements, his clipped rapid-fire sentences held the people's attention whether they agreed with him or not. When he spoke in Leavenworth, the hall was packed with Irishmen who were building the railroad to the West. They hissed when he mentioned woman suffrage, but before long he had won them over and they cheered when he shook his finger at them and shouted, "Every man in Kansas who throws a vote for the Negro and not for women has insulted his mother, his daughter, his sister, and his wife."[200]

George Francis Train

At once the Republican press began a campaign of vilification, calling Train a Copperhead and ridiculing his eccentricities and conceits; and eastern Republicans, fearing they had harmed the Negro amendment in Kansas by their opposition to woman suffrage, tried to make last-minute amends by sending an appeal to Kansas voters to support both amendments. Even Horace Greeley lamely supported them in a Tribune editorial which Susan read with disgust: "It is plain that the experiment of Female Suffrage is to be tried; and, while we regard it with distrust, we are quite willing to see it pioneered by Kansas. She is a young State, and has a memorable history, wherein her women have borne an honorable part.... If, then, a majority of them really desire to vote, we, if we lived in Kansas, should vote to give them the opportunity. Upon a full and fair trial, we believe they would conclude that the right of suffrage for women was, on the whole, rather a plague than a profit, and vote to resign it into the hands of their husbands and fathers...."[201]

These halfhearted appeals were too late, for the political machine in Kansas had already done its work; and Susan, turning her back on such fair-weather friends, cultivated the Democrats even more sedulously. When the Democrat who had promised to accompany George Francis Train on a speaking tour failed him, she took his place. When Train demurred at the strenuous task ahead, she announced she would undertake it alone. Always the gallant gentleman, he accompanied her, and continued with her through the long hard weeks of travel in mail and lumber wagons over rough roads, through mud and rain, to the remotest settlements, far from the railroads. Because it was a necessity, traveling alone with a gentleman whom she hardly knew troubled her not at all, unconventional though it was.

She took charge of the meetings, opening them herself with a short sincere plea for both the woman and Negro suffrage amendments, and then she introduced George Francis Train, who, no matter how late they arrived or how tiring the day, had changed his wrinkled gray traveling suit for his resplendent platform costume. The expectant crowd never failed to respond with a gasp of surprise, and immediately the fun began as Train with his wit and his mimicry entertained them, calling for their support of woman suffrage and advocating as well some of his own pet ideas, such as freeing Ireland from British oppression, paying our national debt in greenbacks, establishing an eight-hour day in industry, and even nominating himself for President.

Amused by his dramatics and often amazed at his conceit, Susan found neither as objectionable as the outright falsehood circulated by opponents of woman suffrage. As the days went by with their continued hardships and increasing fatigue, she marveled at his unfailing courteousness, his pluck, and good cheer, while he in turn admired her courage, her endurance, and her zeal for her cause, and between them a bond of respect and loyalty was built up which could not be destroyed by the pressures of later years.

During the long hours on the road, he entertained her with the story of his life and his travels, an adventure story of a poor boy who had made good. Building clipper ships, introducing American goods in Australia, traveling in India, China, and Russia, promoting street railways in England, and now building the Union Pacific, he had a wealth of information to impart.

Their views on the Negro differed sharply. Rating the whole race as inferior and incapable of improvement, he naturally opposed enfranchising Negroes before women. She, on the other hand, had always regarded Negroes as her equals, and in campaigning with Train, she had to make her choice between Negroes and women. She chose women, just as her abolitionist friends in the East had chosen the Negro; and their indifference and opposition to woman suffrage at this crucial time was as unforgivable to her as was his valuation of the Negro to them. They called him a Copperhead, remembering his southern wife and his hatred of abolitionists, his vocal resistance to the draft, and his demands for immediate unconditional peace. They ignored entirely his defense of the Union in England during the Civil War when he publicly debated with Englishmen who supported the Confederacy. They abused him in their newspapers and he, not to be outdone, ridiculed them in his speeches, shouting, "Where is Wendell Phillips, today? Lost caste everywhere. Inconsistent in all things, cowardly in this. Where is Horace Greeley in this Kansas war for liberty? Pitching the woman suffrage idea out of the Convention and bailing out Jeff Davis. Where is William Lloyd Garrison? Being patted on the shoulders by his employers, our enemies abroad, for his faithful work in trying to destroy our nation. Where is Henry Ward Beecher? Writing a story for Bonner's Ledger...."[202]

They never forgave him this estimate of them, nor did they forgive Susan for associating herself with him.

On one of the last days of the Kansas campaign, while she was driving over the prairie with him, he suddenly asked her why the woman suffrage people did not have a paper of their own. "Not lack of brains, but lack of money," she tersely replied.[203]

They talked for a while about the good such a paper would do, about the people who should edit and write for it, what name it should have. Then he said simply, "I will give you the money."

Because a woman suffrage paper had been her cherished dream for so many years, she did not dare regard this as more than a gallant gesture soon to be forgotten; but to her amazement that very evening she heard Train announce to his audience, "When Miss Anthony gets back to New York, she is going to start a woman suffrage paper. Its name is to be The Revolution: its motto, 'Men their rights, and nothing more; women, their rights and nothing less.' This paper is to be a weekly, price $2. per year; its editors, Elizabeth Cady Stanton and Parker Pillsbury; its proprietor, Susan B. Anthony. Let everybody subscribe for it!"

Election day brought both Susan and Mrs. Stanton back to Leavenworth, to Daniel's home, to learn the verdict of the people of Kansas. As the returns came in, their hope of seeing Kansas become the first woman suffrage state quickly faded. Neither their amendment nor the Negroes' polled enough votes for adoption. Their woman suffrage amendment, however, received only 1,773 votes less than the Republican-sponsored Negro amendment, and to have accomplished this in a hard-fought bitter campaign against powerful opponents gave them confidence in themselves and in their judgment of men and events. No longer need they depend upon Wendell Phillips or other abolitionist leaders for guidance. From now on they would chart their own course. This led, they believed, to Washington, where they must gain support among members of Congress for a federal woman suffrage amendment. Few, if any, Republicans would help them, but already one Democrat had come forward. George Francis Train had offered to pay their expenses if they would join him on a lecture tour on their way East. To Susan, who had to raise every penny spent in her work, this seemed like an answer to prayer, as did his proposal to finance a woman suffrage paper for them.

By this time their abolitionist friends in the East were writing them indignant letters blaming the defeat of the Negro amendment on George Francis Train and warning them not to link woman suffrage with an unbalanced charlatan. Even their devoted friends in Kansas, including Governor Robinson, advised them against further association with Train. They did not make their decision lightly, nor was it easy to go against the judgment of respected friends, but of this they were confident—that with or without Train, they would estrange most of their old friends if they campaigned for woman suffrage now. Without him, their work, limited by lack of funds, would be ineffectual. With his financial backing, they not only had the opportunity of spreading their message in all the principal cities on their way back to New York, but had the promise of a paper, now so desperately needed when other news channels were closed to them. That Train was eccentric they agreed, and they also admitted that possibly some of his financial theories were unsound. They believed he was ahead of his time when he advocated the eight-hour day and the abolition of standing armies; but at least he looked forward, not backward. Susan had found him to be a man of high principles. She had heard him "make speeches on woman's suffrage that could be equalled only by John B. Gough,"[204] the well-known temperance crusader. Train's radical ideas did not disturb her. Her association with antislavery extremists prior to the Civil War had made her impervious to the criticism and accusations of conservatives. She was aware that on this proposed lecture tour Train probably wanted to make use of her executive ability and of Mrs. Stanton's popularity as a speaker; but on the other hand, his generosity to them was beyond anything they had ever experienced.

For Susan there was only one choice—to work for woman suffrage with the financial backing of Train. Mrs. Stanton agreed, and as she expressed it, "I have always found that when we see eye to eye, we are sure to be right, and when we pull together we are strong.... I take my beloved Susan's judgment against the world."[205]

Traveling homeward with George Francis Train, Susan and Mrs. Stanton spoke in Chicago, St. Louis, Louisville, Cincinnati, Cleveland, Buffalo, Rochester, Boston, Hartford, and other important cities where they drew large crowds, which had never before listened to a discussion of woman suffrage. Most of their old friends among the suffragists and abolitionists shunned them, for they had been warned against this folly by their colleagues in the East. The lively meetings rated plenty of publicity, complimentary in the Democratic papers but sarcastic and hostile in the Republican press. Usually "Woman Suffrage" got the headlines, but sometimes it was "Woman Suffrage and Greenbacks" or "Train for President." Handbills, the printing of which Susan supervised, scattered Train's rhymes and epigrams far and wide and carried a notice that the proceeds of all meetings would be turned over to the woman's rights cause. Susan also arranged for the printing of Train's widely distributed pamphlet, The Great Epigram Campaign of Kansas, with this jingle, so uncomplimentary to the eastern abolitionists, on its cover:

The Garrisons, Phillipses, Greeleys, and Beechers,
False prophets, false guides, false teachers and preachers,
Left Mrs. Stanton, Miss Anthony, Brown, and Stone,
To fight the Kansas battle alone;
While your Rosses, Pomeroys, and your Clarkes
Stood on the fence, or basely fled,
While woman was saved by a Copperhead.

Even more unforgivable than this to the abolitionist suffragists were the back-page advertisements of a new woman-suffrage paper, The Revolution, and of woman's rights tracts which could be purchased from Susan B. Anthony, Secretary of the American Equal Rights Association. That Susan would presume to line up this organization in any way with George Francis Train aroused the indignation of Lucy Stone, who felt the cause was being trailed in the dust.

While Susan and Mrs. Stanton traveled homeward, enjoying the comfort of the best hotels and the applause of enthusiastic audiences, a coalition against them was being formed in the East.

"All the old friends with scarce an exception are sure we are wrong," Susan wrote in her diary, January 1, 1868. "Only time can tell, but I believe we are right and hence bound to succeed."[206]

The One Word Of The Hour

"If we women fail to speak the one word of the hour," Susan wrote Anna E. Dickinson, "who shall do it? No man is able, for no man sees or feels as we do. To whom God gives the word, to him or her he says, 'Go preach it.'"[207]

This is just what Susan aimed to do in her new paper, The Revolution. It's name, she believed, expressed exactly the stirring up of thought necessary to establish justice for all—for women, Negroes, workingmen and-women, and all who were oppressed. Her two editors, Elizabeth Cady Stanton and Parker Pillsbury, reliable friends as well as vivid forceful writers, were completely in sympathy with her own liberal ideas and could be counted on to crusade fearlessly for every righteous cause. What did it matter if George Francis Train wanted space in the paper to publish his views and for a financial column, edited by David M. Melliss of the New York World? Brought up on the antislavery platform where free speech was the watchword and where all, even long-winded cranks, were allowed to express their opinions, Susan willingly opened the pages of The Revolution to Train and to Melliss in return for financial backing. When on January 8, 1868, the first issue of her paper came off the press, her heart swelled with pride and satisfaction as she turned over its pages, read its good editorials, and under the frank of Democratic Congressman James Brooks of New York, sent out ten thousand copies to all parts of the country.

The Revolution promised to discuss not only subjects which were of particular concern to her and to Elizabeth Stanton, such as "educated suffrage, irrespective of sex or color," equal pay for women for equal work, and practical education for girls as well as boys, but also the eight-hour day, labor problems, and a new financial policy for America. This new financial policy, the dream of George Francis Train, advocated the purchase of American goods only; the encouragement of immigration to rebuild the South and to settle the country from ocean to ocean; the establishment of the French financing systems, the Crédit Foncier and Crédit Mobilier, to develop our mines and railroads; the issuing of greenbacks; and penny ocean postage "to strengthen the brotherhood of Labor."

All in all it was not a program with wide appeal. Dazzled by the opportunities for making money in this new undeveloped country, people were in no mood to analyze the social order, or to consider the needs of women or labor or the living standards of the masses. Unfamiliar with the New York Stock Exchange, they found little to interest them in the paper's financial department, while speculators and promoters, such as Jay Gould and Jim Fiske, wanted no advice from the lone eagle, George Francis Train, and resented Melliss's columns of Wall Street gossip which often portrayed them in an unfavorable light. Nor did a public-affairs paper edited and published by women carry much weight. None of this, however, mattered much to Susan, who did not aim for a popular paper but "to make public sentiment." It was her hope that just as the Liberator under William Lloyd Garrison had been "the pillar of light and of fire to the slave's emancipation," so The Revolution would become "the guiding star to the enfranchisement of women."[208]

Upon Susan fell the task of building up subscriptions, soliciting advertisements, and getting copy to the printer. As her office in the New York World building, 37 Park Row, was on the fourth floor and the printer was several blocks away on the fifth floor of a building without an elevator, her job proved to be a test of physical endurance. To this was added an ever-increasing financial burden, for Train had sailed for England when the first number was issued, had been arrested because of his Irish sympathies, and had spent months in a Dublin jail, from which he sent them his thoughts on every conceivable subject but no money for the paper. He had left $600 with Susan and had instructed Melliss to make payments as needed, but this soon became impossible, and she had to face the alarming fact that, if the paper were to continue, she must raise the necessary money herself. Because the circulation was small, it was hard to get advertisers, particularly as she was firm in her determination to accept only advertisements of products she could recommend. Patent medicines and any questionable products were ruled out. Subscriptions came in encouragingly but in no sense met the deficit which piled up unrelentingly. Her goal was 100,000 subscribers.

She had gone to Washington at once to solicit subscriptions personally from the President and members of Congress. Ben Wade of Ohio headed the list of Senators who subscribed, and loyal as always to woman suffrage, encouraged her to go ahead and push her cause. "It has got to come," he added, "but Congress is too busy now to take it up." Senator Henry Wilson of Massachusetts greeted her gruffly, telling her that she and Mrs. Stanton had done more to block reconstruction in the last two years than all others in the land, but he subscribed because he wanted to know what they were up to. Although Senator Pomeroy was "sore about Kansas" and her alliance with the Democrats, he nevertheless subscribed, but Senator Sumner was not to be seen. The first member of the House to put his name on her list was her dependable understanding friend, George Julian of Indiana, and many others followed his lead. For two hours she waited to see President Johnson, in an anteroom "among the huge half-bushel-measure spittoons and terrible filth ... where the smell of tobacco and whiskey was powerful." When she finally reached him, he immediately refused her request, explaining that he had a thousand such solicitations every day. Not easily put off, she countered at once by remarking that he had never before had such a request in his life. "You recognize, Mr. Johnson," she continued, "that Mrs. Stanton and myself for two years have boldly told the Republican party that they must give ballots to women as well as to Negroes, and by means of The Revolution we are bound to drive the party to this logical conclusion or break it into a thousand pieces as was the old Whig party, unless we get our rights." This "brought him to his pocketbook," she triumphantly reported, and in a bold hand he signed his name, Andrew Johnson, as much as to say, "Anything to get rid of this woman and break the radical party."[209]

She was proud of her paper, proud of its typography which was far more readable than the average news sheets of the day with their miserably small print. The larger type and less crowded pages were inviting, the articles stimulating. Parker Pillsbury, covering Congressional and political developments and the impeachment trial of President Johnson with which he was not in sympathy, was fearless in his denunciations of politicians, their ruthless intrigue and disregard of the public. During the turbulent days when the impeachment trial was front-page news everywhere, The Revolution proclaimed it as a political maneuver of the Republicans to confuse the people and divert their attention from more important issues, such as corruption in government, high prices, taxation, and the fabulous wealth being amassed by the few. This of course roused the intense disapproval of Wendell Phillips, Theodore Tilton, and Horace Greeley, all of whom regarded Johnson as a traitor and shouted for impeachment. It ran counter to the views of Susan's brother Daniel, who telegraphed Senator Ross of Kansas demanding his vote for impeachment. Although no supporter of President Johnson, Susan was now completely awake to the political manipulations of the radical Republicans and what seemed to her their readiness to sacrifice the good of the nation for the success of their party. She repudiated them all—all but the rugged Ben Wade, always true to woman suffrage, and the tall handsome Chief Justice, Salmon P. Chase, who, she believed, stood for justice and equality.

Both of these men Susan regarded as far better qualified for the Presidency than General Grant, who now was the obvious choice of the Republicans for 1868. "Why go pell-mell for Grant," asked The Revolution, "when all admit that he is unfit for the position? It is not too late, if true men and women will do their duty, to make an honest man like Ben Wade, President. Let us save the Nation. As to the Republican party the sooner it is scattered to the four winds of Heaven the better."[210] Later when Chase was out of the running among Republicans and not averse to overtures from the Democrats, The Revolution urged him as the Democratic candidate with universal suffrage as his slogan. Susan demanded civil rights, suffrage, education, and farms for the Negroes as did the Republicans, but she could not overlook the political corruption which was flourishing under the military control of the South, and she recognized that the Republicans' insistence on Negro suffrage in the South did not stem solely from devotion to a noble principle, but also from an overwhelming desire to insure victory for their party in the coming election. These views were reflected editorially in The Revolution, which, calling attention to the fact that Connecticut, Michigan, Minnesota, Ohio, and Pennsylvania had refused to enfranchise their Negroes, asked why Negro suffrage should be forced on the South before it was accepted in the North.

The Fourteenth Amendment was having hard sledding and The Revolution repudiated it, calling instead for an amendment granting universal suffrage, or in other words, suffrage for women and Negroes. The Revolution also discussed in editorials by Mrs. Stanton other subjects of interest to women, such as marriage, divorce, prostitution, and infanticide, all of which Susan agreed needed frank thoughtful consideration, but which other papers handled with kid gloves.

In still another unpopular field, that of labor and capital, The Revolution also pioneered fearlessly, asking for shorter hours and lower wages for workers, as it pointed out labor's valuable contribution to the development of the country. It also called attention to the vicious contrasts in large cities, where many lived in tumbledown tenements in abject poverty while the few, with more wealth than they knew what to do with, spent lavishly and built themselves palaces. Sentiments such as these increased the indignation of Susan's critics, but she gloried in the output of her two courageous editors just as she had gloried in the evangelistic zeal of the antislavery crusaders. Wisely, however, she added to her list of contributors some of the popular women writers of the day, among them Alice and Phoebe Cary. She ran a series of articles on women as farmers, machinists, inventors, and dentists, secured news from foreign correspondents, mostly from England, and published a Washington letter and woman's rights news from the states. Believing that women should become acquainted with the great women of the past, especially those who fought for their freedom and advancement, she printed an article on Frances Wright and serialized Mary Wollstonecraft's A Vindication of the Rights of Women.

Eagerly Susan looked for favorable notices of her new paper in the press. Much to her sorrow, Horace Greeley's New York Tribune completely ignored its existence, as did her old standby, the Antislavery Standard. The New York Times ridiculed as usual anything connected with woman's rights or woman suffrage. The New York Home Journal called it "plucky, keen, and wide awake, although some of its ways are not at all to our taste." Theodore Tilton in the Congregationalist paper, The Independent, commented in his usual facetious style, which pinned him down neither to praise nor unfriendliness, but Susan was grateful to read, "The Revolution from the start will arouse, thrill, edify, amuse, vex, and non-plus its friends. But it will command attention: it will conquer a hearing." Newspapers were generally friendly. "Miss Anthony's woman's rights paper," declared the Troy (New York) Times, "is a realistic, well-edited, instructive journal ... and its beautiful mechanical execution renders its appearance very attractive." The Chicago Workingman's Advocate observed, "We have no doubt it will prove an able ally of the labor reform movement." Nellie Hutchinson of the Cincinnati Commercial, one of the few women journalists, described sympathetically for her readers the neat comfortable Revolution office and Susan with her "rare" but "genial smile," Susan, "the determined—the invincible ... destined to be Vice-President or Secretary of State...," adding, "The world is better for thee, Susan."[211]

While new friends praised, old friends pleaded unsuccessfully with Mrs. Stanton and Parker Pillsbury to free themselves from Susan's harmful influence. William Lloyd Garrison wrote Susan of his regret and astonishment that she and Mrs. Stanton had so taken leave of their senses as to be infatuated with the Democratic party and to be associated with that "crack-brained harlequin and semi-lunatic," George Francis Train. She published his letter in The Revolution with an answer by Mrs. Stanton which not only pointed out how often the Republicans had failed women but reminded Garrison how he had welcomed into his antislavery ranks anyone and everyone who believed in his ideas, "a motley crew it was." She recalled the label of fanatic which had been attached to him, how he had been threatened and pelted with rotten eggs for expressing his unpopular ideas and for burning the Constitution which he declared sanctioned slavery. With such a background, she told him, he should be able to recognize her right and Susan's to judge all parties and all men on what they did for woman suffrage.[212]

None of these arguments made any impression upon Garrison, or upon Lucy Stone, whose bitter criticism and distrust of Susan's motives wounded Susan deeply. Only a few of her old friends seemed able to understand what she was trying to do, among them Martha C. Wright, who, at first critical of her association with Train, now wrote of The Revolution, "Its vigorous pages are what we need. Count on me now and ever as your true and unswerving friend."[213]

Anna E. Dickinson

Another bright spot was Susan's friendship with Anna E. Dickinson, with whom she carried on a lively correspondence, scratching oft hurried notes to her on the backs of old envelopes or any odd scraps of paper that came to hand. Whenever Anna was in New York, she usually burst into the Revolution office, showered Susan with kisses, and carried on such an animated conversation about her experiences that the whole office force was spellbound, admiring at the same time her stylish costume and jaunty velvet cap with its white feather, very becoming on her short black curls. Repeatedly Susan urged Anna to stay with her in her "plain quarters" at 44 Bond Street or in her "nice hall bedroom" at 116 East Twenty-third Street. That Anna could have risen out of the hardships of her girlhood to such popularity as a lecturer and to such financial success was to Susan like a fairy tale come true. Scarcely past twenty, Anna not only had moved vast audiences to tears, but was sought after by the Republicans as one of their most popular campaign speakers and had addressed Congress with President Lincoln in attendance. Susan had been sadly disappointed that Anna had not seen her way clear to speak a strong word for women in the Kansas campaign, but she hoped that this vivid talented young woman would prove to be "the evangel" who would lead women "into the kingdom of political and civil rights." It never occurred to her that she herself might even now be that "evangel."[214]

By this time Susan had been called on the carpet by some of the officers of the American Equal Rights Association because she had used the Association's office as a base for business connected with the Train lecture tour and the establishment of The Revolution. She was also accused of spending the funds of the Association for her own projects and to advertise Train. Lucy Stone, Henry Blackwell, and Stephen Foster were particularly suspicious of her. Her accounts were checked and rechecked by them and found in good order. However, at the annual meeting of the Association in May 1868, Henry Blackwell again brought the matter up. Deeply hurt by his public accusation, she once more carefully explained that because there had been no funds except those which came out of her own pocket or had been raised by her, she had felt free to spend them as she thought best. This obviously satisfied the majority, many of whom expressed appreciation of her year of hard work for the cause. She later wrote Thomas Wentworth Higginson, "Even if not one old friend had seemed to have remembered the past and it had been swallowed up, overshadowed by the Train cloud, I should still have rejoiced that I have done the work—for no human prejudice or power can rob me of the joy, the compensation, I have stored up therefrom. That it is wholly spiritual, I need but tell you that this day, I have not two hundred dollars more than I had the day I entered upon the public work of woman's rights and antislavery."[215]

What troubled her most at these meetings was not the animosity directed against her by Henry Blackwell and Lucy Stone, but the assertion, made by Frederick Douglass and agreed to by all the men present, that Negro suffrage was more urgent than woman suffrage. When Lucy Stone came to the defense of woman suffrage in a speech whose content and eloquence Susan thought surpassed that of "any other mortal woman speaker," she was willing to forgive Lucy anything, and wrote Thomas Wentworth Higginson, "I want you to know that it is impossible for me to lay a straw in the way of anyone who personally wrongs me, if only that one will work nobly in the cause in their own way and time. They may try to hinder my success but I never theirs."

Realizing that it would be futile for her to spend any more time trying to persuade the American Equal Rights Association to help her with her woman suffrage campaign, she now formed a small committee of her own, headed by Elizabeth Cady Stanton. It included Elizabeth Smith Miller, the liberal wealthy daughter of Gerrit Smith, Abby Hopper Gibbons, the Quaker philanthropist and social worker; and Mary Cheney Greeley, the wife of Horace Greeley, who, in spite of the fact that her husband now opposed woman suffrage, continued to take her stand for it. This committee, with The Revolution as its mouthpiece, was soon acting as a clearing house for woman suffrage organizations throughout the country and called itself the Woman's Suffrage Association of America.

To the national Republican convention in Chicago which nominated General Grant for President, these women sent a carefully worded memorial asking that the rights of women be recognized in the reconstruction. It was ignored. Thereupon Susan turned to the Democrats, attending with Mrs. Stanton a preconvention rally in New York, addressed by Governor Horatio Seymour. Given seats of honor on the platform, they attracted considerable attention and the New York Sun commented editorially that this honor conferred upon them by the Democrats not only committed Miss Anthony and Mrs. Stanton to Governor Seymour's views but also committed the Democrats to incorporate a woman suffrage plank in their platform.

This was too much for some of the officers of the American Equal Rights Association, whose executive committee now adopted a sarcastic resolution proposing that Susan attend the national Democratic convention and prove her confidence in the Democrats by securing a plank in their platform.

Ignoring the unfriendly implications of this resolution and the ridicule heaped upon her by the New York City papers, Susan made plans to attend the Democratic convention, which for the first time since the war was bringing northern

and southern Democrats together for the dedication of their new, imposing headquarters, Tammany Hall, and which was also attracting many liberals who, disgusted by the corruption of the Republicans, were looking for a "new departure" from the Democrats. To the amazement of the delegates, Susan with Mrs. Stanton and several other women walked into the convention when it was well under way and sent a memorial up to Governor Seymour who was presiding. He received it graciously, announcing that he held in his hand a memorial of the women of the United States signed by Susan B. Anthony, and then turned it over to the secretary to be read while the audience shouted and cheered. The sonorous passages demanding the enfranchisement of women rang out through and above the bedlam: "We appeal to you because ... you have been the party heretofore to extend the suffrage. It was the Democratic party that fought most valiantly for the removal of the 'property qualification' from all white men and thereby placed the poorest ditch digger on a political level with the proudest millionaire.... And now you have an opportunity to confer a similar boon on the women of the country and thus ... perpetuate your political power for decades to come...."[216]
To hear these words read in a national political convention was to Susan worth any ridicule she might be forced to endure. She was not allowed to speak to the convention as she had requested, and shouts and jeers continued as her memorial was hurriedly referred to the Resolutions committee where it could be conveniently overlooked.
The Republican press reported the incident with sarcasm and animosity, the Tribune deeply wounding her: "Miss Susan B. Anthony has our sincere pity. She has been an ardent suitor of democracy, and they rejected her overtures yesterday with screams of laughter."[217]
The Democrats' nomination of Horatio Seymour and Frank Blair was as reactionary and unpromising of a "new departure" as was the choice of General Grant and Schuyler Colfax by the Republicans. Thereupon The Revolution called for a new party, a people's party which would be sincerely devoted to the welfare of all the people. So strongly did Susan feel about this that in one of her few signed editorials she declared, "Both the great political parties pretending to save the country are only endeavoring to save themselves.... In their hands humanity has no hope.... The sooner their power is broken as parties the better.... The Revolution calls for construction, not reconstruction.... Who will aid us in our grand enterprise of a nation's salvation?"[218]
To "darling Anna" she wrote more specifically, "Both parties are owned body and soul by the Gold Gamblers of the Nation—and so far as the honest working men and women of the country are concerned, it matters very little which succeeds. Oh that the Gods would inspire men of influence and money to move for a third party—universal suffrage and anti-monopolist of land and gold."[219]

Work, Wages, And The Ballot

In her zeal to promote the welfare of all the people, Susan now turned her attention to the workingwomen of New York, whose low wages, long hours, and unhealthy working and living conditions had troubled her for a long time. Women were being forced out of the home into the factory by a changing and expanding economy, and at last were being paid for their work. However, the women she met on the streets of New York, hurrying to work at dawn and returning late at night, weary, pale, and shabbily dressed, had none of the confidence of the economically independent. They had merely exchanged one form of slavery for another. She saw the ballot as their most powerful ally, and as she told the factory girls of Cohoes, New York, they could compel their employers to grant them a ten-hour day, equal opportunity for advancement, and equal pay, the moment they held the ballot in their hands.[220]
As yet labor unions were few and short-lived. The women tailors of New York had formed a union as early as 1825, but it had not survived, and later attempts to form women's unions had rarely been successful. A few men's unions had weathered the years, but they had not enrolled women, fearing their competition. Women were welcomed only by the National Labor Union, established in Baltimore in 1866 for the purpose of federating all unions.
When the National Labor Union Congress met in New York in September 1868, Susan saw an opportunity for women to take part, and in preparation she called a group of workingwomen together in The Revolution office to form a Workingwomen's Association which she hoped would eventually represent all of the trades. At this meeting, the majority were from the printing trade, typesetters operating the newly invented typesetting machines, press feeders, bookbinders, and clerks, in whom she had become interested through her venture in publishing. She wanted them to call their organization the Workingwomen's Suffrage Association, but they refused, because they feared the public's disapproval of woman suffrage and were convinced they should not seek political rights until they had improved their

working conditions. She could not make them see that they were putting the cart before the horse. They did, however, form Workingwomen's Association No. 1, electing her their delegate to the National Labor Congress.

Next she called a meeting of the women in the sewing trades, and with the help of men from the National Labor Union, persuaded a hundred of them to form Workingwomen's Association No. 2. Most of these women were seamstresses making men's shirts, women's coats, vests, lace collars, hoop skirts, corsets, fur garments, and straw hats, but also represented were women from the umbrella, parasol, and paper collar industry, metal burnishers, and saleswomen. Most of them were young girls who worked from ten to fourteen hours a day, from six in the morning until eight at night, and earned from $4 to $8 a week.

"You must not work for these starving prices any longer ...," Susan told them. "Have a spirit of independence among you, 'a wholesome discontent,' as Ralph Waldo Emerson has said, and you will get better wages for yourselves. Get together and discuss, and meet again and again.... I will come and talk to you...."[221] They elected Mrs. Mary Kellogg Putnam to represent them at the National Labor Congress.

With Mrs. Putnam and Kate Mullaney, the able president of the Collar Laundry Union of Troy, New York, with Mary A. MacDonald of the Women's Protective Labor Union of Mt. Vernon, New York, and Mrs. Stanton, representing the Woman's Suffrage Association of America, Susan knocked at the door of the National Labor Congress. All were welcomed but Mrs. Stanton, who represented a woman suffrage organization and whose acceptance the rank and file feared might indicate to the public that the Labor Congress endorsed votes for women.

The women had a friend in William H. Sylvis of the Iron Molders' Union, who was the driving force behind the National Labor Congress, and he made it clear at once that he welcomed Mrs. Stanton and everyone else who believed in his cause. So strong, however, was the opposition to woman suffrage among union men that eighteen threatened to resign if Mrs. Stanton were admitted as a delegate. The debate continued, giving Susan an opportunity to explain why the ballot was important to workingwomen. "It is the power of the ballot," she declared, "that makes men successful in their strikes."[222] She recommended that both men and women be enrolled in unions, pointing out that had this been done, women typesetters would not have replaced men at lower wages in the recent strike of printers on the New York World. Finally a resolution was adopted, making it clear that Mrs. Stanton's acceptance in no way committed the National Labor Congress to her "peculiar ideas" or to "Female Suffrage."

A committee on female labor was then appointed with Susan as one of its members. At once she tried to show the committee how the vote would help women in their struggle for higher wages. She had at hand a perfect example in the unsuccessful strike of Kate Mullaney's strong, well-organized union of 500 collar laundry workers in Troy, New York. Aware that Kate blamed their defeat on the ruthless newspaper campaign, inspired and paid for by employers, Susan asked her, "If you had been 500 carpenters or 500 masons, do you not think you would have succeeded?"[223] "Certainly," Kate Mullaney replied, adding that the striking bricklayers had won everything they demanded. Susan then reminded her that because the bricklayers were voters, newspapers respected them and would hesitate to arouse their displeasure, realizing that in the next election they would need the votes of all union men for their candidates. "If you collar women had been voters," she told them, "you too would have held the balance of political power in that little city of Troy."

Susan convinced the committee on female labor, and in their strong report to the convention they urged women "to secure the ballot" as well as "to learn the trades, engage in business, join labor unions or form protective unions of their own, ... and use every other honorable means to persuade or force employers to do justice to women by paying them equal wages for equal work." These women also called upon the National Labor Congress to aid the organization of women's unions, to demand the eight-hour day for women as well as men, and to ask Congress and state legislatures to pass laws providing equal pay for women in government employ. The phrase, "to secure the ballot," was quickly challenged by some of the men and had to be deleted before the report was accepted; but this setback was as nothing to Susan in comparison with the friends she had made for woman suffrage among prominent labor leaders and with the fact that a woman, Kate Mullaney of Troy, had been chosen assistant secretary of the National Labor Union and its national organizer of women.[224]

The National Labor Union Congress won high praise in The Revolution as laying the foundation of the new political party of America which would be triumphant in 1872. "The producers, the working-men, the women, the Negroes," The Revolution declared, "are destined to form a triple power that shall speedily wrest the sceptre of government from the non-producers, the land monopolists, the bondholders, and the politicians."[225]

One of the most encouraging signs at this time was the friendliness of the New York World, whose reporters covered the meetings of the Workingwomen's Association with sympathy, arousing much local interest. Reprinting these reports and supplementing them, The Revolution carried their import farther afield, bringing to the attention of many the wisdom and justice of equal pay for equal work, and the need to organize workingwomen and to provide training and trade schools for them. The Revolution continually spurred women on to improve themselves, to learn new skills, and actually to do equal work if they expected equal pay.

When reports reached Susan that women in the printing trade were afraid of manual labor, of getting their hands and fingers dirty, and of lifting heavy galleys, she quickly let them know that she had no patience with this. "Those who stay at home," she told them, "have to wash kettles and lift wash tubs and black stoves until their hands are blackened and hardened. In this spirit, you must go to work on your cases of type. Are these cases heavier than a wash tub filled with water and clothes, or the old cheese tubs?... The trouble is either that girls are not educated to have physical strength or else they do not like to use it. If a union of women is to succeed, it must be composed of strength, nerve, courage, and persistence, with no fear of dirtying their white fingers, but with a determination that when they go into an office they would go through all that was required of them and demand just as high wages as the men....

"Make up your mind," she continued, "to take the 'lean' with the 'fat,' and be early and late at the case precisely as the men are. I do not demand equal pay for any women save those who do equal work in value. Scorn to be coddled by your employers; make them understand that you are in their service as workers, not as women."[226]

Workingwomen's associations now existed in Boston, St. Louis, Chicago, San Francisco and other cities, encouraged and aroused by the efforts at organization in New York. These associations occasionally exchanged ideas, and news of all of them was published in The Revolution. The groups in Boston and in the outlying textile mills were particularly active, and Susan brought to her next suffrage convention in Washington in 1870 Jennie Collins of Lowell who was ably leading a strike against a cut in wages. The newspapers, too, began to notice workingwomen, publishing articles about their working and living conditions.

Trying to amalgamate the various groups in New York, Susan now formed a Workingwomen's Central Association, of which she was elected president. To its meetings she brought interesting speakers and practical reports on wages, hours, and working conditions. She herself picked up a great deal of useful information in her daily round as she talked with this one and that one. On her walks to and from work, in all kinds of weather, she met poorly clad women carrying sacks and baskets in which they collected rags, scraps of paper, bones, old shoes, and anything worth rescuing from "garbage boxes." With friendliness and good cheer, she greeted these ragpickers, sometimes stopping to talk with them about their work, and through her interest brought several into the Workingwomen's Association. Looking forward to surveys on all women's occupations, she started out by appointing a committee to investigate the ragpickers, many of whom lived in tumbledown slab shanties on the rocky land which is now a part of Central Park.

This investigation revealed that more than half of the 1200 ragpickers were women and that it was the one occupation in which women had equal opportunity with men and received equal compensation for their day's work. Average earnings ranged from forty cents a day to ten dollars a week. The report, highly sentimental in the light of today's scientific approach, was a promising beginning, a survey made by women themselves in their own interest—the forerunner of the reports of the Labor Department's Women's Bureau.

Cooperatives appealed to Susan as they did to many labor leaders as the best means of freeing labor. When the Sewing Machine Operators Union tried to establish a shop where their members could share the profits of their labor, she did her best to help them, hoping to see them gain economic independence in a light airy clean shop where wealthy women, eager to help their sisters, would patronize them. However, the wealthy women to whom she appealed to finance this project did not respond, looking upon a cooperative as a first step toward socialism and a threat to their own profits. She was able, however, to arouse a glimmer of interest among the members of the newly formed literary club, Sorosis, in the problems of working women.

She had the satisfaction of seeing women typesetters form their own union in 1869, and this was, according to the Albany Daily Knickerbocker, "the first move of the kind ever made in the country by any class of labor, to place woman on a par with man as regards standing, intelligence, and manual ability."[227] The Revolution encouraged this union by printing notices of its meetings and urging all women compositors to join. In signed articles, Susan pointed out how wages had improved since the union was organized. "A little more Union, girls," she said, "and soon all employers will come up to 45 cents, the price paid men.... So join the Union, girls, and together say Equal Pay for Equal Work."[228]

Eager to bring more women into the printing trade where wages were higher, she tried in every possible way to establish trade schools for them. She looked forward to a printing business run entirely by women, giving employment to hundreds. So obsessed was she by the idea of a trade school for women compositors that when printers in New York went on a strike, she saw an opportunity for women to take their places and appealed by letter and in person to a group of employers "to contribute liberally for the purpose of enabling us to establish a training school for girls in the art of typesetting." Explaining that hundreds of young women, now stitching at starvation wages, were ready and eager to learn the trade, she added, "Give us the means and we will soon give you competent women compositors."[229] Having learned by experience that men always kept women out of their field of labor unless forced by circumstances to admit them, she also urged young women to take the places of striking typesetters at whatever wage they could get. It never occurred to her in her eagerness to bring women into a new occupation that she might be breaking the strike. She saw only women's opportunity to prove to employers that they were able to do the work and to show the Typographical Union that they should admit women as members. Labor men, however, soon let her know how much they disapproved of her strategy. She tried to explain her motives to them, that she was trying to fit these women to earn equal wages with men. She reminded these men of how hard it was for women to get into the printing trade and how they had refused to admit women to their union; and she called their attention to her whole-hearted support of the lately formed Women's Typographical Union.

Some of the men were never convinced and never forgot this misstep, bringing it up at the National Labor Union Congress in Philadelphia in 1869, which Susan attended as a delegate of the New York Workingwomen's Association. Here she found herself facing an unfriendly group without the support of William H. Sylvis, who had recently died. For three days they debated her eligibility as a delegate, first expressing fear that her admission would commit the Labor Congress to woman suffrage. When she won 55 votes against 52 in opposition, Typographical Union No. 6 of New York brought accusations against her which aroused suspicion in the minds of many union members. They pointed out that she belonged to no union, and they called her an enemy of labor because she had encouraged women to take men's jobs during the printers' strike. They could not or would not understand that in urging women to take men's jobs, she had been fighting for women just as they fought for their union, and they completely overlooked how continuously and effectively she had supported the Women's Typographical Union. Her Revolution, they claimed, was printed at less than union rates in a "rat office" and her explanation was not satisfactory. That it was printed on contract outside her office was no answer to satisfy union men who could not realize on what a scant margin her paper operated or how gladly she would have set up a union shop had the funds been available.

Not only were these accusations repeated again and again, they were also carried far and wide by the press, with the result that Susan was not only kept out of the Labor Congress but was even sharply criticized by some members of her Workingwomen's Association.

"As to the charges which were made by Typographical Union No. 6," she reported to this Association, "no one believes them; and I don't think they are worth answering. I admit that this Workingwomen's Association is not a trade organization; and while I join heart and hand with the working people in their trades unions, and in everything else by which they can protect themselves against the oppression of capitalists and employers, I say that this organization of ours is more upon the broad platform of philosophizing on the general questions of labor, and to discuss what can be done to ameliorate the condition of working people generally."[230]

She was not without friends in the ranks of labor, however, the New England delegates giving her their support. The New York World, very fair in its coverage of the heated debates, declared, "Of her devotion to the cause of workingwomen, there can be no question."[231]

The activities of the Workingwomen's Association had by this time begun to irk employers, and some of them threatened instant dismissal of any employee who reported her wages or hours to these meddling women. Fear of losing their jobs now hung over many while others were forbidden by their fathers, husbands, and brothers to have anything to do with strong-minded Susan B. Anthony.

To counteract this disintegrating influence and to bring all classes of women together in their fight for equal rights, Susan persuaded the popular lecturer, Anna E. Dickinson, to speak for the Workingwomen's Association at Cooper Union. This, however, only added fuel to the flames, for Anna, in an emotional speech, "A Struggle for Life," told the tragic story of Hester Vaughn, a workingwoman who had been accused of murdering her illegitimate child. Found in a critical condition with her dead baby beside her, Hester Vaughn had been charged with infanticide, tried without proper defense, and convicted by a prejudiced court, although there was no proof that she had deliberately killed her child. At Susan's instigation, the Workingwomen's Association sent a woman physician, Dr. Clemence Lozier, and the well-known author, Eleanor Kirk, to Philadelphia to investigate the case. Both were convinced of Hester Vaughn's innocence.

With the aid of Elizabeth Cady Stanton's courageous editorials in The Revolution, Susan made such an issue of the conviction of Hester Vaughn that many newspapers accused her of obstructing justice and advocating free love, and this provided a moral weapon for her critics to use in their fight against the growing independence of women. Eventually her efforts and those of her colleagues won a pardon for Hester Vaughn. At the same time the publicity given this case served to educate women on a subject heretofore taboo, showing them that poverty and a double standard of morals made victims of young women like Hester Vaughn. Susan also made use of this case to point out the need for women jurors to insure an unprejudiced trial. She even suggested that Columbia University Law School open its doors to women so that a few of them might be able to understand their rights under the law and bring aid to their less fortunate sisters.

Under Susan's guidance, the Workingwomen's Association continued to hold meetings as long as she remained in New York. In its limited way, it carried on much-needed educational work, building up self-respect and confidence among workingwomen, stirring up "a wholesome discontent," and preparing the way for women's unions. The public responded. At Cooper Union, telegraphy courses were opened to women; the New York Business School, at Susan's instigation, offered young women scholarships in bookkeeping; and there were repeated requests for the enrollment of women in the College of New York.

Living in the heart of this rapidly growing, sprawling city, Susan saw much to distress her and pondered over the disturbing social conditions, looking for a way to relieve poverty and wipe out crime and corruption. She saw luxury, extravagance, and success for the few, while half of the population lived in the slums in dilapidated houses and in damp cellars, often four or five to a room. Immigrants, continually pouring in from Europe, overtaxed the already inadequate housing, and unfamiliar with our language and customs, were the easy prey of corrupt politicians. Many were homeless, sleeping in the streets and parks until the rain or cold drove them into police stations for warmth and shelter. Susan longed to bring order and cleanliness, good homes and good government to this overcrowded city, and again and again she came to the conclusion that votes for women, which meant a voice in the government, would be the most potent factor for reform.

Yet she did not close her mind to other avenues of reform. Seeing reflected in the life of the city the excesses, the injustice, and the unsoundness of laissez-faire capitalism, she spoke out fearlessly in The Revolution against its abuses, such as the fortunes made out of the low wages and long hours of labor, or the Wall Street speculation to corner the gold market, or the efforts to take over the public lands of the West through grants to the transcontinental railroads. Her active mind also sought a solution of the complicated currency problem. In fact there was no public question which she hesitated to approach, to think out or attempt to solve. She did not keep her struggle for woman suffrage aloof from the pressing problems of the day. Instead she kept it abreast of the times, keenly alive to social, political, and economic issues, and involved in current public affairs.

The Inadequate Fifteenth Amendment

The Fourteenth Amendment had been ratified in July 1868, but Republicans found it inadequate because it did not specifically enfranchise Negroes. More than ever convinced that they needed the Negro vote in order to continue in power, they prepared to supplement it by a Fifteenth Amendment, which Susan hoped would be drafted to enfranchise women as well as Negroes. Immediately through her Woman's Suffrage Association of America, she petitioned Congress to make no distinction between men and women in any amendment extending or regulating suffrage.

She and Elizabeth Stanton also persuaded their good friends, Senator Pomeroy of Kansas and Congressman Julian of Indiana, to introduce in December 1868 resolutions providing that suffrage be based on citizenship, be regulated by Congress, and that all citizens, native or naturalized, enjoy this right without distinction of race, color, or sex. Before the end of the month, Senator Wilson of Massachusetts and Congressman Julian had introduced other resolutions to enfranchise women in the District of Columbia and in the territories. Even the New York Herald could see no reason why "the experiment" of woman suffrage should not be tried in the District of Columbia.[232]

To focus attention on woman suffrage at this crucial time, Susan, in January 1869, called together the first woman suffrage convention ever held in Washington. No only did it attract women from as far west as Illinois, Missouri, and Kansas, but Senator Pomeroy lent it importance by his opening speech, and through the detailed and respectful reporting of the New York World and of Grace Greenwood of the Philadelphia Press it received nationwide notice. Congress, however, gave little heed to women's demands. "The experiment" of woman suffrage in the District of Columbia was not tried and nothing came of the resolutions for universal suffrage introduced by Pomeroy, Julian, and Wilson. In spite of all Susan's efforts to have the word "sex" added to the Fifteenth Amendment, she soon faced the bitter disappointment of seeing a version ignoring women submitted to the states for ratification: "The right of citizens of the United States to vote shall not be denied or abridged by the United States or by any State on account of race, color, or previous condition of servitude."

The blatant omission of the word "sex" forced Susan and Mrs. Stanton to initiate an amendment of their own, a Sixteenth Amendment, and again Congressman Julian came to their aid, although he too regarded Negro suffrage as more "immediately important and absorbing"[233] than suffrage for women. On March 15, 1869, at one of the first sessions of the newly elected Congress, he introduced an amendment to the Constitution, providing that the right of suffrage be based on citizenship without any distinction or discrimination because of sex. This was the first federal woman suffrage amendment ever proposed in Congress.

Opportunity to campaign for this amendment was now offered Susan and Elizabeth Stanton as they addressed a series of conventions in Ohio, Illinois, Wisconsin, and Missouri. Press notices were good, a Milwaukee paper describing Susan as "an earnest enthusiastic, fiery woman—ready, apt, witty and what a politician would call sharp ... radical in the strongest sense," making "radical everything she touches."[234] She found woman suffrage sentiment growing by leaps and bounds in the West and western men ready to support a federal woman suffrage amendment.

With a lighter heart than she had had in many a day and with new subscriptions to The Revolution, Susan returned to New York. She moved the Revolution office to the first floor of the Women's Bureau, a large four-story brownstone house at 49 East Twenty-third Street, near Fifth Avenue, which had been purchased by a wealthy New Yorker, Mrs. Elizabeth Phelps, who looked forward to establishing a center where women's organizations could meet and where any woman interested in the advancement of her sex would find encouragement and inspiration. Susan's hopes were high for the Women's Bureau, and in this most respectable, fashionable, and even elegant setting, she expected her Revolution, in spite of its inflammable name, to live down its turbulent past and win new friends and subscribers.[235]

She made one last effort to resuscitate the American Equal Rights Association, writing personal letters to old friends, urging that past differences be forgotten and that all rededicate themselves to establishing universal suffrage by means of the Sixteenth Amendment. She was optimistic as she prepared for a convention in New York, particularly as one obstacle to unity had been removed. George Francis Train had voluntarily severed all connections with The Revolution to devote himself to freeing Ireland. She soon found, however, that the misunderstandings between her and her old antislavery friends were far deeper than George Francis Train, although he would for a long time be blamed for them. The Fifteenth Amendment was still a bone of contention and The Revolution's continued editorials against it widened the breach.

The fireworks were set off in the convention of the American Equal Rights Association by Stephen S. Foster, who objected to the nomination of Susan and Mrs. Stanton as officers of the Association because they had in his opinion repudiated its principles. When asked to explain further, he replied that not only had they published a paper advocating educated suffrage while the Association stood for universal suffrage but they had shown themselves unfit by collaboration with George Francis Train who ridiculed Negroes and opposed their enfranchisement.

Trying to pour oil on the troubled waters, Mary Livermore, the popular new delegate from Chicago, asked whether it was quite fair to bring up George Francis Train when he had retired from The Revolution.

To this Stephen Foster sternly replied, "If The Revolution which has so often endorsed George Francis Train will repudiate him because of his course in respect to the Negro's rights, I have nothing further to say. But they do not repudiate him. He goes out; but they do not cast him out."[236]

"Of course we do not," Susan instantly protested.

Mr. Foster then objected to the way Susan had spent the funds of the Association, accusing her of failing to keep adequate accounts.

This she emphatically denied, explaining that she had presented a full accounting to the trust fund committee, that it had been audited, and she had been voted $1,000 to repay her for the amount she had personally advanced for the work.

Unwilling to accept her explanation and calling it unreliable, he continued his complaints until interrupted by Henry Blackwell who corroborated Susan's statement, adding that she had refused the $1,000 due her because of the dissatisfaction expressed over her management. Declaring himself completely satisfied with the settlement and confident of the purity of Susan's motives even if some of her expenditures were unwise, Henry Blackwell continued, "I will agree that many unwise things have been written in The Revolution by a gentleman who furnished part of the means by which the paper has been carried on. But that gentleman has withdrawn, and you, who know the real opinions of Miss Anthony and Mrs. Stanton on the question of Negro suffrage, do not believe that they mean to create antagonism between the Negro and woman question...."

To Susan's great relief Henry Blackwell's explanation satisfied the delegates, who gave her and Mrs. Stanton a vote of confidence. Not so easily healed, however, were the wounds left by the accusations of mismanagement and dishonesty. The atmosphere was still tense, for differences of opinion on policy remained. Most of the old reliable workers stood unequivocally for the Fifteenth Amendment, which they regarded as the crowning achievement of the antislavery movement, and they heartily disapproved of forcing the issue of woman suffrage on Congress and the people at this time. Although they had been deeply moved by the suffering of Negro women under slavery and had used this as a telling argument for emancipation, they now gave no thought to Negro women, who, even more than Negro men, needed the vote to safeguard their rights. Believing with the Republicans that one reform at a time was all they could expect, they did not want to hear one word about woman suffrage or a Sixteenth Amendment until male Negroes were safely enfranchised by the Fifteenth Amendment.

Offering a resolution endorsing the Fifteenth Amendment, Frederick Douglass quoted Julia Ward Howe as saying, "I am willing that the Negro shall get the ballot before me," and he added, "I cannot see how anyone can pretend that there is the same urgency in giving the ballot to women as to the Negro."

Quick as a flash, Susan was on her feet, challenging his statements, and as the dauntless champion of women debated the question with the dark-skinned fiery Negro, the friendship and warm affection built up between them over the years occasionally shone through the sharp words they spoke to each other.

"The old antislavery school says that women must stand back," declared Susan, "that they must wait until male Negroes are voters. But we say, if you will not give the whole loaf of justice to an entire people, give it to the most intelligent first."

Here she was greeted with applause and continued, "If intelligence, justice, and morality are to be placed in the government, then let the question of woman be brought up first and that of the Negro last.... Mr. Douglass talks about the wrongs of the Negro, how he is hunted down ..., but with all the wrongs and outrages that he today suffers, he would not exchange his sex and take the place of Elizabeth Cady Stanton."

"I want to know," shouted Frederick Douglass, "if granting you the right of suffrage will change the nature of our sexes?"

"It will change the pecuniary position of woman," Susan retorted before the shouts of laughter had died down. "She will not be compelled to take hold of only such employments as man chooses for her."

Lucy Stone, who so often in her youth had pleaded with Susan and Frederick Douglass for both the Negro and women, now entered the argument. She had matured, but her voice had lost none of its conviction or its power to sway an audience. Disagreeing with Douglass's assertion that Negro suffrage was more urgent than woman suffrage, she pointed out that white women of the North were robbed of their children by the law just as Negro women had been by slavery.

This was balm to Susan's soul, but with Lucy's next words she lost all hope that her old friend would cast her lot wholeheartedly with women at this time. "Woman has an ocean of wrongs too deep for any plummet," Lucy continued, "and the Negro too has an ocean of wrongs that cannot be fathomed. But I thank God for the Fifteenth Amendment, and hope that it will be adopted in every state. I will be thankful in my soul if anybody can get out of the terrible pit....

"I believe," she admitted, "that the national safety of the government would be more promoted by the admission of women as an element of restoration and harmony than the other. I believe that the influence of woman will save the country before every other influence. I see the signs of the times pointing to this consummation. I believe that in some parts of the country women will vote for the President of these United States in 1872."

Susan grew impatient as Lucy shifted from one side to the other, straddling the issue. Her own clear-cut approach, earning for her the reputation of always hitting the nail on the head, made Lucy's seem like temporizing.

The men now took control, criticizing the amount of time given to the discussion of woman's rights, and voted endorsement of the Fifteenth Amendment. Nevertheless, a small group of determined women continued their fight, Susan declaring with spirit that she protested against the Fifteenth Amendment because it was not Equal Rights and would put 2,000,000 more men in the position of tyrants over 2,000,000 women who until now had been the equals of the Negro men at their side.[237]

It was now clear to Susan and to the few women who worked closely with her that they needed a strong organization of their own and that it was folly to waste more time on the Equal Rights Association. Western delegates, disappointed in the convention's lack of interest in woman suffrage, expressed themselves freely. They had been sorely tried by the many speeches on extraneous subjects which cluttered the meetings, the heritage of a free-speech policy handed down by antislavery societies.

"That Equal Rights Association is an awful humbug," exploded Mary Livermore to Susan. "I would not have come on to the anniversary, nor would any of us, if we had known what it was. We supposed we were coming to a woman suffrage convention."[238]

At a reception for all the delegates held at the Women's Bureau at the close of the convention, this dissatisfaction culminated in a spontaneous demand for a new organization which would concentrate on woman suffrage and the Sixteenth Amendment. Alert to the possibilities, Susan directed this demand into concrete action by turning the reception temporarily into a business meeting. The result was the formation of the National Woman Suffrage Association by women from nineteen states, with Mrs. Stanton as president and Susan as a member of the executive committee. The younger women of the West, trusting the judgment of Susan and Mrs. Stanton, looked to them for leadership, as did a few of the old workers in the East—Ernestine Rose, always in the vanguard, Paulina Wright Davis, Elizabeth Smith Miller, Lucretia Mott, who although holding no office in the new organization gave it her support, Martha C. Wright, and Matilda Joslyn Gage who never wavered in her allegiance. Lucy Stone, who would have found it hard even to step into the Revolution office, did not attend the reception at the Women's Bureau or take part in the formation of the new woman suffrage organization.

Paulina Wright Davis

Aided and abetted by her new National Woman Suffrage Association, Susan continued her opposition in The Revolution to the Fifteenth Amendment until it was ratified in 1870.

So incensed was the Boston group by The Revolution's opposition to the Fifteenth Amendment, so displeased was Lucy Stone by the formation of the National Woman Suffrage Association without consultation with her, one of the oldest workers in the field, that they began to talk of forming a national woman suffrage organization of their own. They charged Susan with lust for power and autocratic control. Mrs. Stanton they found equally objectionable because of her radical views on sex, marriage, and divorce, expressed in The Revolution in connection with the Hester Vaughn case. They sincerely felt that the course of woman suffrage would run more smoothly, arouse less antagonism, and make more progress without these two militants who were forever stirring things up and introducing extraneous subjects. During these trying days of accusations, animosity, and rival factions, Mrs. Stanton's unwavering support was a great comfort to Susan as was the joy of having a paper to carry her message.

In addition to all the responsibilities connected with publishing her weekly paper, advertising, subscriptions, editorial policy, and raising the money to pay the bills, Susan was also holding successful conventions in Saratoga and Newport where men and women of wealth and influence gathered for the summer; she was traveling out to St. Louis, Chicago, and other western cities to speak on woman suffrage, making trips to Washington to confer with Congressmen, getting petitions for the Sixteenth Amendment circulated, and through all this, building up the National Woman Suffrage Association.

The Revolution office became the rallying point for a forward-looking group of women, many of whom contributed to the hard-hitting liberal sheet. Elizabeth Tilton, the lovely dark-haired young wife of the popular lecturer and editor of the Independent, selected the poetry. Alice and Phoebe Cary gladly offered poems and a novel; and when Susan was away, Phoebe Cary often helped Mrs. Stanton get out the paper. Elizabeth Smith Miller gave money, encouragement, and invaluable aid with her translations of interesting letters which The Revolution received from France and Germany. Laura Curtis Bullard, the heir to the Dr. Winslow-Soothing-Syrup fortune, who traveled widely in Europe, sent letters from abroad and took a lively interest in the paper. Another new recruit was Lillie Devereux Blake, who was gaining a reputation as a writer and who soon proved to be a brilliant orator and an invaluable worker in the New

York City suffrage group. Dr. Clemence S. Lozier, unfailingly gave her support, and her calm assurance strengthened Susan. The wealthy Paulina Wright Davis of Providence, Rhode Island, who followed Parker Pillsbury as editor, when he felt obliged to resign for financial reasons, gave the paper generous financial backing.

Isabella Beecher Hooker

It was Mrs. Davis who brought into the fold the half sister of Henry Ward Beecher, Isabella Beecher Hooker, a queenly woman, one of the elect of Hartford, Connecticut. Hoping to break down Mrs. Hooker's prejudice against Susan and Mrs. Stanton, which had been built up by New England suffragists, Mrs. Davis invited the three women to spend a few days with her. After this visit, Mrs. Hooker wrote to a friend in Boston, "I have studied Miss Anthony day and night for nearly a week.... She is a woman of incorruptible integrity and the thought of guile has no place in her heart. In unselfishness and benevolence she has scarcely an equal, and her energy and executive ability are bounded only by her physical power, which is something immense. Sometimes she fails in judgment, according to the standards of others, but in right intentions never, nor in faithfulness to her friends.... After attending a two days' convention in Newport, engineered by her in her own fashion, I am obliged to accept the most favorable interpretation of her which prevails generally, rather than that of Boston. Mrs. Stanton too is a magnificent woman.... I hand in my allegiance to both as leaders and representatives of the great movement."[239]
From then on, Mrs. Hooker did her best to reconcile the Boston and New York factions, hoping to avert the formation of a second national woman suffrage organization.

A House Divided

"I think we need two national associations for woman suffrage so that those who do not oppose the Fifteenth Amendment, nor take the tone of The Revolution may yet have an organization with which they can work in harmony."[240] So wrote Lucy Stone to many of her friends during the summer of 1869, and some of these letters fell into Susan's hands.
"The radical abolitionists and the Republicans could never have worked together but in separate organizations both did good service," Lucy further explained. "There are just as distinctly two parties to the woman movement.... Each organization will attract those who naturally belong to it—and there will be harmonious work."
When the ground had been prepared by these letters, Lucy asked old friends and new to sign a call to a woman suffrage convention, to be held in Cleveland, Ohio, in November 1869, "to unite those who cannot use the methods which Mrs. Stanton and Susan use...."[241]
Those feeling as she did eagerly signed the call, while others who knew little about the controversy in the East added their names because they were glad to take part in a convention sponsored by such prominent men and women as Julia Ward Howe, George William Curtis, Henry Ward Beecher, Thomas Wentworth Higginson, and William Lloyd Garrison. Still others who did not understand the insurmountable differences in temperament and policy between the two groups hoped that a new truly national organization would unite the two factions. Even Mary Livermore, who had been active in the formation of the National Woman Suffrage Association, was by this time responding to overtures from the Boston group, writing William Lloyd Garrison, "I have been repelled by some of the idiosyncrasies of our New York

friends, as have others. Their opposition to the Fifteenth Amendment, the buffoonery of George F. Train, the loose utterances of the Revolution on the marriage and dress questions—and what is equally potent hindrance to the cause, the fearful squandering of money at the New York headquarters—all this has tended to keep me on my own feet, apart from those to whom I was at first attracted.... I am glad at the prospect of an association that will be truly national and which promises so much of success and character."[242]

Neither Susan nor Mrs. Stanton received a notice of the Cleveland convention, but Susan, scanning a copy of the call sent her by a solicitous friend, was deeply disturbed when she saw the signatures of Lydia Mott, Amelia Bloomer, Myra Bradwell, Gerrit Smith, and other good friends.

The New York World, at once suspecting a feud, asked, "Where are those well-known American names, Susan B. Anthony, Parker Pillsbury, and Elizabeth Cady Stanton? It is clear that there is a division in the ranks of the strong-minded and that an effort is being made to ostracize The Revolution which has so long upheld the cause of Suffrage, through evil report and good...."[243]

The Rochester Democrat, loyal to Susan, put this question, "Can it be possible that a National Woman's Suffrage Convention is called without Susan's knowledge or consent?... A National Woman's Suffrage Association without speeches from Susan B. Anthony and Mrs. Stanton will be a new order of things. The idea seems absurd."[244]

To Susan it also seemed both absurd and unrealistic, for she remembered how almost single-handed she had held together and built up the woman suffrage movement during the years when her colleagues had been busy with family duties. She was appalled at the prospect of a division in the ranks at this time when she believed victory possible through the action of a strong united front.

Confident that many who signed the call were ignorant of or blind to the animus behind it, she did her best to bring the facts before them. She put the blame for the rift entirely upon Lucy Stone, believing that without Lucy's continual stirring up, past differences in policy would soon have been forgotten. The antagonism between the two burned fiercely at this time. Susan was determined to fight to the last ditch for control of the movement, convinced that her policies and Mrs. Stanton's were forward-looking, unafraid, and always put women first.

Susan now also had to face the humiliating possibility that she might be forced to give up The Revolution. Not only was the operating deficit piling up alarmingly, but there were persistent rumors of a competitor, another woman suffrage paper to be edited by Lucy Stone and Julia Ward Howe.

Susan had assumed full financial responsibility for The Revolution because Mrs. Stanton and Parker Pillsbury, both with families to consider, felt unable to share this burden. Mrs. Stanton had always contributed her services and Parker Pillsbury had been sadly underpaid, while Susan had drawn out for her salary only the most meager sums for bare living expenses.

With a maximum of 3,000 subscribers, the paper could not hope to pay its way even though she had secured a remarkably loyal group of advertisers.[245] Reluctantly she raised the subscription price from $2 to $3 a year. Her friends and family were generous with gifts and loans, but these only met the pressing needs of the moment and in no way solved the overall financial problem of the paper.

Appealing once again to her wealthy and generous Quaker cousin, Anson Lapham, she wrote him in desperation, "My paper must not, shall not go down. I am sure you believe in me, in my honesty of purpose, and also in the grand work which The Revolution seeks to do, and therefore you will not allow me to ask you in vain to come to the rescue. Yesterday's mail brought 43 subscribers from Illinois and 20 from California. We only need time to win financial success. I know you will save me from giving the world a chance to say, 'There is a woman's rights failure; even the best of women can't manage business!' If only I could die, and thereby fail honorably, I would say, 'Amen,' but to live and fail—it would be too terrible to bear."[246] He came to her aid as he always had in the past.

Susan's sister Mary not only lent her all her savings, but spent her summer vacation in New York in 1869, working in The Revolution office while Susan, busy with woman suffrage conventions in Newport, Saratoga, Chicago, and Ohio, was building up good will and subscriptions for her paper. Concerned for her welfare, Mary repeatedly but unsuccessfully urged her to give up. Daniel added his entreaties to Mary's, begging Susan not to go further into debt, but to form a stock company if she were determined to continue her paper. She considered his advice very seriously for he was a practical businessman and yet appreciated what she was trying to do. For a time the formation of a stock company seemed possible, for the project appealed to three women of means, Paulina Wright Davis, Isabella Beecher Hooker, and Laura Curtis Bullard, but it never materialized.

With the financial problem of The Revolution still unsolved, Susan decided to make her appearance at Lucy Stone's convention in Cleveland, Ohio, on November 24, 1869. Not only did she want to see with her own eyes and hear with her own ears all that went on, but she was determined to walk the second mile with Lucy and her supporters, or even to turn the other cheek, if need be, for the sake of her beloved cause.

Seeing her in the audience, Judge Bradwell of Chicago moved that she be invited to sit on the platform, but Thomas Wentworth Higginson, who was presiding, replied that he thought this unnecessary as a special invitation had already been extended to all desiring to identify themselves with the movement. Judge Bradwell would not be put off, his motion was carried, and as Susan walked up to the platform to join the other notables, she was greeted with hearty applause. Sitting there among her critics, she wondered what she could possibly say to persuade them to forget their differences for the sake of the cause. After listening to Lucy Stone plead for renewed work for woman suffrage and for petitions for a Sixteenth Amendment, she spontaneously rose to her feet and asked permission to speak. "I hope," she began, "that the work of this association, if it be organized, will be to go in strong array up to the Capitol at Washington to demand a Sixteenth Amendment to the Constitution. The question of the admission of women to the ballot would not then be left to the mass of voters in every State, but would be submitted by Congress to the several legislatures of the States for ratification, and ... be decided by the most intelligent portion of the people. If the question is left to the vote of the rank and file, it will be put off for years.[247]

"So help me, Heaven!" she continued with emotion. "I care not what may come out of this Convention, so that this great cause shall go forward to its consummation! And though this Convention by its action shall nullify the National Association of which I am a member, and though it shall tread its heel upon The Revolution, to carry on which I have struggled as never mortal woman or mortal man struggled for any cause ... still, if you will do the work in Washington so that this Amendment will be proposed, and will go with me to the several Legislatures and compel them to adopt it, I will thank God for this Convention as long as I have the breath of life."

Loud and continuous applause greeted these earnest words. However, instead of pledging themselves to work for a Sixteenth Amendment, the newly formed American Woman Suffrage Association, blind to the exceptional opportunity at this time for Congressional action on woman suffrage, decided to concentrate on work in the states where suffrage bills were pending. Instead of electing an outstanding woman as president, they chose Henry Ward Beecher, boasting that this was proof of their genuine belief in equal rights. Lucy Stone headed the executive committee.

Divisions soon began developing among the suffragists in the field. Many whose one thought previously had been the cause now spent time weighing the differences between the two organizations and between personalities, and antagonisms increased.

Hardest of all for Susan to bear was the definite announcement of a rival paper, the Woman's Journal, to be issued in Boston in January 1870 under the editorship of Lucy Stone, Mary A. Livermore, and Julia Ward Howe, with Henry Blackwell as business manager. Mary Livermore, who previously had planned to merge her paper, the Agitator, with The Revolution now merged it with the Woman's Journal. Financed by wealthy stockholders, all influential Republicans, the Journal, Susan knew, would be spared the financial struggles of The Revolution, but would be obliged to conform to Republican policy in its support of woman's rights. Had not the Woman's Journal been such an obvious affront to the heroic efforts of The Revolution and a threat to its very existence, she could have rejoiced with Lucy over one more paper carrying the message of woman suffrage.

More determined than ever to continue The Revolution, Susan redoubled her efforts, announcing an imposing list of contributors for 1870, including the British feminist, Lydia Becker, and as a special attraction, a serial by Alice Cary. Through the efforts of Mrs. Hooker, Harriet Beecher Stowe was persuaded to consider serving as contributing editor provided the paper's name was changed to The True Republic or to some other name satisfactory to her.[248]

Having struggled against the odds for so long, Susan had no intention of being stifled now by Mrs. Stowe's more conservative views, nor would she give her crusading sheet an innocuous name. However, the decision was taken out of her hands by The Revolution's coverage of the sensational McFarland-Richardson murder case, which so shocked both Mrs. Hooker and Mrs. Stowe that they gave up all thought of being associated in a publishing venture with Susan or Mrs. Stanton.

The whole country was stirred in December 1869 by the fatal shooting in the Tribune office of the well-known journalist, Albert D. Richardson, by Daniel McFarland, to whose divorced wife Richardson had been attentive. When just before his death, Richardson was married to the divorced Mrs. McFarland by Henry Ward Beecher with Horace Greeley as a witness, the press was agog. So strong was the feeling against a divorced woman that Henry Ward Beecher was severely condemned for officiating at the marriage, and Mrs. Richardson was played up in the press and in court as the villain, although her divorce had been granted because of the brutality and instability of McFarland.

Indignant at the sophistry of the press and the general acceptance of a double standard of morals, The Revolution not only spoke out fearlessly in defense of Mrs. Richardson but in an editorial by Mrs. Stanton frankly analyzed the tragic human relations so obvious in the case. With Susan's full approval, Mrs. Stanton wrote, "I rejoice over every slave that escapes from a discordant marriage. With the education and elevation of women we shall have a mighty sundering of the unholy ties that hold men and women together who loathe and despise each other...."[249] When the court acquitted McFarland, giving him the custody of his twelve-year-old son, Susan called a protest meeting which attracted an audience of two thousand.

Such words and such activities disturbed many who sympathized with Mrs. Richardson but saw no reason for flaunting exultant approval of divorce in a woman suffrage paper, and they turned to the Woman's Journal as more to their taste. Susan, however, reading the first number of the Woman's Journal, found its editorials lacking fire. She rebelled at Julia Ward Howe's counsel, "to lay down all partisan warfare and organize a peaceful Grand Army of the Republic of Women ... not ... as against men, but as against all that is pernicious to men and women."[250] Susan's fight had never been against men but against man-made laws that held women in bondage. There had always been men willing to help her. Experience had taught her that the struggle for woman's rights was no peaceful academic debate, but real warfare which demanded political strategy, self-sacrifice, and unremitting labor. She was prouder than ever of her Revolution and its liberal hard-hitting policy.

Convinced that the National Woman Suffrage Association must publicize its existence and its value, Susan began the year 1870 with a convention in Washington which even Senator Sumner praised as exceeding in interest anything he had ever witnessed there. Its striking demonstration of the vitality and intelligence of the National Association was the best answer she could possibly have given to the accusations and criticism aimed at her and her organization.

Jessie Benton Frémont, watching the delegates enter the dining room of the Arlington Hotel, called Susan over to her table and said with a twinkle in her eyes, "Now, tell me, Miss Anthony, have you hunted the country over and picked out and brought to Washington a score of the most beautiful women you could find?"[251]

They were a fine-looking and intelligent lot—Paulina Wright Davis, Isabella Beecher Hooker, Josephine Griffin of the Freedman's Bureau, Charlotte Wilbour, Matilda Joslyn Gage, Martha C. Wright, and Olympia Brown; Phoebe Couzins and Virginia Minor from Missouri, Madam Annekè from Wisconsin, and best of all to Susan, Elizabeth Cady Stanton. Their presence, their friendship and allegiance were a source of great pride and joy. Elizabeth Stanton had come from St. Louis, interrupting her successful lecture tour, when she much preferred to stay away from all conventions. She had written Susan, "Of course, I stand by you to the end. I would not see you crushed by rivals even if to prevent it required my being cut into inch bits.... No power in heaven, hell or earth can separate us, for our hearts are eternally wedded together."[252]

Also at this convention to show his support of Susan and her program, was her faithful friend of many years, the Rev. Samuel J. May of Syracuse. Clara Barton, ill and unable to attend, sent a letter to be read, an appeal to her soldier friends for woman suffrage.

Not only did the large and enthusiastic audiences show a growing interest in votes for women, but two great victories for women in 1869, one in Great Britain and the other in the United States, brought to the convention a feeling of confidence. Women taxpayers had been granted the right to vote in municipal elections in England, Scotland, and Wales, through the efforts of Jacob Bright. In the Territory of Wyoming, during the first session of its legislature, women had been granted the right to vote, to hold office, and serve on juries, and married women had been given the right to their separate property and their earnings. This progressive action by men of the West turned Susan's thoughts hopefully to the western territories, and early in 1870 when the Territory of Utah enfranchised its women, she had further cause for rejoicing.

To celebrate these victories for which her twenty years' work for women had blazed the trail, some of her friends held a reception for her in New York at the Women's Bureau on her fiftieth birthday. She was amazed at the friendly attention her birthday received in the press. "Susan's Half Century," read a headline in the Herald. The World called her the Moses of her sex. "A Brave Old Maid," commented the Sun. But it was to the Tribune that she turned with special interest, always hoping for a word of approval from Horace Greeley and finding at last this faint ray of praise: "Careful readers of the Tribune have probably succeeded in discovering that we have not always been able to applaud the course of Miss Susan B. Anthony. Indeed, we have often felt, and sometimes said that her methods were as unwise as we thought her aims undesirable. But through these years of disputation and struggling. Miss Anthony has thoroughly impressed friends and enemies alike with the sincerity and earnestness of her purpose...."[253]

To Anna E. Dickinson, far away lecturing, Susan confided, "Oh, Anna, I am so glad of it all because it will teach the young girls that to be true to principle—to live an idea, though an unpopular one—that to live single—without any man's name—may be honorable."[254]

A few of Susan's younger colleagues still insisted that a merger of the National and American Woman Suffrage Associations might be possible. Again Theodore Tilton undertook the task of mediation and Lucretia Mott, who had retired from active participation in the woman's rights movement, tried to help work out a reconciliation. Susan was skeptical but gave them her blessing. Representatives of the American Association, however, again made it plain that they were unwilling to work with Susan and Mrs. Stanton.[255]

By this time The Revolution had become an overwhelming financial burden. For some months Mrs. Stanton had been urging Susan to give it up and turn to the lecture field, as she had done, to spread the message of woman's rights. Susan hesitated, unwilling to give up The Revolution and not yet confident that she could hold the attention of an audience for a whole evening. However, she found herself a great success when pushed into several Lyceum lecture engagements in Pennsylvania by Mrs. Stanton's sudden illness. "Miss Anthony evidently lectures not for the purpose of receiving applause," commented the Pittsburgh Commercial, "but for the purpose of making people understand and be convinced. She takes her place on the stage in a plain and unassuming manner and speaks extemporaneously and fluently, too, reminding one of an old campaign speaker, who is accustomed to talk simply for the purpose of converting his audience to his political theories. She used plain English and plenty of it.... She clearly evinced a quality that many politicians lack—sincerity."[256]

For each of these lectures on "Work, Wages, and the Ballot," she received a fee of $75 and was able as well to get new subscribers for The Revolution. She now saw the possibilities for herself and the cause in a Lyceum tour, and when the Lyceum Bureau, pleased with her reception in Pennsylvania wanted to book her for lectures in the West, she accepted, calling Parker Pillsbury back to The Revolution to take charge. All through Illinois she drew large audiences and her fees increased to $95, $125, and $150. In two months she was able to pay $1,300 of The Revolution's debt.

When she returned to New York, she realized that she could not continue to carry The Revolution alone, in spite of increased subscriptions. Its $10,000 debt weighed heavily upon her. Parker Pillsbury's help could only be temporary; Mrs. Stanton's strenuous lecture tour left her little time to give to the paper; and Susan's own friends and family were unable to finance it further.

Fortunately the idea of editing a paper appealed strongly to the wealthy Laura Curtis Bullard, who had the promise of editorial help from Theodore Tilton. Susan now turned the paper over to them completely, receiving nothing in return but shares of stock, while she assumed the entire indebtedness.

Giving up the control of her beloved paper was one of the most humiliating experiences and one of the deepest sorrows she ever faced. The Revolution had become to her the symbol of her crusade for women. Overwhelmed by a sense of failure, she confided to her diary on the date of the transfer, "It was like signing my own death warrant," and to a friend she wrote, "I feel a great, calm sadness like that of a mother binding out a dear child that she could not support."[257]

She made a valiant announcement of the transfer in The Revolution of May 26, 1870, expressing her delight that the paper had at last found financial backing and a new, enthusiastic editor. "In view of the active demand for conventions, lectures, and discussions on Woman Suffrage," she added, "I have concluded that so far as my own personal efforts are concerned, I can be more useful on the platform than in a newspaper. So, on the 1st of June next, I shall cease to be the sole proprietor of The Revolution, and shall be free to attend public meetings where ever so plain and matter of fact an old worker as I am can secure a hearing."[258]

Financial backing, however, did not put The Revolution on its feet, although its forthright editorials and articles were replaced by spicy and brilliant observations on pleasant topics which offended no one. Before the year was up, Mrs. Bullard was making overtures to Susan to take the paper back. Susan wanted desperately "to keep the Old Ship Revolution's colors flying"[259] and to bring back Mrs. Stanton's stinging editorials. She also feared that Mrs. Bullard on Theodore Tilton's advice might turn the paper over to the Boston group to be consolidated with the Woman's Journal. As no funds were available, she had to turn her back on her beloved paper and hope for the best. "I suppose there is a wise Providence in my being stripped of power to go forward," she wrote at this time. "At any rate, I mean to try and make good come out of it."[260]

For one more year, The Revolution struggled on under the editorship of Mrs. Bullard and Theodore Tilton and then was taken over by the Christian Enquirer. The $10,000 debt, incurred under Susan's management, she regarded as her responsibility, although her brother Daniel and many of her friends urged bankruptcy proceedings. "My pride for women, to say nothing of my conscience," she insisted, "says no."[261]

A New Slant On The Fourteenth Amendment

While Susan was lecturing in the West, hoping to earn enough to pay off The Revolution's debt, she was pondering a new approach to the enfranchisement of women which had been proposed by Francis Minor, a St. Louis attorney and the husband of her friend, Virginia Minor.

Francis Minor contended that while the Constitution gave the states the right to regulate suffrage, it nowhere gave them the power to prohibit it, and he believed that this conclusion was strengthened by the Fourteenth Amendment which provided that "no State shall make or enforce any law which shall abridge the privileges or immunities of citizens of the United States."

To claim the right to vote under the Fourteenth Amendment made a great appeal to both Susan and Elizabeth Stanton. Susan published Francis Minor's arguments in The Revolution and also his suggestion that some woman test this interpretation of the Fourteenth Amendment by attempting to vote at the next election; while Mrs. Stanton used this new approach as the basis of her speech before a Congressional committee in 1870.

With such a fresh and thrilling project to develop, Susan looked forward to the annual woman suffrage convention to be held in Washington in January 1871. So heavy was her lecture schedule that she reluctantly left preparations for the convention in the willing hands of Isabella Beecher Hooker, who was confident she could improve on Susan's meetings and guide the woman's rights movement into more ladylike and aristocratic channels, winning over scores of men and women who hitherto had remained aloof. At the last moment, however, she appealed in desperation to Susan for help, and Susan, canceling important lecture engagements, hurried to Washington. Here she found the newspapers full of Victoria C. Woodhull and her Memorial to Congress on woman suffrage, which had been presented by Senator Harris of Louisiana and Congressman Julian of Indiana. Capitalizing on the new approach to woman suffrage, Mrs. Woodhull based her arguments on the Fourteenth and Fifteenth Amendments, praying Congress to enact legislation to enable women to exercise the right to vote vested in them by these amendments. A hearing was scheduled before the House judiciary committee the very morning the convention opened.

Victoria C. Woodhull

Convinced that she and her colleagues must attend that hearing, Susan consulted with her friends in Congress and overrode Mrs. Hooker's hesitancy about associating their organization with so questionable a woman as Victoria Woodhull. She engaged a constitutional lawyer, Albert G. Riddle,[262] to represent the 30,000 women who had petitioned Congress for the franchise. Then she and Mrs. Hooker attended the hearing and asked for prompt action on woman suffrage. This was the first Congressional hearing on federal enfranchisement. Previous hearings had considered trying the experiment only in the District of Columbia.

Susan had never before seen Victoria Woodhull. Early in 1870, however, she had called at the brokerage office which Victoria and her sister, Tennessee Claflin, had opened in New York on Broad Street. The press had been full of amused comments regarding the lady bankers, and Susan had wanted to see for herself what kind of women they were. Here she met and talked with Tennessee Claflin, publishing their interview in The Revolution, and also an advertisement of Woodhull, Claflin & Co., Bankers and Brokers.[263]

About six weeks later, these prosperous "lady brokers" had established their own paper, Woodhull & Claflin's Weekly, an "Organ of Social Regeneration and Constructive Reform," but Susan had barely noticed its existence, so burdened had she been by the impending loss of her own paper and by pressing lecture engagements. She was therefore unaware that this new weekly explored a field wider than finance, advocating as well woman suffrage and women's advancement, spiritualism, radical views on marriage, love, and sex, and the nomination of Victoria C. Woodhull for President of the United States.

Now in a committee room of the House of Representatives, Susan listened carefully as the dynamic beautiful Victoria Woodhull read her Memorial and her arguments to support it, in a clear well-modulated voice. Simply dressed in a dark blue gown, with a jaunty Alpine hat perched on her curls, she gave the impression of innocent earnest youth, and she captivated not only the members of the judiciary committee, but the more critical suffragists as well. For the moment at least she seemed an appropriate colleague of the forthright crusader, Susan B. Anthony, and her fashionable friends, Isabella Beecher Hooker and Paulina Wright Davis. They invited Victoria and her sister, Tennessee Claflin, to their convention, and asked her to repeat her speech for them.

At this convention Susan, encouraged by the favorable reception among politicians of the Woodhull Memorial, mapped out a new and militant campaign, based on her growing conviction that under the Fourteenth Amendment women's rights as citizens were guaranteed. She urged women to claim their rights as citizens and persons under the Fourteenth Amendment, to register and prepare to vote at the next election, and to bring suit in the courts if they were refused.

So enthusiastic had been the reception of this new approach to woman suffrage, so favorable had been the news from those close to leading Republicans, that Susan was unprepared for the adverse report of the judiciary committee on the Woodhull Memorial. She now studied the favorable minority report issued by Benjamin Butler of Massachusetts and William Loughridge of Iowa. Their arguments seemed to her unanswerable; and hurriedly and impulsively in the midst of her western lecture tour, she dashed off a few lines to Victoria Woodhull, to whom she willingly gave credit for bringing out this report. "Glorious old Ben!" she wrote. "He surely is going to pronounce the word that will settle the woman question, just as he did the word 'contraband' that so summarily settled the Negro question.... Everybody here chimes in with the new conclusion that we are already free."[264]

Far from New York where Victoria's activities were being aired by the press, Susan thought of her at this time only in connection with the Memorial and its impact on the judiciary committee. To be sure, she heard stories crediting Benjamin Butler with the authorship of the Woodhull Memorial, and rumors reached her of Victoria's unorthodox views on love and marriage and of her girlhood as a fortune teller, traveling about like a gypsy and living by her wits. Even so, Susan was ready to give Victoria the benefit of the doubt until she herself found her harmful to the cause, for long ago she had learned to discount attacks on the reputations of progressive women. In fact, Victoria Woodhull provided Susan and her associates with a spectacular opportunity to prove the sincerity of their contention that there should not be a double standard of morals—one for men and another for women.

Returning to New York in May 1871, to a convention of the National Woman Suffrage Association, Susan found that Mrs. Hooker, Mrs. Stanton, and Mrs. Davis had invited Victoria Woodhull to address that convention and to sit on the platform between Lucretia Mott and Mrs. Stanton.

Through them and others more critical, Susan was brought up to date on the sensational story of Victoria Woodhull, who had been drawing record crowds to her lectures and whose unconventional life continuously provided reporters with interesting copy. Victoria's home at 15 East Thirty-eighth Street, resplendent and ornate with gilded furniture and bric-a-brac, housed not only her husband, Colonel Blood, and herself but her divorced husband and their children as well, and also all of her quarrelsome relatives. Here many radicals, social reformers, and spiritualists gathered, among them Stephen Pearl Andrews, who soon made use of Victoria and her Weekly to publicize his dream of a new world order, the Pantarchy, as he called it. Victoria, herself, was an ardent spiritualist, controlled by Demosthenes of the spirit world to whom she believed she owed her most brilliant utterances and by whom she was guided to announce herself as a presidential candidate in 1872. Needless to say, with such a background, Victoria Woodhull became a very controversial figure among the suffragists.

In New York only a few days, it was hard for Susan to separate fact from fiction, truth from rumor and animosity. Even Demosthenes did not seem too ridiculous to her, for many of her most respected friends were spiritualists. Nor did Victoria's presidential aspirations trouble her greatly. Presidential candidates had been nothing to brag of, and willingly would she support the right woman for President. If Victoria lived up to the high standard of the Woodhull

Memorial, then even she might be that woman. After all, it was an era of radical theories and Utopian dreams, of extravagances of every sort. Almost anything could happen.

Whatever doubts the suffragists may have had when they saw Victoria Woodhull on the platform at the New York meeting of the National Association, she swept them all along with her when, as one inspired, she made her "Great Secession" speech. "If the very next Congress refuses women all the legitimate results of citizenship," she declared, "we shall proceed to call another convention expressly to frame a new constitution and to erect a new government.... We mean treason; we mean secession, and on a thousand times grander scale than was that of the South. We are plotting revolution; we will overthrow this bogus Republic and plant a government of righteousness in its stead...."[265]

Susan, who felt deeply her right to full citizenship, who herself had talked revolution, and who had so often listened to the extravagant antislavery declarations of William Lloyd Garrison, Wendell Phillips, and Parker Pillsbury, was not offended by these statements. She was, however, troubled by the attitude of the press, particularly of the Tribune which labeled this gathering the "Woodhull Convention" and accused the suffragists of adopting Mrs. Woodhull's free-love theories.

Having experienced so recently the animosity stirred up by her alliance with George Francis Train, Susan resolved to be cautious regarding Victoria Woodhull and was beginning to wonder if Victoria was not using the suffragists to further her own ambitions. Yet many trusted friends, who had talked with Mrs. Woodhull far more than she had the opportunity to do, were convinced that she was a genius and a prophet who had risen above the sordid environment of her youth to do a great work for women and who had the courage to handle subjects which others feared to touch. Free love, for example, Susan well knew was an epithet hurled indiscriminately at anyone indiscreet enough to argue for less stringent divorce laws or for an intelligent frank appraisal of marriage and sex. Was it for this reason, Susan asked herself, that Mrs. Woodhull was called a "free-lover," or did she actually advocate promiscuity?

With these questions puzzling her, she left for Rochester and the West. Almost immediately the papers were full of Victoria Woodhull and her family quarrels which brought her into court. This was a disillusioning experience for the National Woman Suffrage Association which had so recently featured Victoria Woodhull as a speaker, and Susan began seriously to question the wisdom of further association with this strange controversial character. Nevertheless, Victoria still had her ardent defenders among the suffragists, particularly Isabella Beecher Hooker and Paulina Wright Davis. Even the thoughtful judicious Martha C. Wright wrote Mrs. Hooker at this time, "It is not always 'the wise and prudent' to whom the truth is revealed; tho' far be it from me to imply aught derogatory to Mrs. Woodhull. No one can be with her, see her gentle and modest bearing and her spiritual face, without feeling sure that she is a true woman, whatever unhappy surroundings may have compromised her. I have never met a stranger toward whom I felt more tenderly drawn, in sympathy and love."[266]

Elizabeth Cady Stanton spoke her mind in Theodore Tilton's new paper, The Golden Age: "Victoria C. Woodhull stands before us today a grand, brave woman, radical alike in political, religious and social principles. Her face and form indicate the complete triumph in her nature of the spiritual over the sensuous. The processes of her education are little to us; the grand result everything."[267]

Victoria was in dire need of defenders, for the press was venomous, goading her on to revenge. Susan, now traveling westward, lecturing in one state after another, thinking of ways to interest the people in woman suffrage, was too busy and too far away to follow Victoria Woodhull's court battles.

Mrs. Stanton met Susan in Chicago late in May 1871, to join her on a lecture tour of the far West. Together they headed for Wyoming and Utah, eager to set foot in the states which had been the first to extend suffrage to women. The long leisurely days on the train gave these two old friends, Susan now fifty-one and Mrs. Stanton, fifty-six, ample time to talk and philosophize, to appraise their past efforts for women, and plan their speeches for the days ahead. While their main theme would always be votes for women, they decided that from now on they must also arouse women to rebel against their legal bondage under the "man marriage," as they called it, and to face frankly the facts about sex, prostitution, and the double standard of morals. In Utah, in the midst of polygamy fostered by the Mormon Church, they would encounter still another sex problem.

After an enthusiastic welcome in Denver, they moved on to Laramie, Wyoming, where one hundred women greeted them as the train pulled in. From this first woman suffrage state, Susan exultingly wrote, "We have been moving over the soil, that is really the land of the free and the home of the brave.... Women here can say, 'What a magnificent country is ours, where every class and caste, color and sex, may find freedom....'"[268]

They reached Salt Lake City just after the Godbe secession by which a group of liberal Mormons abandoned polygamy. As guests of the Godbes for a week, they had every opportunity to become acquainted with the Mormons, to observe women under polygamy, and to speak in long all-day sessions to women alone.

Susan tried to show her audiences in Utah that her point of attack under both monogamy and polygamy was the subjection of women, and that to remedy this the self-support of women was essential. In Utah she found little opportunity for women to earn a living for themselves and their children, as there was no manufacturing and there were no free schools in need of teachers. "Women here, as everywhere," she declared, "must be able to live honestly and honorably without the aid of men, before it can be possible to save the masses of them from entering into polygamy or prostitution, legal or illegal."[269]

Susan B. Anthony

Some of Susan's' critics at home felt she was again besmirching the suffrage cause by setting foot in polygamous Utah, but this was of no moment to her, for she saw the crying need of the right kind of missionary work among Mormon women, "no Phariseeism, no shudders of Puritanic horror, ... but a simple, loving fraternal clasp of hands with these struggling women" to encourage them and point the way.

Hearing that Susan and Mrs. Stanton were in the West en route to California, Leland Stanford, Governor of California and president of the recently completed Central Pacific Railway, sent them passes for their journey. They reached San Francisco with high hopes that they could win the support of western men for their demand for woman suffrage under the Fourteenth Amendment. Their welcome was warm and the press friendly. An audience of over 1,200 listened with real interest to Mrs. Stanton. Then the two crusaders made a misstep. Eager to learn the woman's side of the case in the recent widely publicized murder of the wealthy attorney, Alexander P. Crittenden, by Laura Fair, they visited Laura Fair in prison. Immediately the newspapers reported this move in a most critical vein, with the result that an uneasy audience crowded into the hall where Susan was to speak on "The Power of the Ballot." As she proceeded to prove that women needed the ballot to protect themselves and their work and could not count on the support and protection of men, she cited case after case of men's betrayal of women. Then bringing home her point, she declared with vigor, "If all men had protected all women as they would have their own wives and daughters protected, you would have no Laura Fair in your jail tonight."[270]

Boos and hisses from every part of the hall greeted this statement; but Susan, trained on the antislavery platform to hold her ground whatever the tumult, waited patiently until this protest subsided, standing before the defiant audience, poised and unafraid. Then, in a clear steady voice, she repeated her challenging words. This time, above the hisses, she heard a few cheers, and for the third time she repeated, "If all men had protected all women as they would have their own wives and daughters protected, you would have no Laura Fair in your jail tonight."

Now the audience, admiring her courage, roared its applause. "I declare to you," she concluded, "that woman must not depend upon the protection of man, but must be taught to protect herself, and here I take my stand."

Reading the newspapers the next morning, she found herself accused not only of defending Laura Fair, but of condoning the murder of Crittenden. This story was republished throughout the state and eagerly picked up by New York newspapers.

As it was now impossible for her or for Mrs. Stanton to draw a friendly audience anywhere in California, they took refuge in the Yosemite Valley for the next few weeks. Susan was inconsolable. These slanders on top of the loss of The Revolution and the split in the suffrage ranks seemed more than she could bear. "Never in all my hard experience have I been under such fire," she confided to her diary. "The clouds are so heavy over me.... I never before was so cut down."[271]

Not until she had spent several days riding horseback in the Yosemite Valley on "men's saddles" in "linen bloomers," over long perilous exhausting trails, did the clouds begin to lift. Gradually the beauty and grandeur of the mountains and the giant redwoods brought her peace and refreshment, putting to flight "all the old six-days story and the 6,000 jeers."

Bearing the brunt of the censure in California, Susan expected Mrs. Stanton to come to her defense in letters to the newspapers. When she did not do so, Susan was deeply hurt, for in the past she had so many times smoothed the way for her friend. Even now, on their return to San Francisco, where she herself did not yet dare lecture, she did her best to build up audiences for Mrs. Stanton and to get correct transcripts of her lectures to the papers. Disillusioned and heartsick, she was for the first time sadly disappointed in her dearest friend.

Moving on to Oregon to lecture at the request of the pioneer suffragist, Abigail Scott Duniway, she wrote Mrs. Stanton, who had left for the East, "As I rolled on the ocean last week feeling that the very next strain might swamp the ship, and thinking over all my sins of omission and commission, there was nothing undone which haunted me like the failure to speak the word at San Francisco again and more fully. I would rather today have the satisfaction of having said the true and needful thing on Laura Fair and the social evil, with the hisses and hoots of San Francisco and the entire nation around me, than all that you or I could possibly experience from their united eulogies with that one word unsaid."[272]

So far Susan's western trip had netted her only $350. This was disappointing in so far as she had counted upon it to reduce substantially her Revolution debt. She now hoped to build her earnings up to $1,000 in Oregon and Washington. Everywhere in these two states people took her to their hearts and the press with a few exceptions was complimentary. The beauty of the rugged mountainous country compensated her somewhat for the long tiring stage rides over rough roads and for the cold uncomfortable lonely nights in poor hotels. Only occasionally did she enjoy the luxury of a good cup of coffee or a clean bed in a warm friendly home.

At first in Oregon she was apprehensive about facing an audience because of her San Francisco experience, and she wrote Mrs. Stanton, "But to the rack I must go, though another San Francisco torture be in store for me."[273] She spoke on "The Power of the Ballot," on women's right to vote under the Fourteenth Amendment, on the need of women to be self-supporting, and clearly and logically she marshaled her facts and her arguments. Occasionally she obliged with a temperance speech, or gathered women together to talk to them about the social evil, relieved when they responded to this delicate subject with earnestness and gratitude. Practice soon made her an easy, extemporaneous speaker. Yet she was only now and then satisfied with her efforts, recording in her diary, "Was happy in a real Patrick Henry speech."[274]

The proceeds from her lectures were disappointing, as money was scarce in the West that winter, and she had just decided to return to the East to spend Christmas with her mother and sisters when she was urged to accept lecture engagements in California. Putting her own personal longings behind her, she took the stage to California, sitting outside with the driver so that she could better enjoy the scenery and learn more about the people who had settled this new lonely overpowering country. "Horrible indeed are the roads," she wrote her mother, "miles and miles of corduroy and then twenty miles ... of black mud.... How my thought does turn homeward, mother."[275]

This time she was warmly received in San Francisco. The prejudice, so vocal six months before, had disappeared. "Made my Fourteenth Amendment argument splendidly," she wrote in her diary. "All delighted with it and me—and it is such a comfort to have the friends feel that I help the good work on."[276]

She was gaining confidence in herself and wrote her family, "I miss Mrs. Stanton. Still I can not but enjoy the feeling that the people call on me, and the fact that I have an opportunity to sharpen my wits a little by answering questions and doing the chatting, instead of merely sitting a lay figure and listening to the brilliant scintillations as they emanate from her never-exhausted magazine. There is no alternative—whoever goes into a parlor or before an audience with that woman does it at a cost of a fearful overshadowing, a price which I have paid for the last ten years, and that cheerfully, because I felt our cause was most profited by her being seen and heard, and my best work was making the way clear for her."[277]

Starting homeward through Wyoming and Nevada where she also had lecture engagements, she wrote in her diary on January 1, 1872, "6 months of constant travel, full 8000 miles, 108 lectures. The year's work full 13,000 miles travel—170 meetings." On the train she met the new California Senator, Aaron A. Sargent, his wife Ellen, and their children. A warm friendship developed on this long journey during which the train was stalled in deep snow drifts. "This is indeed a fearful ordeal, fastened here ... midway of the continent at the top of the Rocky mountains," she recorded. "The railroad has supplied the passengers with soda crackers and dried fish.... Mrs. Sargent and I have made tea and carried it throughout the train to the nursing mothers."[278] The Sargents had brought their own food for the journey and shared it with Susan. This and the good conversation lightened the ordeal for her, especially as both Senator and Mrs. Sargent believed heartily in woman's rights, and Senator Sargent in his campaign for the Senate had boldly announced his endorsement of woman suffrage.

This friendly attitude among western men toward votes for women was the most encouraging development in Susan's long uphill fight. These men, looking upon women as partners who had shared with them the dangers and hardships of the frontier, recognized at once the justice of woman suffrage and its benefit to the country.

Susan traveled directly from Nevada to Washington instead of breaking her journey by a visit with her brothers in Kansas, as she had hoped to do. She even omitted Rochester so that she might be in time for the national woman suffrage convention in Washington in January 1872, for which Mrs. Hooker, Mrs. Davis, and Mrs. Stanton were preparing. She found Victoria Woodhull with them, her presence provoking criticism and dissension.

Impulsively she came to Victoria's defense at the convention: "I have been asked by many, 'Why did you drag Victoria Woodhull to the front?' Now, bless your souls, she was not dragged to the front. She came to Washington with a powerful argument. She presented her Memorial to Congress and it was a power.... She had an interview with the judiciary committee. We could never secure that privilege. She was young, handsome, and rich. Now if it takes youth, beauty, and money to capture Congress, Victoria is the woman we are after."[279]

"I was asked by an editor of a New York paper if I knew Mrs. Woodhull's antecedents," she continued. "I said I didn't and that I did not care any more for them than I do about those of the members of Congress.... I have been asked along the Pacific coast, 'What about Woodhull? You make her your leader?' Now we don't make leaders; they make themselves."

Victoria, however, did not prove to be the leading light of this convention, although she made one of her stirring fiery speeches calling upon her audience to form an Equal Rights party and nominate her for President of the United States. By this time, Susan had concluded that Victoria Woodhull for President did not ring true and she would have nothing to do with her self-inspired candidacy. Quickly she steered the convention away from Victoria Woodhull for President toward the consideration of the more practical matter of woman's right to vote under the Fourteenth and Fifteenth Amendments.

This time it was Susan, not Victoria, who was granted a hearing before the Senate judiciary committee. "At the close of the war," Susan reminded the Senators, "Congress lifted the question of suffrage for men above State power, and by the amendments prohibited the deprivation of suffrage to any citizen by any State. When the Fourteenth Amendment was first proposed ... we rushed to you with petitions praying you not to insert the word 'male' in the second clause. Our best friends ... said to us: 'The insertion of that word puts no new barrier against women; therefore do not embarrass us but wait until we get the Negro question settled.' So the Fourteenth Amendment with the word 'male' was adopted.[280]

"When the Fifteenth was presented without the word 'sex,'" she continued, "we again petitioned and protested, and again our friends declared that the absence of the word was no hindrance to us, and again begged us to wait until they had finished the work of the war, saying, 'After we have enfranchised the Negro, we will take up your case.'

"Have they done as they promised?" she asked. "When we come asking protection under the new guarantees of the Constitution, the same men say to us ... to wait the action of Congress and State legislatures in the adoption of a Sixteenth Amendment which shall make null and void the word 'male' in the Fourteenth and supply the want of the word 'sex' in the Fifteenth. Such tantalizing treatment imposed upon yourselves or any class of men would have caused rebellion and in the end a bloody revolution...."

Unconvinced of the urgency or even the desirability of votes for women, the Senate judiciary committee promptly issued an adverse report, but Susan was assured that her cause had a few persistent supporters in Congress when Benjamin Butler presented petitions to the House for a declaratory act for the Fourteenth Amendment and Congressman Parker of Missouri introduced a bill granting women the right to vote and hold office in the territories. Susan now turned to the more sympathetic West to take her plea for woman suffrage directly to the people. Speaking almost daily in Kansas, Nebraska, Iowa, and Illinois, she had little time to think of the work in the East; the glamor of Victoria Woodhull faded, and she realized that her own hard monotonous spade work would in the long run do more for the cause than the meteoric rise of a vivid personality who gave only part of herself to the task.

When letters came from Mrs. Stanton and Mrs. Hooker showing plainly that they were falling in with Victoria's plans to form a new political party, Susan at once dashed off these lines of warning: "We have no element out of which to make a political party, because there is not a man who would vote a woman suffrage ticket if thereby he endangered his Republican, Democratic, Workingmen's, or Temperance party, and all our time and words in that direction are simply thrown away. My name must not be used to call any such meeting."[281]

Then she added, "Mrs. Woodhull has the advantage of us because she has the newspaper, and she persistently means to run our craft into her port and none other. If she were influenced by women spirits ... I might consent to be a mere sail-hoister for her; but as it is she is wholly owned and dominated by men spirits and I spurn the whole lot of them...."

A few weeks later, as she looked over the latest copy of Woodhull & Claflin's Weekly, she was horrified to find her name signed to a call to a political convention sponsored by the National Woman Suffrage Association. Immediately she telegraphed Mrs. Stanton to remove her name and wrote stern indignant letters begging her and Mrs. Hooker not to involve the National Association in Victoria Woodhull's presidential campaign. Although she herself had often called for a new political party while she was publishing The Revolution, she was practical enough to recognize that a party formed under Victoria Woodhull's banner was doomed to failure.

Returning to New York, she found both Mrs. Stanton and Mrs. Hooker still completely absorbed in Victoria's plans. Bringing herself up to date once more on the latest developments in the colorful life of Victoria Woodhull, she found that she had been lecturing on "The Impending Revolution" to large enthusiastic audiences and that she had again been called into court by her family. Goaded to defiance by an increasingly virulent press, Victoria had also begun to blackmail suffragists who she thought were her enemies, among them Mrs. Bullard, Mrs. Blake, and Mrs. Phelps. This made Susan take steps at once to free the National Association of her influence.

When Victoria Woodhull, followed by a crowd of supporters, sailed into the first business session of the National Woman Suffrage Association in New York, announcing that the People's convention would hold a joint meeting with the suffragists, Susan made it plain that they would do nothing of the kind, as Steinway Hall had been engaged for a woman suffrage convention. With relief, she watched Victoria and her flock leave for a meeting place of their own. Disgruntled at what she called Susan's intolerance, Mrs. Stanton then asked to be relieved of the presidency. Elected to take her place, Susan was now free to cope with Victoria, should this again become necessary.

Not to be outmaneuvered by Susan, Victoria made a surprise appearance near the end of the evening session and moved that the convention adjourn to meet the next morning in Apollo Hall with the people's convention. Quickly one of her colleagues seconded the motion. Susan refused to put this motion, standing quietly before the excited audience, stern and somber in her steel-gray silk dress. Beside her on the platform, Victoria, intense and vivid, put the motion herself, and it was overwhelmingly carried by her friends scattered among the suffragists. Declaring this out of order because neither Victoria nor many of those voting were members of the National Association, Susan in her most commanding voice adjourned the convention to meet in the same place the next morning. Victoria, however, continued her demands until Susan ordered the janitor to turn out the lights. Then the audience dispersed in the darkness.

With these drastic measures, Susan rescued the National Woman Suffrage Association from Victoria Woodhull, who had her own triumph later at Apollo Hall, where, surrounded by wildly cheering admirers, she was nominated for President of the United States by the newly formed Equal Rights party.

Reading about Victoria's nomination in the morning papers, Susan breathed a prayer of gratitude for a narrow escape, recording in her diary, "There never was such a foolish muddle—all come of Mrs. S. [Stanton] consulting and conceding to Woodhull & calling a People's Con[vention].... All came near being lost.... I never was so hurt with the folly of Stanton.... Our movement as such is so demoralized by letting go the helm of ship to Woodhull—though we rescued it—it was as by a hair breadth escape." She was surprised to find no condemnation of her actions in Woodhull & Claflin's Weekly but only the implication that the suffragists were too slow for Victoria's great work.[282]

The attitude of some of the leading suffragists toward Victoria Woodhull remained a problem. Fortunately Mrs. Stanton came back into line, but both Mrs. Hooker and Mrs. Davis seemed bound to drift under Victoria's influence, and the promising young lawyer, Belva Lockwood, campaigned for the Equal Rights party and its candidate Victoria Woodhull. While Victoria Woodhull's fortunes were speedily dropping from the sublime heights of a presidential nomination to the humiliation of financial ruin, the loss of her home, and the suspended publication of her Weekly, Susan was knocking at the doors of the Republican and Democratic national conventions. She had previously appealed to the liberal Republicans, among whose delegates were her old friends George W. Julian, B. Gratz Brown, and Theodore Tilton, but they had ignored woman suffrage and had nominated for President, Horace Greeley, now a persistent opponent of votes for women. The Democrats did no better. Faced with Grant as the strong Republican nominee, they too nominated Horace Greeley with B. Gratz Brown as his running mate, hoping by this coalition to achieve victory. The

Republicans, still unwilling to go the whole way for woman suffrage by giving it the recognition of a plank in their platform, did, however, offer women a splinter at which Susan grasped eagerly because it was the first time an important, powerful political party had ever mentioned women in their platform.

"The Republican party," read the splinter, "is mindful of its obligations to the loyal women of America for their noble devotion to the cause of freedom; their admission to wider fields of usefulness is received with satisfaction; and the honest demands of any class of citizens for equal rights should be treated with respectful consideration."[283]

Thankful to have escaped involvement with Victoria Woodhull and her Equal Rights party just at this time when the Republicans were ready to smile upon women, Susan basked in an aura of respectability thrown around her by her new political allies. She was even hopeful that the two woman-suffrage factions could now forget their differences and work together for "the living, vital issue of today—freedom to women."

She at once began speaking for the Republican party, looking forward to carrying the discussion of woman suffrage into every school district and every ward meeting. In the beginning the Republicans were generous with funds, giving her $1,000 for women's meetings in New York, Philadelphia, Rochester, and other large cities. For speakers she sought both Lucy Stone and Anna E. Dickinson, but Lucy made it plain in letters to Mrs. Stanton that she would take no part in Republican rallies conducted by Susan, and Anna responded with a torrent of false accusations.[284] Only Mary Livermore of the American Association consented to speak at Susan's Republican rallies; but with Mrs. Stanton, Mrs. Gage, and Olympia Brown to call upon, Susan did not lack for effective orators.

In an Appeal to the Women of America, financed by the Republicans and widely circulated, she urged the election of Grant and Wilson and the defeat of Horace Greeley, whom she described as women's most bitter opponent. "Both by tongue and pen," she declared, "he has heaped abuse, ridicule, and misrepresentation upon our leading women, while the whole power of the Tribune had been used to crush our great reform...."[285]

Beyond this she was unwilling to go in criticizing her one-time friend. In fact her sense of fairness recoiled at the ridicule and defamation heaped upon Horace Greeley in the campaign. "I shall not join with the Republicans," she wrote Mrs. Stanton, "in hounding Greeley and the Liberals with all the old war anathemas of the Democracy.... My sense of justice and truth is outraged by the Harper's cartoons of Greeley and the general falsifying tone of the Republican press. It is not fair for us to join in the cry that everybody who is opposed to the present administration is either a Democrat or an apostate."[286]

Susan sensed a change in the Republicans' attitude toward women, as they grew increasingly confident of victory. Not only did they refuse further financial aid, but criticized Susan roundly because in her speeches she emphasized woman suffrage rather than the virtues of the Republican party. She ignored their complaints, and wrote Mrs. Stanton, "If you are willing to go forth ... saying that you endorse the party on any other point ... than that of its recognition of woman's claim to vote, I am not...."[287]

Testing The Fourteenth Amendment

Susan preached militancy to women throughout the presidential campaign of 1872, urging them to claim their rights under the Fourteenth and Fifteenth Amendments by registering and voting in every state in the Union.

Even before Francis Minor had called her attention to the possibilities offered by these amendments, she had followed with great interest a similar effort by Englishwomen who, in 1867 and 1868, had attempted to prove that the "ancient legal rights of females" were still valid and entitled women property holders to vote for representatives in Parliament, and who claimed that the word "man" in Parliamentary statutes should be interpreted to include women. In the case of the 5,346 householders of Manchester, the court held that "every woman is personally incapable" in a legal sense.[288] This legal contest had been fully reported in The Revolution, and disappointing as the verdict was, Susan looked upon this attempt to establish justice as an indication of a great awakening and uprising among women.

There had also been heartening signs in her own country, which she hoped were the preparation for more successful militancy to come. She had exulted in The Revolution in 1868 over the attempt of women to vote in Vineland, New Jersey. Encouraged by the enfranchisement of women in Wyoming in 1869, Mary Olney Brown and Charlotte Olney French had cast their votes in Washington Territory. A young widow, Marilla Ricker, had registered and voted in New Hampshire in 1870, claiming this right as a property holder, but her vote was refused. In 1871, Nannette B. Gardner and Catherine Stebbins in Detroit, Catherine V. White in Illinois, Ellen R. Van Valkenburg in Santa Cruz, California, and

Carrie S. Burnham in Philadelphia registered and attempted to vote. Only Mrs. Gardner's vote was accepted. That same year, Sarah Andrews Spencer, Sarah E. Webster, and seventy other women marched to the polls to register and vote in the District of Columbia. Their ballots refused, they brought suit against the Board of Election Inspectors, carrying the case unsuccessfully to the Supreme Court of the United States.[289] Another test case based on the Fourteenth Amendment had also been carried to the Supreme Court by Myra Bradwell, one of the first women lawyers, who had been denied admission to the Illinois bar because she was a woman.

With the spotlight turned on the Fourteenth Amendment by these women, lawyers here and there throughout the country were discussing the legal points involved, many admitting that women had a good case. Even the press was friendly.

Susan had looked forward to claiming her rights under the Fourteenth and Fifteenth Amendments and was ready to act. She had spent the thirty days required of voters in Rochester with her family and as she glanced through the morning paper of November 1, 1872, she read these challenging words, "Now Register!... If you were not permitted to vote you would fight for the right, undergo all privations for it, face death for it...."[290]

This was all the reminder she needed. She would fight for this right. She put on her bonnet and coat, telling her three sisters what she intended to do, asked them to join her, and with them walked briskly to the barber shop where the voters of her ward were registering. Boldly entering this stronghold of men, she asked to be registered. The inspector in charge, Beverly W. Jones, tried to convince her that this was impossible under the laws of New York. She told him she claimed her right to vote not under the New York constitution but under the Fourteenth Amendment, and she read him its pertinent lines. Other election inspectors now joined in the argument, but she persisted until two of them, Beverly W. Jones and Edwin F. Marsh, both Republicans, finally consented to register the four women.

This mission accomplished, Susan rounded up twelve more women willing to register. The evening papers spread the sensational news, and by the end of the registration period, fifty Rochester women had joined the ranks of the militants.

On election day, November 5, 1872, Susan gleefully wrote Elizabeth Stanton, "Well, I have gone and done it!!— positively voted the Republican ticket—Strait—this a.m. at 7 o'clock—& swore my vote in at that.... All my three sisters voted—Rhoda deGarmo too—Amy Post was rejected & she will immediately bring action against the registrars.... Not a jeer not a word—not a look—disrespectful has met a single woman.... I hope the mornings telegrams will tell of many women all over the country trying to vote.... I hope you voted too."[291]

Election day did not bring the general uprising of women for which Susan had hoped. In Michigan, Missouri, Ohio, and Connecticut, as in Rochester, a few women tried to vote. In New York City, Lillie Devereux Blake and in Fayetteville, New York, Matilda Joslyn Gage had courageously gone to the polls only to be turned away. Elizabeth Stanton did not vote on November 5, 1872, and her lack of enthusiasm about a test case in the courts was very disappointing to Susan. However, the fact that Susan B. Anthony had voted won immediate response from the press in all parts of the country. Newspapers in general were friendly, the New York Times boldly declaring, "The act of Susan B. Anthony should have a place in history," and the Chicago Tribune venturing to suggest that she ought to hold public office. The cartoonists, however, reveling in a new and tempting subject, caricatured her unmercifully, the New York Graphic setting the tone. Some Democratic papers condemned her, following the line of the Rochester Union and Advertiser which flaunted the headline, "Female Lawlessness," and declared that Miss Anthony's lawlessness had proved women unfit for the ballot.

Before she voted, Susan had taken the precaution of consulting Judge Henry R. Selden, a former judge of the Court of Appeals. After listening with interest to her story and examining the arguments of Benjamin Butler, Francis Minor, and Albert G. Riddle in support of the claim that women had a right to vote under the Fourteenth and Fifteenth Amendments, he was convinced that women had a good case and consented to advise her and defend her if necessary. Judge Selden, now retired from the bench because of ill health, was practicing law in Rochester where he was highly respected. A Republican, he had served as lieutenant governor, member of the Assembly, and state senator. Susan had known him as one of the city's active abolitionists, a friend of Frederick Douglass who had warned him to flee the country after the raid on Harper's Ferry and the capture of John Brown. Such a man she felt she could trust.

All was quiet for about two weeks after the election and it looked as if the episode might be forgotten in the jubilation over Grant's election. Then, on November 18, the United States deputy marshal rang the doorbell at 7 Madison Street and asked for Miss Susan B. Anthony. When she greeted him, he announced with embarrassment that he had come to arrest her.

"Is this your usual manner of serving a warrant?" she asked in surprise.[292]

He then handed her papers, charging that she had voted in violation of Section 19 of an Act of Congress, which stipulated that anyone voting knowingly without having the lawful right to vote was guilty of a crime, and on conviction would be punished by a fine not exceeding $500, or by imprisonment not exceeding three years.

This was a serious development. It had never occurred to Susan that this law, passed in 1870 to halt the voting of southern rebels, could actually be applicable to her. In fact, she had expected to bring suit against election inspectors for refusing to accept the ballots of women. Now charged with crime and arrested, she suddenly began to sense the import of what was happening to her.

When the marshal suggested that she report alone to the United States Commissioner, she emphatically refused to go of her own free will and they left the house together, she extending her wrists for the handcuffs and he ignoring her gesture. As they got on the streetcar and the conductor asked for her fare, she further embarrassed the marshal by loudly announcing, "I'm traveling at the expense of the government. This gentleman is escorting me to jail. Ask him for my fare." When they arrived at the commissioner's office, he was not there, but a hearing was set for November 29.

On that day, in the office where a few years before fugitive slaves had been returned to their masters, Susan was questioned and cross-examined, and she felt akin to those slaves. Proudly she admitted that she had voted, that she had conferred with Judge Selden, that with or without his advice she would have attempted to vote to test women's right to the franchise.[293]

"Did you have any doubt yourself of your right to vote?" asked the commissioner.

"Not a particle," she replied.

On December 23, 1872, in Rochester's common council chamber, before a large curious audience, Susan, the other women voters, and the election inspectors were arraigned. People expecting to see bold notoriety-seeking women were surprised by their seriousness and dignity. "The majority of these law-breakers," reported the press, "were elderly, matronly-looking women with thoughtful faces, just the sort one would like to see in charge of one's sick-room, considerate, patient, kindly."[294]

The United States Commissioner fixed their bail at $500 each. All furnished bail but Susan, who through her counsel, Henry R. Selden, applied for a writ of habeas corpus, demanding immediate release and challenging the lawfulness of her arrest. When a writ of habeas corpus was denied and her bail increased to $1,000 by United States District Judge Nathan K. Hall, sitting in Albany, Susan was more than ever determined to resist the interference of the courts in her constitutional right as a citizen to vote. She refused to give bail, emphatically stating that she preferred prison.

Seeing no heroism but only disgrace in a jail term for his client and unwilling to let her bring this ignominy upon herself. Henry Selden chivalrously assured her that this was a time when she must be guided by her lawyer's advice, and he paid her bail. Ignorant of the technicalities of the law, she did not realize the far-reaching implications of this well-intentioned act until they left the courtroom and in the hallway met tall vigorous John Van Voorhis of Rochester who was working on the case with Judge Selden. With the impatience of a younger man, eager to fight to the finish, he exclaimed, "You have lost your chance to get your case before the Supreme Court by writ of habeas corpus!"[295]

Aghast, Susan rushed back to the courtroom, hoping to cancel the bond, but it was too late. Bitterly disappointed, she remonstrated with Henry Selden, but he quietly replied, "I could not see a lady I respected in jail." She never forgave him for this, in spite of her continued appreciation of his keen legal mind, his unfailing kindness, and his willingness to battle for women.

Within a few days she appeared before the Federal Grand Jury in Albany and was indicted on the charge that she "did knowingly, wrongfully and unlawfully vote for a Representative in the Congress of the United States...."[296] Her trial was set for the term of the United States District Court, beginning May 13, 1873, in Rochester, New York.

Judge Henry R. Selden

During these difficult days in Albany, Susan found comfort and courage, as in the past, in the friendliness of Lydia Mott's home. Here she planned the steps by which to win public approval and financial aid for her test case. She addressed the commission which was revising New York's constitution on woman's right to vote under the Fourteenth and Fifteenth Amendments, pointing out that the law limiting suffrage to males was nullified by this new interpretation. Eager to spread the truth about her own legal contest, she distributed printed copies of Judge Selden's argument. Then traveling to New York and Washington, she personally presented copies to newspaper editors and Congressmen. To one of these men she wrote, "It is not for myself—but for all womanhood—yes and all manhood too—that I most rejoice in the appeal to the legal mind of the Nation. It is no longer whether women wish to vote, or men are willing, but it is woman's Constitutional right."[297]

In spite of the fact that Susan was technically in the custody of the United States Marshal, who objected to her leaving Rochester, she managed to carry out a full schedule of lectures in Ohio, Indiana, and Illinois, and also the usual annual Washington and New York woman suffrage conventions at which she told the story of her voting, her arrest, and her pending trial, and where she received enthusiastic support.

Because she wanted the people to understand the legal points on which she based her right to vote, Susan spoke on "The Equal Right of All Citizens to the Ballot" in every district in Monroe County. So thorough and convincing was she that the district attorney asked for a change of venue, fearing that any Monroe County jury, sitting in Rochester, would be prejudiced in her favor. When her case was transferred to the United States Circuit Court in Canandaigua, to be heard a month later, she immediately descended upon Ontario County with her speech, "Is It a Crime for a Citizen of the United States to Vote?" and Matilda Joslyn Gage joined her, speaking on "The United States on Trial, Not Susan B. Anthony."

On the lecture platform Susan wore a gray silk dress with a soft, white lace collar. Her hair, now graying, was smoothed back and twisted neatly into a tight knot. Everything about her indicated refinement and sincerity, and most of her audiences felt this.

"Our democratic-republican government is based on the idea of the natural right of every individual member thereof to a voice and vote in making and executing the laws," she declared as she looked into the faces of the men and women who had gathered to hear her, farmers, storekeepers, lawyers, and housewives, rich and poor, a cross section of America.

Repeating to them salient passages from the Declaration of Independence and the Preamble to the Constitution, she added, "It was we, the people, not we, the white male citizens, nor yet we, the male citizens: but we the whole people, who formed this Union. And we formed it, not to give the blessings of liberty, but to secure them; not to the half of ourselves and the half of our posterity, but to the whole people—women as well as men."[298]

She asked, "Is the right to vote one of the privileges or immunities of citizens? I think the disfranchised ex-rebels, and the ex-state prisoners will agree with me that it is not only one of them, but the one without which all the others are nothing."[299]

Quoting for them the Fifteenth Amendment, she told them it had settled forever the question of the citizen's right to vote. The Fifteenth Amendment, she reasoned, applies to women, first because women are citizens and secondly because of their "previous condition of servitude." Defining a slave as a person robbed of the proceeds of his labor and subject to the will of another, she showed how state laws relating to married women had placed them in the position of slaves.

As she analyzed the Thirteenth, Fourteenth, and Fifteenth Amendments and cited authorities for her conclusions, she left little doubt in the minds of those who heard her that women were persons and citizens whose privileges and immunities could not be abridged.

On this note she concluded: "We ask the juries to fail to return verdicts of 'guilty' against honest, law-abiding, tax-paying United States citizens for offering their votes at our elections ... We ask the judges to render true and unprejudiced opinions of the law, and wherever there is room for doubt to give its benefit on the side of liberty and equal rights to women, remembering that 'the true rule of interpretation under our national constitution, especially since its amendments, is that anything for human rights is constitutional, everything against human rights unconstitutional.' And it is on this line that we propose to fight our battle for the ballot—all peaceably, but nevertheless persistently through to complete triumph, when all United States citizens shall be recognized as equals before the law."

Speaking twenty-one nights in succession was arduous. "So few see or feel any special importance in the impending trial," she jotted down in her diary. In towns, such as Geneva, where she had old friends, like Elizabeth Smith Miller, she was assured of a friendly welcome and a good audience.[300]

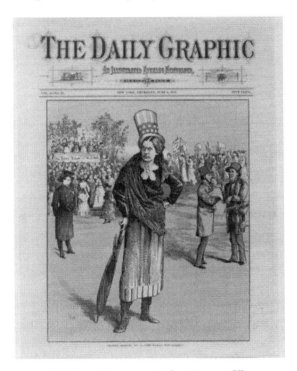

"The Woman Who Dared"

As the collections, taken up after her lectures, were too small to pay her expenses, her financial problems weighed heavily. The notes she had signed for The Revolution were in the main still unpaid, and one of her creditors was growing impatient. She had recently paid her counsel, Judge Selden, $200 and John Van Voorhis, $75, leaving only $3.45 in her defense fund, but as usual a few of her loyal friends came to her aid, and both Judge Selden and John Van Voorhis, deeply interested in her courageous fight, gave most of their time without charge.[301]

If this campaign was a problem financially, it was a success in the matter of nation-wide publicity. The New York Herald exulted in hostile gibes at women suffrage and published fictitious interviews, ridiculing Susan as a homely aggressive old maid, but the New York Evening Post prophesied that the court decision would likely be in her favor. The Rochester Express championed her warmly: "All Rochester will assert—at least all of it worth heeding—that Miss Anthony holds here the position of a refined and estimable woman, thoroughly respected and beloved by the large circle of staunch friends who swear by her common sense and loyalty, if not by her peculiar views." In fact the consensus of opinion in Rochester was much like that of the woman who remarked, "No, I am not converted to what these women advocate. I am too cowardly for that; but I am converted to Susan B. Anthony."[302]

This, however, was far from the attitude of Lucy Stone's Woman's Journal, which had ignored Susan's voting in November 1872 because it was out of sympathy with this militant move and with her interpretation of the Fourteenth and Fifteenth Amendments. Later, as her case progressed in the courts, the Journal did give it brief notice as a news item, but in 1873 when it listed as a mark of honor the women who had worked wisely for the cause, Susan B. Anthony's name was not among them, and this did not pass unnoticed by Susan; nor did the fact that she was snubbed by the Congress of Women, meeting in New York and sponsored by Mary A. Livermore, Julia Ward Howe, and Maria Mitchell. This drawing away of women hurt her far more than newspaper gibes. In fact she was sadly disappointed in women's response to the herculean effort she was making for them.

Even more disconcerting was the adverse decision of the Supreme Court on the Myra Bradwell case, which at once shattered the confidence of most of her legal advisors. The court held that Illinois had violated no provision of the federal Constitution in refusing to allow Myra Bradwell to practice law because she was a woman and declared that the right to practice law in state courts is not a privilege or an immunity of a citizen of the United States, nor is the power of a state to prescribe qualifications for admission to the bar affected by the Fourteenth Amendment. Chief Justice Salmon P. Chase, filing a dissenting opinion, lived up to Susan's faith in him, but Benjamin Butler wrote her, "I do not believe anybody in Congress doubts that the Constitution authorizes the right of women to vote, precisely as it authorizes trial by jury and many other like rights guaranteed to citizens. But the difficulty is, the courts long since decided that the constitutional provisions do not act upon the citizens, except as guarantees, ex proprio vigore, and in order to give force to them there must be legislation.... Therefore, the point is for the friends of woman suffrage to get congressional legislation."[303]

Susan, however, never wavered in her conviction that she as a citizen had a constitutional right to vote and that it was her duty to test this right in the courts.

"Is It A Crime For A Citizen ... To Vote?"

Charged with the crime of voting illegally, Susan was brought to trial on June 17, 1873, in the peaceful village of Canandaigua, New York. Simply dressed and wearing her new bonnet faced with blue silk and draped with a dotted veil,[304] she stoically climbed the court-house steps, feeling as if on her shoulders she carried the political destiny of American women. With her were her counsel, Henry R. Selden and John Van Voorhis, her sister, Hannah Mosher, most of the women who had voted with her in Rochester, and Matilda Joslyn Gage, whose interest in this case was akin to her own.

In the courtroom on the second floor, seated behind the bar, Susan watched the curious crowd gather and fill every available seat. She wondered, as she calmly surveyed the all-male jury, whether they could possibly understand the humiliation of a woman who had been arrested for exercising the rights of a citizen. The judge, Ward Hunt, did not promise well, for he had only recently been appointed to the bench through the influence of his friend and townsman, Roscoe Conkling, the undisputed leader of the Republican party in New York and a bitter opponent of woman suffrage. She tried to fathom this small, white-haired, colorless judge upon whose fairness so much depended. Prim and stolid, he sat before her, faultlessly dressed in a suit of black broadcloth, his neck wound with an immaculate white neckcloth. He ruled against her at once, refusing to let her testify on her own behalf.

She was completely satisfied, however, as she listened to Henry Selden's presentation of her case. Tall and commanding, he stood before the court with nobility and kindness in his face and eyes, bringing to mind a handsome cultured Lincoln. So logical, so just was his reasoning, so impressive were his citations of the law that it seemed to her they must convince the jury and even the expressionless judge on the bench.

Pointing out that the only alleged ground of the illegality of Miss Anthony's vote was that she was a woman, Henry Selden declared, "If the same act had been done by her brother under the same circumstances, the act would have been not only innocent and laudable, but honorable; but having been done by a woman it is said to be a crime.... I believe this is the first instance in which a woman has been arraigned in a criminal court, merely on account of her sex."[305] He claimed that Miss Anthony had voted in good faith, believing that the United States Constitution gave her the right to vote, and he clearly outlined her interpretation of the Fourteenth and Fifteenth Amendments, declaring that she stood arraigned as a criminal simply because she took the only step possible to bring this great constitutional question before the courts.

After he had finished, Susan followed closely for two long hours the arguments of the district attorney, Richard Crowley, who contended that whatever her intentions may have been, good or bad, she had by her voting violated a law of the United States and was therefore guilty of crime.

At the close of the district attorney's argument, Judge Hunt without leaving the bench drew out a written document, and to her surprise, read from it as he addressed the jury. "The right of voting or the privilege of voting," he declared, "is a right or privilege arising under the constitution of the State, not of the United States.[306]

"The Legislature of the State of New York," he continued, "has seen fit to say, that the franchise of voting shall be limited to the male sex.... If the Fifteenth Amendment had contained the word 'sex,' the argument of the defendant would have been potent.... The Fourteenth Amendment gives no right to a woman to vote, and the voting of Miss Anthony was in violation of the law....

"There was no ignorance of any fact," he added, "but all the facts being known, she undertook to settle a principle in her own person.... To constitute a crime, it is true, that there must be a criminal intent, but it is equally true that knowledge of the facts of the case is always held to supply this intent...."

Then hesitating a moment, he concluded, "Upon this evidence I suppose there is no question for the jury and that the jury should be directed to find a verdict of guilty."

Immediately Henry Selden was on his feet, addressing the judge, requesting that the jury determine whether or not the defendant was guilty of crime.

Judge Hunt, however, refused and firmly announced, "The question, gentlemen of the jury, in the form it finally takes, is wholly a question or questions of law, and I have decided as a question of law, in the first place, that under the Fourteenth Amendment which Miss Anthony claims protects her, she was not protected in a right to vote.

"And I have decided also," he continued, "that her belief and the advice which she took does not protect her in the act which she committed. If I am right in this, the result must be a verdict on your part of guilty, and therefore I direct that you find a verdict of guilty."

Again Henry Selden was on his feet. "That is a direction," he declared, "that no court has power to make in a criminal case."

The courtroom was tense. Susan, watching the jury and wondering if they would meekly submit to his will, heard the judge tersely order, "Take the verdict, Mr. Clerk."

"Gentlemen of the jury," intoned the clerk, "hearken to your verdict as the Court has recorded it. You say you find the defendant guilty of the offense whereof she stands indicted, and so say you all."

Claiming exception to the direction of the Court that the jury find a verdict of guilty in this a criminal case. Henry Selden asked that the jury be polled.

To this, Judge Hunt abruptly replied, "No. Gentlemen of the jury, you are discharged."

That night Susan recorded her estimate of Judge Hunt's verdict in her diary in one terse sentence, "The greatest outrage History ever witnessed."[307]

The New York Sun, the Rochester Democrat and Chronicle, and the Canandaigua Times were indignant over Judge Hunt's failure to poll the jury. "Judge Hunt," commented the Sun, "allowed the jury to be impanelled and sworn, and to hear the evidence; but when the case had reached the point of rendering the verdict, he directed a verdict of guilty. He thus denied a trial by jury to an accused party in his court; and either through malice, which we do not believe, or through ignorance, which in such a flagrant degree is equally culpable in a judge, he violated one of the most important provisions of the Constitution of the United States.... The privilege of polling the jury has been held to be an absolute right in this State and it is a substantial right ..."[308]

Claiming that the defendant had been denied her right of trial by jury. Henry Selden the next day moved for a new trial. Judge Hunt denied the motion, and, ordering the defendant to stand up, asked her, "Has the prisoner anything to say why sentence shall not be pronounced."[309]

"Yes, your honor," Susan replied, "I have many things to say; for in your ordered verdict of guilty, you have trampled underfoot every vital principle of our government. My natural rights, my civil rights, my political rights, my judicial rights, are all alike ignored...."

Impatiently Judge Hunt protested that he could not listen to a rehearsal of arguments which her counsel had already presented.

"May it please your honor," she persisted, "I am not arguing the question but simply stating the reasons why sentence cannot in justice be pronounced against me. Your denial of my citizen's right to vote is the denial of my right of consent as one of the governed, the denial of my right of representation as one of the taxed, the denial of my right to a trial by a jury of my peers ..."

"The Court cannot allow the prisoner to go on," interrupted Judge Hunt; but Susan, ignoring his command to sit down, protested that her prosecutors and the members of the jury were all her political sovereigns.

Again Judge Hunt tried to stop her, but she was not to be put off. She was pleading for all women and her voice rang out to every corner of the courtroom.

"The Court must insist," declared Judge Hunt, "the prisoner has been tried according to established forms of law."

"Yes, your honor," admitted Susan, "but by forms of law all made by men, interpreted by men, administered by men, in favor of men, and against women...."

"The Court orders the prisoner to sit down," shouted Judge Hunt. "It will not allow another word."

Unheeding, Susan continued, "When I was brought before your honor for trial, I hoped for a broad and liberal interpretation of the Constitution and its recent amendments, that should declare all United States citizens under its protecting aegis—that should declare equality of rights the national guarantee to all persons born or naturalized in the United States. But failing to get this justice—failing, even, to get a trial by a jury not of my peers—I ask not leniency at your hands—but rather the full rigors of the law."

Once more Judge Hunt tried to stop her, and acquiescing at last, she sat down, only to be ordered by him to stand up as he pronounced her sentence, a fine of $100 and the costs of prosecution.

"May it please your honor," she protested, "I shall never pay a dollar of your unjust penalty. All the stock in trade I possess is a $10,000 debt, incurred by publishing my paper—The Revolution ... the sole object of which was to educate all women to do precisely as I have done, rebel against your man-made, unjust, unconstitutional forms of law, that tax, fine, imprison, and hang women, while they deny them the right of representation in the government.... I shall earnestly and persistently continue to urge all women to the practical recognition of the old revolutionary maxim that 'Resistance to tyranny is obedience to God.'"

Pouring cold water on this blaze of oratory, Judge Hunt tersely remarked that the Court would not require her imprisonment pending the payment of her fine.

This shrewd move, obviously planned in advance, made it impossible to carry the case to the United States Supreme Court by writ of habeas corpus.

That same afternoon, Susan was on hand for the trial of the three election inspectors. This time Judge Hunt submitted the case to the jury but with explicit instructions that the defendants were guilty. The jury returned a verdict of guilty, and the inspectors, denied a new trial, were each fined $25 and costs. Two of them, Edwin F. Marsh and William B. Hall, refused to pay their fines and were sent to jail. Susan appealed on their behalf to Senator Sargent in Washington, who eventually secured a pardon for them from President Grant. He also presented a petition to the Senate, in January 1874, to remit Susan's fine, as did William Loughridge of Iowa to the House, but the judiciary committees reported adversely.

Because neither of these cases had been decided on the basis of national citizenship and the right of a citizen to vote, Susan was heartsick. To have them relegated to the category of election fraud was as if her high purpose had been trailed in the dust. Wishing to spread reliable information about her trial and the legal questions involved, she had 3,000 copies of the court proceedings printed for distribution.[310]

It was hard for her to concede that justice for women could not be secured in the courts, but there seemed to be no way in the face of the cold letter of the law to take her case to the Supreme Court of the United States. This would have been possible on writ of habeas corpus had Judge Hunt sentenced her to prison for failure to pay her fine, but this he carefully avoided.

Even that intrepid fighter, John Van Voorhis, could find no loophole, and another of her loyal friends in the legal profession, Albert G. Riddle, wrote her, "There is not, I think, the slightest hope from the courts and just as little from the politicians. They will never take up this cause, never! Individuals will, parties never—till the thing is done.... The trouble is that man can govern alone, and that, though woman has the right, man wants to do it, and if she wait for him to ask her, she will never vote.... Either man must be made to see and feel ... the need of woman's help in the great field of human government, and so demand it; or woman must arise and come forward as she never has, and take her place."[311]

The case of Virginia Minor of St. Louis still held out a glimmer of hope. She had brought suit against an election inspector for his refusal to register her as a voter in the presidential election of 1872, and the case of Minor vs.

Happersett reached the United States Supreme Court in 1874. An adverse decision, on March 29, 1875, delivered by Chief Justice Waite, a friend of woman suffrage, was a bitter blow to Susan and to all those who had pinned their faith on a more liberal interpretation of the Fourteenth and Fifteenth Amendments.

Carefully studying the decision, Susan tried to fathom its reasoning, so foreign to her own ideas of justice. "Sex," she read, "has never been made of one of the elements of citizenship in the United States.... The XIV Amendment did not affect the citizenship of women any more than it did of men.... The direct question is, therefore, presented whether all citizens are necessarily voters."[312]

She read on: "The Constitution does not define the privileges and immunities of citizens.... In this case we need not determine what they are, but only whether suffrage is necessarily one of them. It certainly is nowhere made so in express terms....

"When the Constitution of the United States was adopted, all the several States, with the exception of Rhode Island, had Constitutions of their own.... We find in no State were all citizens permitted to vote.... Women were excluded from suffrage in nearly all the States by the express provision of their constitutions and laws ... No new State has ever been admitted to the Union which has conferred the right of suffrage upon women, and this has never been considered valid objection to her admission. On the contrary ... the right of suffrage was withdrawn from women as early as 1807 in the State of New Jersey, without any attempt to obtain the interference of the United States to prevent it. Since then the governments of the insurgent States have been reorganized under a requirement that, before their Representatives could be admitted to seats in Congress, they must have adopted new Constitutions, republican in form. In no one of these Constitutions was suffrage conferred upon women, and yet the States have all been restored to their original position as States in the Union ... Certainly if the courts can consider any question settled, this is one....

"Our province," concluded Chief Justice Waite, "is to decide what the law is, not to declare what it should be.... Being unanimously of the opinion that the Constitution of the United States does not confer the right of suffrage upon any one, and that the Constitutions and laws of the several States which commit that important trust to men alone are not necessarily void, we affirm the judgment of the Court below."

"A states-rights document," Susan called this decision and she scored it as inconsistent with the policies of a Republican administration which, through the Civil War amendments, had established federal control over the rights and privileges of citizens. If the Constitution does not confer the right of suffrage, she asked herself, why does it define the qualifications of those voting for members of the House of Representatives? How about the enfranchisement of Negroes by federal amendment or the enfranchisement of foreigners? Why did the federal government interfere in her case, instead of leaving it in the hands of the state of New York?

Like most abolitionists, Susan had always regarded the principles of the Declaration of Independence as underlying the Constitution and as the essence of constitutional law. In her opinion, the interpretation of the Constitution in the Virginia Minor case was not only out of harmony with the spirit of the Declaration of Independence, but also contrary to the wise counsel of the great English jurist, Sir Edward Coke, who said, "Whenever the question of liberty runs doubtful, the decision must be given in favor of liberty."[313]

In the face of such a ruling by the highest court in the land, she was helpless. Women were shut out of the Constitution and denied its protection. From here on there was only one course to follow, to press again for a Sixteenth Amendment to enfranchise women.

Social Purity

Militancy among the suffragists continued to flare up here and there in resistance to taxation without representation. Abby Kelley Foster's home in Worcester was sold for taxes for a mere fraction of its worth, while in Glastonbury, Connecticut, Abby and Julia Smith's cows and personal property were seized for taxes. Both Dr. Harriot K. Hunt in Boston and Mary Anthony in Rochester continued their tax protests. Much as Susan admired this spirited rebellion, she recognized that these militant gestures were but flames in the wind unless they had behind them a well-organized, sustained campaign for a Sixteenth Amendment, and this she could not undertake until The Revolution debt was paid. Nor was there anyone to pinch-hit for her since Ernestine Rose had returned to England and Mrs. Stanton gave all her time to Lyceum lectures.

At the moment the prospect looked bleak for woman suffrage. In Congress, there was not the slightest hope of the introduction of or action on a Sixteenth Amendment. In the states, interest was kept alive by woman suffrage bills before the legislatures, and year by year, with more people recognizing the inherent justice of the demand, the margin of defeat grew smaller. Whenever these state contests were critical, Susan managed to be on hand, giving up profitable lecture engagements to speak without fees; in Michigan in 1874 and in Iowa in 1875, she made new friends for the cause but was unable to stem the tide of prejudice against granting women the vote. After the defeat in Michigan, she wrote in her diary, "Every whisky maker, vendor, drinker, gambler, every ignorant besotted man is against us, and then the other extreme, every narrow, selfish religious bigot."[314]

A new militant movement swept the country in 1874, starting in small Ohio towns among women who were so aroused over the evil influence of liquor on husbands, sons, fathers, and brothers, that they gathered in front of saloons to sing and pray, hoping to persuade drunkards to reform and saloon keepers to close their doors. Out of this uprising, the Women's Christian Temperance Union developed, and within the next few years was organized into a powerful reform movement by a young schoolteacher from Illinois, Frances E. Willard.

A lifelong advocate of temperance, Susan had long before reached the conclusion that this reform could not be achieved by a strictly temperance or religious movement, but only through the votes of women. Nevertheless, she lent a helping hand to the Rochester women who organized a branch of the W.C.T.U., but she told them just how she felt: "The best thing this organization will do for you will be to show you how utterly powerless you are to put down the liquor traffic. You can never talk down or sing down or pray down an institution which is voted into existence. You will never be able to lessen this evil until you have votes."[315]

As she traveled through the West for the Lyceum Bureau, she did what she could to stimulate interest in a federal woman suffrage amendment, speaking out of a full heart and with sure knowledge on "Bread and the Ballot" and "The Power of the Ballot," earning on the average $100 a week, which she applied to the Revolution debt.

Lyceum lecturers were now at the height of their popularity,—particularly in the West, where in the little towns scattered across the prairies there were few libraries and theaters, and the distribution of books, magazines, and newspapers in no way met the people's thirst for information or entertainment. Men, women, and children rode miles on horseback or drove over rough roads in wagons to see and hear a prominent lecturer. Susan was always a drawing card, for a woman on the lecture platform still was a novelty and almost everyone was curious about Susan B. Anthony. Many, to their surprise, discovered she was not the caricature they had been led to believe. She looked very ladylike and proper as she stood before them in her dark silk platform dress, a little too stern and serious perhaps, but frequently her face lighted up with a friendly smile. She spoke to them as equals and they could follow her reasoning. Her simple conversational manner was refreshing after the sonorous pretentious oratory of other lecturers.

Continuous travel in all kinds of weather was difficult. Branch lines were slow and connections poor. Often trains were delayed by blizzards, and then to keep her engagements she was obliged to travel by sleigh over the snowy prairies. There were long waits in dingy dirty railroad stations late at night. Even there she was always busy, reading her newspapers in the dim light or dashing off letters home on any scrap of paper she had at hand, thinking gratefully of her sister Mary who in addition to her work as superintendent of the neighborhood public school, supervised the household at 7 Madison Street. Hotel rooms were cold and drab, the food was uninviting, and only occasionally did she find to her delight "a Christian cup of coffee."[316] She often felt that the Lyceum Bureau drove her unnecessarily hard, routed her inefficiently, and profited too generously from her labors. Now and then she dispensed with their services, sent out her own circulars soliciting engagements, and arranged her own tours, proving to her satisfaction that a woman could be as businesslike as a man and sometimes more so.[317]

Weighed down by worry over the illness of her sisters, Guelma and Hannah, she felt a lack of fire and enthusiasm in her work. Anxiously she waited for letters from home, and when none reached her she was in despair. At such times, hotel rooms seemed doubly lonely and she reproached herself for being away from home and for putting too heavy a burden on her sister Mary. Yet there was nothing else to be done until the Revolution debt was paid, for some of her creditors were becoming impatient.

As often as possible Susan returned to Rochester to be with her family, and was able to nurse Guelma through the last weeks of her illness. Heartbroken when she died, in November 1873, she resolved to take better care of Hannah, sending her out to Colorado and Kansas for her health. She then tried to spend the summer months at home so that Mary could visit Hannah in Colorado and Daniel and Merritt in Kansas.

These months at home with her mother whom she dearly loved were a great comfort to them both. They enjoyed reading aloud, finding George Eliot's Middlemarch and Hawthorne's Scarlet Letter of particular interest as Susan was searching for the answers to many questions which had been brought into sharp focus by the Beecher-Tilton case, now filling the newspapers. Like everyone else, she read the latest developments in this tragic involvement of three of her good friends. She was especially concerned about Elizabeth and Theodore Tilton, in whose home she had so often visited and toward whom she felt a warm motherly affection. Her sympathy went out to Elizabeth Tilton, whose help and loyalty during the difficult days of The Revolution she never forgot. Although she had often differed with Theodore, whose quick changes of policy and temperament she could not understand, he had won her gratitude many times by befriending the cause. The same was true of Henry Ward Beecher, who had found time in his busy life to say a good word for woman's rights.

Susan was close to the facts, for in desperation a few years before, Elizabeth Tilton had confided in her. Unfortunately both Elizabeth and Theodore had made confidants of others less wise than Susan. Mrs. Stanton had passed the story along to Victoria Woodhull, who late in 1872 had revived her Weekly for a crusade on what she called "the social question" and had published her expose, "The Beecher-Tilton Scandal Case." As a result the lives of all involved were being ruined by merciless publicity.

The Beecher-Tilton story as it unfolded revealed three admirable people caught in a tangled web of human relationships. Henry Ward Beecher, for years a close friend and benefactor of his young parishioners, Theodore and Elizabeth Tilton, had been accused by Theodore of immoral relations with Elizabeth. Accusations and denials continued while intrigue and negotiations deepened the confusion. The whole matter burst into flame in 1874 in the trial of Henry Ward Beecher before a committee of Plymouth Church, which exonerated him. Reading Beecher's statement in her newspaper, Susan impulsively wrote Isabella Beecher Hooker, "Wouldn't you think if God ever did strike anyone dead for telling a lie, he would have struck then?"[318]

When early in 1875 the Beecher-Tilton case reached the courts in a suit brought by Theodore Tilton against Henry Ward Beecher for the alienation of his wife's affections, it became headline news throughout the country. The press, greedy for sensation, published anything and everything even remotely connected with the case. Reporters hounded Susan, who by this time was again lecturing in the West, and she seldom entered a train, bus, or hotel without finding them at her heels, as if by their very persistence they meant to force her to express her opinion regarding the guilt or innocence of Henry Ward Beecher. They never caught her off guard and she steadfastly refused to reveal to them, or to the lawyers of either side, who astutely approached her, the story which Elizabeth Tilton had told her in confidence. Yet in spite of her continued silence, she was twice quoted by the press, once through the impulsiveness of Mrs. Stanton, who expressed herself frankly at every opportunity, and again when the New York Graphic without Susan's consent published her letter to Mrs. Hooker.

The sympathy of the public was generally with Henry Ward Beecher, whose popularity and prestige were tremendous. A dynamic preacher, whose sermons drew thousands to his church and whose written word carried religion and comfort to every part of the country, he could not suddenly be ruined by the circulation of a scandal or even by a sensational trial. Behind him were all those who were convinced that the future of the Church and Morality demanded his vindication. On his side, also, as Susan well knew, was the powerful, behind-the-scenes influence of the financial interests who profited from Plymouth Church real estate, from the earnings of Beecher's paper, Christian Union, and from his book the Life of Christ, now in preparation and for which he had already been paid $20,000.

Susan and Mrs. Stanton paid the penalty of being on the unpopular side. When Elizabeth Tilton was not allowed to testify in her own defense, they accused Beecher and Tilton of ruthlessly sacrificing her to save their own reputations. In fact, Susan and Mrs. Stanton knew far too much about the case for the comfort of either Beecher or Tilton, and to discredit them, a whispering campaign, and then a press campaign was initiated against them. They and their National Woman Suffrage Association were again accused of upholding free love. Their previous association with Victoria Woodhull was held against them, as were the frank discussions of marriage and divorce published in The Revolution six years before.

Actually Susan's views on marriage were idealistic. "I hate the whole doctrine of 'variety' or 'promiscuity,'" she wrote John Hooker, the husband of her friend Isabella. "I am not even a believer in second marriages after one of the parties is dead, so sacred and binding do I consider the marriage relation."[319]

Although in public Susan uttered not one word relating to the guilt or innocence of Henry Ward Beecher, she did confide her real feelings to her diary. She believed that to save himself Beecher was withholding the explanation which the situation demanded. "It is almost an impossibility," she wrote in her diary, "for a man and a woman to have a close sympathetic friendship without the tendrils of one soul becoming fastened around the other, with the result of infinite pain and anguish." Then again she wrote, "There is nothing more demoralizing than lying. The act itself is scarcely so base as the lie which denies it."[320]

Susan's silence probably brought her more notoriety than anything she could have said on this much discussed subject, and it heightened her reputation for honesty and integrity. "Miss Anthony," commented the New York Sun, "is a lady whose word will everywhere be believed by those who know anything of her character." The Rochester Democrat and Chronicle had this to say: "Whether she will make any definite revelations remains to be seen, but whatever she does say will be received by the public with that credit which attaches to the evidence of a truthful witness. Her own character, known and honored by the country, will give importance to any utterances she may make."[321]

She was not called as a witness by either side during the 112 days of trial which ended in July 1875 with the jury unable to agree on a verdict.

Realizing that many taboos were being broken down by the lurid nation-wide publicity on the Beecher-Tilton case and that as a result people were more willing to consider subjects which hitherto had not been discussed in polite society, Susan began to plan a lecture on "Social Purity."

She was familiar with the public protest Englishwomen under the leadership of Josephine Butler were making against the state regulation of vice. Following with interest and admiration their courageous fight for the repeal of the Contagious Diseases Acts, which placed women suspected of prostitution under police power, Susan found encouragement in the support these reformers had received from such men as John Stuart Mill and Jacob Bright. Such legislation, she resolved, must not gain a foothold in her country, because it not only disregarded women's right to personal liberty but showed a dangerous callousness toward men's share of responsibility for prostitution.

She was awake to the problems prostitution presented in cities like New York and Washington, its prevalence, the police protection it received, the political corruption it fostered and the reluctance of the public to face the situation, the majority of men regarding it as a necessity, and most women closing their eyes to its existence.

During the winter of 1875, while the Beecher-Tilton case was being tried in Brooklyn, she delivered her speech on "Social Purity" at the Chicago Grand Opera House, in the Sunday dime-lecture course, facing with trepidation the immense crowd which gathered to hear her. Even the daring Mrs. Stanton had warned her that she would never be asked to speak in Chicago again, and with this the manager of the Slayton Lecture Bureau agreed. But they were wrong. The people were hungry for the truth and for a constructive policy. In the past they had heard the "social evil" described and denounced in vivid thunderous words by eloquent men and by the dramatic Anna E. Dickinson. Now an earnest woman with graying hair, one of their own kind, talked to them without mincing matters, calmly and logically, and offered them a remedy.

Calling their attention to the daily newspaper reports of divorce and breach-of-promise suits, of wife murders and "paramour" shootings, of abortions and infanticide, she told them that the prevalence of these evils showed clearly that men were incapable of coping with them successfully and needed the help of women. She cited statistics, revealing 20,000 prostitutes in the city of New York, where a foundling hospital during the first six months of its existence rescued 1,300 waifs laid in baskets on its doorstep. She courageously mentioned the prevalence of venereal disease and spoke out against England's Contagious Diseases Acts which were repeatedly suggested for New York and Washington and which she described as licensed prostitution, men's futile and disastrous attempt to deal with social corruption.

Declaring that the poverty and economic dependence of women as well as the passions of men were the causes of prostitution, she quoted more statistics which showed a great increase in the poverty of women. Work formerly done in the household, she explained, was being gradually taken over by factories, with the result that women in order to earn a living had been forced to follow it out of the home and were supporting themselves wholly or in part at a wage inadequate to meet their needs. No wonder many were tempted by food, clothes, and comfortable shelter into an immoral life.

Her solution was "to lift this vast army of poverty-stricken women who now crowd our cities, above the temptation, the necessity, to sell themselves in marriage or out, for bread and shelter." "Women," she told them, "must be educated out of their unthinking acceptance of financial dependence on man into mental and economic independence. Girls like boys must be educated to some lucrative employment. Women like men must have an equal chance to earn a living."[322]

"Whoever controls work and wages," she continued, "controls morals. Therefore we must have women employers, superintendents, committees, legislators; wherever girls go to seek the means of subsistence, there must be some woman. Nay, more; we must have women preachers, lawyers, doctors—that wherever women go to seek counsel—spiritual, legal, physical—there, too, they will be sure to find the best and noblest of their own sex to minister to them."

Then she added, "Marriage, to women as to men, must be a luxury, not a necessity; an incident of life, not all of it.... Marriage never will cease to be a wholly unequal partnership until the law recognizes the equal ownership in the joint earnings and possessions."

She asked for the vote so that women would have the power to help make the laws relating to marriage, divorce, adultery, breach of promise, rape, bigamy, infanticide, and so on. These laws, she reminded them, have not only been framed by men, but are administered by men. Judges, jurors, lawyers, all are men, and no woman's voice is heard in our courts except as accused or witness, and in many cases the married woman is denied the right to testify as to her guilt or innocence.

Never before had the audience heard the case for social purity presented in this way and they listened intently. When the applause was subsiding, Susan saw Parker Pillsbury and Bronson Alcott, fellow-lecturers on the Lyceum circuit, coming toward her, smiling approval. They were generous in their praise, Bronson Alcott declaring, "You have stated here this afternoon, in a fearless manner, truths that I have hardly dared to think, much less to utter."[323]

She repeated this lecture in St. Louis, in Wisconsin, and in Kansas, and while most city newspapers, acknowledging the need of facing the issues, praised her courage, small-town papers were frankly disturbed by a spinster's public discussion of the "social evil," one paper observing, "The best lecture a woman can give the community ... on the sad 'evil' ... is the sincerity of her profound ignorance on the subject."[324]

Having bravely done her bit for social purity, Susan with relief turned again to her favorite lecture, "Bread and the Ballot." Her message fell on fertile ground. These western men and women saw justice in her reasoning. Having broken with tradition by leaving the East for the frontier, they could more easily drop old ways for new. Western men also recognized the influence for good that women had brought to lonely bleak western towns—better homes, cleanliness, comfort, then schools, churches, law and order—and many of them were willing to give women the vote. All they needed was prodding to translate that willingness into law.

As she continued her lecturing, she kept her watchful eye on her family and the annual New York and Washington conventions, attending to many of the routine details herself. Finally, on May 1, 1876, she recorded in her diary, "The day of Jubilee for me has come. I have paid the last dollar of the Revolution debt."[325]

Even the press took notice, the Chicago Daily News commenting, "By working six years and devoting to the purpose all the money she could earn, she has paid the debt and interest. And now, when the creditors of that paper and others who really know her, hear the name of Susan B. Anthony, they feel inclined to raise their hats in reverence."[326]

A Federal Woman Suffrage Amendment

Like everyone else in the United States in 1876, Susan now turned her attention to the Centennial Exposition in Philadelphia, which was proclaiming to the world the progress this new country had made. Susan pointed out, however, that one hundred years after the signing of the Declaration of Independence, women were still deprived of basic citizenship rights.

As an afterthought, a Woman's Pavilion had been erected on the exposition grounds and exhibited here she found only women's contribution to the arts but nothing which would in any way show the part women had played in building up the country or developing industry. She longed to explain so that all could hear how the skilled work of women had contributed to the prosperous textile and shoe industries, to the manufacture of cartridges and Waltham watches, and countless other products. Could she have had her way, she would have made the Woman's Pavilion an eloquent appeal for equal rights, but unable to do this, she established a center of rebellion for the National Woman Suffrage Association at 1431 Chestnut Street, in parlors on the first floor. Here she spent many happy hours directing the work, often sleeping on the sofa so that she could work late and save money for the cause.

Philadelphia had always been a friendly city because of Lucretia Mott. Now Lucretia came almost daily to the women's headquarters, bringing a comforting sense of support, approval, and friendship. When Mrs. Stanton, free at last from her lecture engagements, joined them in June, Susan's happiness was complete and she confided to her diary, "Glad enough to see her and feel her strength come in."[327]

Susan and Mrs. Stanton now sent the Republican and Democratic national conventions well-written memorials pointing out the appropriateness of enfranchising women in this centennial year. But no woman suffrage plank was adopted by either party. Susan put Mrs. Stanton and Mrs. Gage to work on a Women's Declaration of 1876, and so "magnificent" a document did they produce that she not only had many copies printed for distribution but had one beautifully engrossed on parchment for presentation to President Grant at the Fourth of July celebration in Independence Square.

Unable to secure permission to present this declaration, she made plans of her own. For herself, she managed to get a press card as reporter for her brother's paper, the Leavenworth Times. Mrs. Stanton and Lucretia Mott refused to attend the celebration, so indignant were they over the snubs women had received from the Centennial Commission, and they held a women's meeting at the First Unitarian Church. When at the last minute four tickets were sent Susan by the Centennial Commission, she gave them to the most militant of her colleagues, Matilda Joslyn Gage, Lillie Devereux Blake, Sarah Andrews Spencer, and Phoebe Couzins. With Susan in the lead, they pushed through the jostling crowd to Independence Square on that bright hot Fourth of July and were seated among the elect on the platform.

By this time they had learned that Thomas W. Ferry of Michigan, Acting Vice President, would substitute for President Grant at the ceremony. Because he was a good friend of woman suffrage, Phoebe Couzins made one more effort for orderly procedure, sending him a note asking for permission to present the Women's Declaration. This failed, and rather than take part in creating a disturbance, she withdrew, leaving her four friends on the platform.

"We ... sat there waiting ..." reported Mrs. Blake. "The heat was frightful.... Amid such a throng it was difficult to hear anything ... We decided that our presentation should take place immediately after Mr. Richard Lee of Virginia, grandson of the Signer, had read the Declaration of Independence. He read it from the original document, and it was an impressive moment when that time-honored parchment was exposed to the view of the wildly cheering crowd.... Mr. Lee's voice was inaudible, but at last I caught the words, 'our sacred honors,' and cried, 'Now is the time.'

"We all four rose, Miss Anthony first, next Mrs. Gage, bearing our engrossed Declaration, and Mrs. Spencer and myself following with hundreds of printed copies in our hands. There was a stir in the crowd just at the time, and General Hawley who had been keeping a wary eye on us, had relaxed his vigilance for a moment, as he signed to the band to resume playing. He did not see us advancing until we reached the Vice President's dais. There Miss Anthony, taking the parchment from Mrs. Gage, stepped forward and presented it to Mr. Ferry, saying, 'I present to you a Declaration of Rights from the women citizens of the United States.'"[328]

Nonplussed, Mr. Ferry bowed low and received the Declaration without a word. Then the four intrepid women filed out, distributing printed copies of their declaration while General Hawley boomed out, "Order! Order!"

Leaving the square and mounting a platform erected for musicians in front of Independence Hall, they waited until a curious crowd had gathered around them. Then while Mrs. Gage held an umbrella over Susan to shield her from the hot sun, she read the Women's Declaration in a loud clear voice that carried far.

"We do rejoice in the success, thus far, of our experiment of self-government," she began. "Our faith is firm and unwavering in the broad principles of human rights proclaimed in 1776, not only as abstract truths, but as the cornerstones of a republic. Yet we cannot forget, even in this glad hour, that while all men of every race, and clime, and condition, have been invested with the full rights of citizenship under our hospitable flag, all women still suffer the degradation of disfranchisement."[329]

Then she enumerated women's grievances and the crowd applauded as she drove home point after point.

"Woman," she continued, "has shown equal devotion with man to the cause of freedom and has stood firmly by his side in its defense. Together they have made this country what it is.... We ask our rulers, at this hour, no special favors, no special privileges.... We ask justice, we ask equality, we ask that all civil and political rights that belong to the citizens of the United States be guaranteed to us and our daughters forever."

Stepping down from the platform into the applauding crowd which eagerly reached for printed copies of the declaration, she and her four companions hurried to the First Unitarian Church where an eager audience awaited their report and hailed their courage.

Aaron A. Sargent

The New York Tribune, commenting on Susan's militancy, prophesied that it foreshadowed "the new forms of violence and disregard of order which may accompany the participation of women in active partisan politics."[330]

Nor was Congress impressed by Susan's centennial publicity demanding a federal woman suffrage amendment. She had gathered petitions from twenty-six states with 10,000 signatures which were presented to the Senate in 1877. The majority of the Senators found these petitions uproariously funny, and Susan in the visitors' gallery at the time of their presentation was infuriated by the mirth and disrespect of these men. "A few read the petitions as they would any other, with dignity and without comment," reported the popular journalist, Mary Clemmer, in her weekly Washington column, "but the majority seemed intensely conscious of holding something unutterably funny in their hands.... The entire Senate presented the appearance of a laughing school practicing sidesplitting and ear-extended grins." After a few humorous and sarcastic remarks the petitions were referred to the Committee on Public Lands. Only one Senator, Aaron A. Sargent of California, was "man enough and gentleman enough to lift the petitions from this insulting proposition.... He ... demanded for the petition of more than 10,000 women at least the courtesy which would be given any other."[331]

Although his words did not deter the Senators, Susan was proud of this tall vigorous white-haired Californian and grateful for his spontaneous support in this humiliating situation. He had been a trusted friend and counselor ever since she had shared with him and his family the long snowy journey from Nevada in 1872. She looked forward to the time when woman suffrage would have more such advocates in the Congress and when she would find there new faces and a more liberal spirit.

Disappointment only drove Susan into more intensive activity. Between lectures she now nursed her sister Hannah who was critically ill in Daniel's home in Leavenworth. After Hannah's death in May 1877, Susan worked off her grief in Colorado, where the question of votes for women was being referred to the people of the state.

The suffragists in Colorado were headed by Dr. Alida Avery, who had left her post as resident physician at the new woman's college, Vassar, to practice medicine in Denver. Making Dr. Avery's home her headquarters, Susan carried her plea for the ballot to settlements far from the railroads, traveling by stagecoach over rough lonely roads through magnificent scenery. Holding meetings wherever she could, she spoke in schoolhouses, in hotel dining rooms, and even in saloons, when no other place was available, and always she was treated with respect and listened to with interest. Occasionally only a mere handful gathered to hear her, but in Lake City she spoke to an audience of a thousand or more from a dry-goods box on the court-house steps. She was equal to anything, but the mining towns depressed her, for they were swarming with foreigners who had been welcomed as naturalized, enfranchised citizens and who almost to a man opposed extending the vote to women. This precedence of foreign-born men over American women was not only galling to her but menaced, she believed, the growth of American democracy.

Woman suffrage was defeated in Colorado in 1877, two to one. With the Chinese coming into the state in great numbers to work in the mines, the specter that stalked through this campaign was the fear of putting the ballot into the hands of Chinese women.

From Colorado, Susan moved on to Nebraska with a new lecture, "The Homes of Single Women." Although she much preferred to speak on "Woman and the Sixteenth Amendment" or "Bread and the Ballot," she realized that, in order to be assured of return engagements, she must occasionally vary her subjects, but she was unwilling to wander far afield while women's needs still were so great. By means of this new lecture she hoped to dispel the widespread, deeply ingrained fallacy that single women were unwanted helpless creatures wholly dependent upon some male relative for a home and support. Aware that this mistaken estimate was slowly yielding in the face of a changing economic order, she believed she could help lessen its hold by presenting concrete examples of independent self-supporting single women who had proved that marriage was not the only road to security and a home. She told of Alice and Phoebe Cary, whose home in New York City was a rendezvous for writers, artists, musicians, and reformers; of Dr. Clemence Lozier, the friend of women medical students; of Mary L. Booth, well established through her income as editor of Harper's Bazaar; and of her beloved Lydia Mott, whose home had been a refuge for fugitive slaves and reformers.[332]

In Nebraska, she made a valuable new friend for the cause, Clara Bewick Colby, whose zeal and earnest, intelligent face at once attracted her. Within a few years, Mrs. Colby established in Beatrice, Nebraska, a magazine for women, the Woman's Tribune, which to Susan's joy spoke out for a federal woman suffrage amendment.

Because Susan's contract with the Slayton Lecture Bureau allowed no break in her engagements, she was obliged to leave the Washington convention of the National Woman Suffrage Association in the hands of others in 1878. It was much on her mind as she traveled through Dakota, Minnesota, Missouri, and Kansas, and she sent a check for $100 to help with the expenses of the convention. Particularly on her mind was a federal woman suffrage amendment, for since 1869 when a Sixteenth Amendment enfranchising women had been introduced in Congress and ignored, no further efforts along that line had been made. Now good news came from Mrs. Stanton, who had attended the convention. She had persuaded Senator Sargent to introduce in the Senate, on January 10, 1878, a new draft of a Sixteenth Amendment, following the wording of the Fifteenth. It read, "The right of citizens of the United States to vote shall not be denied or abridged by the United States or by any State on account of sex."[333]

Clara Bewick Colby

During the next few years the Sixteenth Amendment made little headway, although the complexion of Congress changed, the Democrats breaking the Republicans' hold and winning a substantial majority. Encouraging as was the more liberal spirit of the new Congress and the defeat of several implacable enemies, Susan found California's failure to return Senator Sargent an irreparable loss. In addition she now had to face a newly formed group of anti-suffragists under the leadership of Mrs. Dahlgren, Mrs. Sherman, and Almira Lincoln Phelps, who sang the refrain which Congressmen loved to hear, that women did not want the vote because it would wreck marriage and the home. Hoping to counteract this adverse influence by increased pressure for the Sixteenth Amendment, Susan once more appealed for help to the American Woman Suffrage Association through her old friends, William Lloyd Garrison and Wendell Phillips. Garrison replied that her efforts for a federal amendment were premature and "would bring the movement into needless contempt." This she found strange advice from the man who had fearlessly defied public opinion to crusade against slavery. Wendell Phillips did better, writing, "I think you are on the right track—the best method to agitate the question, and I am with you, though between you and me, I still think the individual States must lead off, and that this reform must advance piecemeal, State by State. But I mean always to help everywhere and everyone."[334]

The American Association continued to follow the state-by-state method, and this holding back aroused Susan to the boiling point, for experience had taught her that in state elections woman suffrage faced the prejudiced opposition of an ever-increasing number of naturalized immigrants, who had little understanding of democratic government or sympathy with the rights of women. A federal amendment, on the other hand, depending for its adoption upon Congress and ratifying legislatures, was in the hands of a far more liberal, intelligent, and preponderantly American group. "We have puttered with State rights for thirty years," she sputtered, "without a foothold except in the territories."[335]

Year by year she continued her Washington conventions, convinced that these gatherings in the national capital could not fail to impress Congressmen with the seriousness of their purpose. As women from many states lobbied for the Sixteenth Amendment, reporting a growing sentiment everywhere for woman suffrage, as they received in the press respectful friendly publicity, Congressmen began to take notice. At the large receptions held at the Riggs House, through the generosity of the proprietors, Jane Spofford and her husband, Congressmen became better acquainted with the suffragists, finding that they were not cranks, as they had supposed, but intelligent women and socially charming.

Mrs. Stanton's poise as presiding officer and the warmth of her personality made her the natural choice for president of the National Woman Suffrage Association through the years. Her popularity, now well established throughout the country after her ten years of lecturing on the Lyceum circuit, lent prestige to the cause. To Susan, her presence brought strength and the assurance that "the brave and true word" would be spoken.[336] A new office had been created for Susan, that of vice-president at large, and in that capacity she guided, steadied, and prodded her flock. The subjects which the conventions discussed covered a wide field going far beyond their persistent demands for a federal woman suffrage amendment. Not only did they at this time urge an educational qualification for voters to combat the argument that woman suffrage would increase the ignorant vote, but they also protested the counting of women in the basis of representation so long as they were disfranchised. They criticized the church for barring women from the ministry and from a share in church government. They took up the case of Anna Ella Carroll,[337] who had been denied recognition and a pension for her services to her country during the Civil War, and they urged pensions for all women who had nursed soldiers during the war. They welcomed to their conventions Mormon women from Utah who came to Washington to protest efforts to disfranchise them as a means of discouraging polygamy.

Susan injected international interest into these conventions by reading Alexander Dumas's arguments for woman suffrage, letters from Victor Hugo and English suffragists, and a report by Mrs. Stanton's son, Theodore, now a journalist, of the International Congress in Paris in 1878, which discussed the rights of women. Occasionally foreign-born women, now making new homes for themselves in this country, joined the ranks of the suffragists, and a few of them, like Madam Anneké and Clara Heyman from Germany contributed a great deal through their eloquence and wider perspective. These contacts with the thoughts and aspirations of men and women of other countries led Susan to dream of an international conference of women in the not too distant future.[338]

Recording Women's History

Recording women's history for future generations was a project that had been in the minds of both Susan and Mrs. Stanton for a long time. Both looked upon women's struggle for a share in government as a potent force in strengthening democracy and one to be emphasized in history. Men had always been the historians and had as a matter of course extolled men's exploits, passing over women's record as negligible. Susan intended to remedy this and she was convinced that if women close to the facts did not record them now, they would be forgotten or misinterpreted by future historians. Already many of the old workers had died, Martha C. Wright, Lydia Mott, whom Susan had nursed in her last illness, Lucretia Mott, and William Lloyd Garrison. There was no time to be lost.[339]

In the spring of 1880, Susan's mother died, and it was no longer necessary for her to fit into her schedule frequent visits in Rochester. Her sister Mary, busy with her teaching, was sharing her home with her two widowed brothers-in-law and two nieces whose education she was supervising.[340] Mrs. Stanton had just given up the strenuous life of a

Lyceum lecturer and welcomed work that would keep her at home. Susan, who had managed to save $4,500 out of her lecture fees, felt she could afford to devote at least a year to the history.

She now shipped several boxes of letters, clippings, and documents to the Stanton home in Tenafly, New Jersey.[341] As they planned their book, it soon became obvious that the one volume which they had hoped to finish in a few months would extend to two or three volumes and take many years to write. They called in Matilda Joslyn Gage to help them, and the three of them signed a contract to share the work and the profits.

The history presented a publishing problem as well as a writing ordeal, and Susan, interviewing New York publishers, found the subject had little appeal. Finally, however, she signed a contract with Fowler & Wells under which the authors agreed to pay the cost of composition, stereotyping, and engravings; and as usual she raised the necessary funds.[342]

Matilda Joslyn Gage Matilda Joslyn Gage

Returning to Tenafly as to a second home, Susan usually found Mrs. Stanton beaming a welcome from the piazza and Margaret and Harriot running to the gate to meet her. The Stanton children were fond of Susan. It was a comfortable happy household, and Susan, thoroughly enjoying Mrs. Stanton's companionship, attacked the history with vigor.

Sitting opposite each other at a big table in the sunny tower room, they spent long hours at work. Susan, thin and wiry, her graying hair neatly smoothed back over her ears, sat up very straight as she rapidly sorted old clippings and letters and outlined chapters, while Mrs. Stanton, stout and placid, her white curls beautifully arranged, wrote steadily and happily, transforming masses of notes into readable easy prose.[343]

Having sent appeals for information to colleagues in all parts of the country, Susan, as the contributions began to come in, struggled to decipher the often almost illegible, handwritten manuscripts, many of them careless and inexact about dates and facts. To their request for data about her, Lucy Stone curtly replied, "I have never kept a diary or any record of my work, and so am unable to furnish you the required dates.... You say 'I' must be referred to in the history you are writing.... I cannot furnish a biographical sketch and trust you will not try to make one. Yours with ceaseless regret that any 'wing' of suffragists should attempt to write the history of the other."[344]

The greater part of the writing fell upon Mrs. Stanton, but Matilda Joslyn Gage contributed the chapters, "Preceding Causes," "Women in Newspapers," and "Women, Church, and State." Susan carefully selected the material and checked the facts. She helped with the copying of the handwritten manuscript and with the proofreading. Believing that pictures of the early workers were almost as important for the History as the subject matter itself, she tried to provide them, but they presented a financial problem with which it was hard to cope, for each engraving cost $100.[345]

When the first volume of the History of Woman Suffrage came off the press in May 1881, she proudly and lovingly scanned its 878 pages which told the story of women's progress in the United States up to the Civil War.

She was well aware that the History was not a literary achievement, but the facts were there, as accurate as humanly possible; all the eloquent, stirring speeches were there, a proof of the caliber and high intelligence of the pioneers; and out of the otherwise dull record of meetings, conventions, and petitions, a spirit of independence and zeal for freedom shone forth, highlighted occasionally by dramatic episodes. As Mrs. Stanton so aptly expressed it, "We have furnished the bricks and mortar for some future architect to rear a beautiful edifice."[346]

The distribution of the book was very much on Susan's mind, for she realized that it would not be in great demand because of its cost, bulk, and subject matter. Nor could she at this time present it to libraries, as she wished, for she had already spent her savings on the illustrations. "It ought to be in every school library," she wrote Amelia Bloomer, "where every boy and girl of the nation could see and read and learn what women have done to secure equality of rights and chances for girls and women...."[347]

So much material had been collected while Volume I was in preparation that both Susan and Mrs. Stanton felt they should immediately undertake Volume II. After a summer of lecturing to help finance its publication, Susan returned to Tenafly to the monotonous work of compilation. "I am just sick to death of it," she wrote her young friend Rachel Foster. "I had rather wash or whitewash or do any possible hard work than sit here and go there digging into the dusty records of the past—that is, rather make history than write it."[348]

Yet she never entirely gave up making history, for she was always planning for the future and Rachel Foster was now her able lieutenant, relieving her of details, doing the spade work for the annual Washington conventions, and arranging for an occasional lecture engagement. Susan would not leave Tenafly for a lecture fee of less than $50.

She took this intelligent young girl to her heart as she had Anna E. Dickinson in the past. Rachel, however, had none of Anna's dramatic temperament or love of the limelight, but in her orderly businesslike way was eager to serve Susan, whom she had admired ever since as a child she had heard her speak for woman suffrage in her mother's drawing room.

While Susan was pondering the ways and means of financing another volume of the History, the light broke through in a letter from Wendell Phillips, announcing the astonishing news that she and Lucy Stone had inherited approximately $25,000 each for "the woman's cause" under the will of Eliza Eddy, the daughter of their former benefactor, Francis Jackson. Although the legacy was not paid until 1885 because of litigation, its promise lightened considerably Susan's financial burden and she knew that Volumes II and III were assured. Her gratitude to Eliza Eddy was unbounded, and better still, she read between the lines the good will of Wendell Phillips who had been Eliza Eddy's legal advisor. That he, whom she admired above all men, should after their many differences still regard her as worthy of this trust, meant as much to her as the legacy itself.

In May 1882 she had the satisfaction of seeing the second volume of the History of Woman Suffrage in print, carrying women's record through 1875. Volume III was not completed until 1885.

Women's response to their own history was a disappointment. Only a few realized its value for the future, among them Mary L. Booth, editor of Harper's Bazaar. The majority were indifferent and some even critical. When Mrs. Stanton offered the three volumes to the Vassar College library, they were refused.[349] Nevertheless, every time Susan looked at the three large volumes on her shelves, she was happy, for now she was assured that women's struggle for citizenship and freedom would live in print through the years. To libraries in the United States and Europe, she presented well over a thousand copies, grateful that the Eliza Eddy legacy now made this possible.

In 1883, Susan surprised everyone by taking a vacation in Europe. Soon after Volume II of the History had been completed, Mrs. Stanton had left for Europe with her daughter Harriot.[350] Her letters to Susan reported not only Harriot's marriage to an Englishman, William Henry Blatch, but also encouraging talks with the forward-looking women of England and France whom she hoped to interest in an international organization. Repeatedly she urged Susan to join her, to meet these women, and to rest for a while from her strenuous labors. The possibility of forming an international organization of women was a greater attraction to Susan than Europe itself, and when Rachel Foster suggested that she make the journey with her, she readily consented.

"She goes abroad a republican Queen," observed the Kansas City Journal, "uncrowned to be sure, but none the less of the blood royal, and we have faith that the noblest men and women of Europe will at once recognize and welcome her as their equal."[351]

In London, Susan met Mrs. Stanton, "her face beaming and her white curls as lovely as ever." Then after talking with English suffragists and her two old friends, William Henry Channing and Ernestine Rose, now living in England, Susan traveled with Rachel through Italy, Switzerland, Germany, and France, where a whole new world opened before her. She thoroughly enjoyed its beauty; yet there was much that distressed her and she found herself far more interested in the people, their customs and living conditions than in the treasures of art. "It is good for our young civilization," she wrote Daniel, "to see and study that of the old world and observe the hopelessness of lifting the masses into freedom and freedom's industry, honesty and integrity. How any American, any lover of our free institutions, based on equality of rights for all, can settle down and live here is more than I can comprehend. It will only be by overturning the powers that education and equal chances ever can come to the rank and file. The hope of the world is indeed our republic...." To a friend she reported, "Amidst it all my head and heart turn to our battle for women at home. Here in the old world, with ... its utter blotting out of women as an equal, there is no hope, no possibility of changing her condition; so I look to our own land of equality for men, and partial equality for women, as the only one for hope or work."[352]

Back in London again, she allowed herself a few luxuries, such as an expensive India shawl and more social life than she had had in many a year, and she longed to have Mary enjoy it all with her. She visited suffragists in Scotland and Ireland as well as in England and occasionally spoke at their meetings.[353] Here as in America suffragists differed over the best way to win the vote, and even the most radical among them were more conservative and cautious than American women, but she admired them all and tried to understand the very different problems they faced. Gradually she interested a few of them in an international conference of women, and before she sailed back to America with Mrs. Stanton in November 1883, she had their promise of cooperation.

The newspapers welcomed her home. "Susan B. Anthony is back from Europe," announced the Cleveland Leader, "and is here for a winter's fight on behalf of woman suffrage. She seems remarkably well, and has gained fifteen pounds since she left last spring. She is sixty-three, but looks just the same as twenty years ago. There is perhaps an extra wrinkle in her face, a little more silver in her hair, but her blue eyes are just as bright, her mouth as serious and her step as active as when she was forty. She would attract attention in any crowd."[354]

Susan came back to an indifferent Congress. "All would fall flat and dead if someone were not here to keep them in mind of their duty to us," she wrote a friend at this time, and to her diary she confided, "It is perfectly disheartening that no member feels any especial interest or earnest determination in pushing this question of woman suffrage, to all men only a side issue."[355]

Impetus From The West

"My heart almost stands still. I hope against hope, but still I hope," Susan wrote in her diary in 1885, as she waited for news from Oregon Territory regarding the vote of the people on a woman suffrage amendment.[356] Woman suffrage was defeated in Oregon; and in Washington Territory, where in 1883 it had carried, a contest was being waged in the courts to invalidate it. In Nebraska it had also been defeated in 1882. Since the victories in Wyoming and Utah in 1869 and 1870, not another state or territory had written woman suffrage into law.

In spite of these setbacks, Susan still saw great promise in the West and resumed her lecturing there. She knew the rapidly growing young western states and territories as few easterners did, and she understood their people. Here women were making themselves indispensable as teachers, and state universities, now open to them, graduated over two thousand women a year. The Farmers' Alliance, the Grange, and the Prohibition party, all distinctly western in origin, admitted women to membership and were friendly to woman suffrage. School suffrage had been won in twelve western states as against five in the East, and Kansas women were now voting in municipal elections. In a sense, woman suffrage was becoming respectable in the West, and a woman was no longer ostracized by her friends for working with Susan B. Anthony.

Still critical of her own speaking, Susan was often discouraged over her lectures, but her vitality, her naturalness, and her flashes of wit seldom failed to win over her audiences. Her nephew, Daniel Jr., a student at the University of Michigan, hearing her speak, wrote his parents, "At the beginning of her lecture, Aunt Susan does not do so well; but when she is in the midst of her argument and all her energies brought into play, I think she is a very powerful speaker."[357]

On these trips through the West, she kept in close touch with her brothers Daniel and Merritt in Kansas, frequently visiting in their homes and taking her numerous nieces to Rochester. She valued Daniel's judgment highly, and he, well-to-do and influential, was a great help to her in many ways, investing her savings and furnishing her with railroad passes which greatly reduced her ever-increasing traveling expenses.

Everywhere she met active zealous members of the Women's Christian Temperance Union. Since the Civil War, temperance had become a vigorous movement in the Middle West, doing its utmost to counteract the influence of the many large new breweries and saloons. Through the Prohibition party, organized on a national basis in 1872, temperance was now a political issue in Kansas, Iowa, and the Territory of Dakota, and through the W.C.T.U. women waged an effective total-abstinence campaign. Brought into the suffrage movement by Frances Willard under the slogan, "For God and Home and Country," these women quickly sensed the value of their votes to the temperance cause. Nor was Susan slow to recognize their importance to her and her work, for they represented an entirely new group, churchwomen, who heretofore had been suspicious of and hostile toward woman's rights. Through them, she anticipated a powerful impetus for her cause.

With admiration she had watched Frances Willard's career.[358] This vivid consecrated young woman was a born leader, quick to understand woman's need of the vote and eager to lead women forward. It was a disappointment, however, when she joined the American rather than the National Woman Suffrage Association. The reasons for this, Susan readily understood, were Frances Willard's warm friendship with Mary Livermore and her own preference for the American's state-by-state method, similar to that she had so successfully followed in her W.C.T.U. Yet Frances Willard, whenever she could, cooperated with Susan whom she admired and loved; and through the years these two great leaders valued and respected each other, even though they frequently differed over policy and method.

Susan, for example, was often troubled because women suffrage and temperance were more and more linked together in the public mind, thus confusing the issues and arousing the hostility of those who might have been friendly toward woman suffrage had they not feared that women's votes would bring in prohibition. She did her best to make it clear to her audiences that she did not ask for the ballot in order that women might vote against saloons and for prohibition. She demanded only that women have the same right as men to express their opinions at the polls. Such an attitude was hard for many temperance women to understand and to forgive.

Over women's support of specific political parties, Susan and Frances Willard were never able to agree. Susan had never been willing to ally herself with a minority party. Therefore, to Frances Willard's disappointment, she withheld her support from the Prohibition party in 1880, although their platform acknowledged woman's need of the ballot and directed them to use it to settle the liquor question, and in 1884 when they recommended state suffrage for women. Finding women eager to support the Prohibitionists in gratitude for these inadequate planks, Susan even issued a statement urging them to support the Republicans, who held out the most hope to them even if woman suffrage had not been mentioned in their platform. Her experience in Washington had proved to her the friendliness and loyalty of individual Republicans, and she was unwilling to jeopardize their support.

Her judgment was confirmed during the next few years when friendly Republicans spoke for woman suffrage in the Senate, and when in 1887 the woman suffrage amendment was debated and voted on in the Senate. In the Senate gallery eagerly listening, Susan took notice that the sixteen votes cast for the amendment were those of Republicans.[359]

Still hoping to win Susan's endorsement of the Prohibition party in 1888, Frances Willard asked her to outline what kind of plank would satisfy her.

"Do you mean so satisfy me," Susan replied, "that I would work, and recommend to all women to work ... for the success of the third party ticket?... Not until a third party gets into power ... which promises a larger per cent of representatives, on the floor of Congress, and in the several State legislatures, who will speak and vote for women's enfranchisement, than does the Republican, shall I work for it. You see, as yet there is not a single Prohibitionist in Congress while there are at least twenty Republicans on the floor of the United States Senate, besides fully one-half of the members of the House of Representatives who are in favor of woman suffrage.... I do not propose to work for the defeat of the party which thus far has furnished nearly every vote in that direction."[360]

Nor was she lured away when, in 1888, the Prohibition party endorsed woman suffrage and granted Frances Willard the honor of addressing its convention and serving on the resolutions committee.

The temperance issue also cropped up in the annual Washington conventions of the National Woman Suffrage Association, preparations for which Susan now left to Rachel Foster, May Wright Sewall, a capable young recruit from Indiana, and Jane Spofford. However, she still supervised these conventions, prodding and interfering, in what she called her most Andrew Jackson-like manner. She always returned to Washington with excitement and pleasure, and with the hope of some outstanding victory, and the suite at the Riggs House, given her by generous Jane Spofford, was a delight after months of hard travel in the West. "I shall come both ragged and dirty," she wrote Mrs. Spofford in 1887. "Though the apparel will be tattered and torn, the mind, the essence of me, is sound to the core. Please tell the little milliner to have a bonnet picked out for me, and get a dressmaker who will patch me together so that I shall be presentable."[361]

Open to all women irrespective of race or creed, the National Woman Suffrage Association attracted fearless independent devoted members. They welcomed Mormon women into the fold, and when the bill to disfranchise Mormon women as a punishment for polygamy was before Congress in 1887, they did their utmost to help Mormon women retain the vote, but were defeated.

They welcomed as well many temperance advocates. A few delegates, however, among them Mrs. Stanton, Mrs. Gage, and Mrs. Colby, scorned what they called the "singing and praying" temperance group and protested that temperance and religion were getting too strong a hold on the organization. Abigail Duniway from Oregon contended that suffragists should not join forces with temperance groups and blamed the defeat of woman suffrage in Oregon, Idaho, and Washington, in 1887, on men's fear that women would vote for prohibition.

Often Susan was obliged to act as arbiter between the temperance and nontemperance groups. She did not underestimate the momentum which the well-organized W.C.T.U. had already given the suffrage cause, particularly in states where the National Association had only a few and scattered workers. She needed and wanted the help of these temperance women and of Frances Willard's forceful and winning personality. She also saw the importance of breaking down with Frances Willard's aid the slow-yielding opposition of the church.

Occasionally enthusiastic workers undertook projects which to her seemed unwise. She told them frankly how she felt and left it at that, but most of them had to learn by experience. When Belva Lockwood, one of her most able colleagues in Washington, accepted the nomination for President of the United States, offered her by the women of California in 1884 and by the women of Iowa in 1888 through their Equal Rights party, she did not lend her support or that of the National Association, but followed her consistent policy of no alignment with a minority party. Nevertheless, she heartily believed in women's right and ability to hold the highest office in the land.

Ever since her trip to Europe in 1883, Susan had been planning for an international gathering of women. Interest in this project was kept alive among European women by Mrs. Stanton during her frequent visits with her daughter Harriot in England and her son Theodore in France. It was Susan, however, who put the machinery in motion through the National Woman Suffrage Association and issued a call for an international conference in Washington, in March 1888, to commemorate the fortieth anniversary of the first woman's rights convention. Ten thousand invitations were sent out to organizations of women in all parts of the world, to professional, business, and reform groups as well as to those advocating political and civil rights for women, and an ambitious program was prepared. Most of the work for the conference and the raising of $13,000 to finance it fell upon the shoulders of Susan, Rachel Foster, and May Wright Sewall, but they also had the enthusiastic cooperation of Frances Willard, who, with her nation-wide contacts, was of inestimable value in arousing interest among the many and varied women's organizations and the labor groups. Another happy development was Clara Colby's decision to publish her Woman's Tribune in Washington during the conference. Mrs. Colby's Tribune, established in Beatrice, Nebraska, in 1883, had since then met in a measure Susan's need for a paper for the National Association and she welcomed its transfer to Washington.[362]

Women from all parts of the world assembled in Albaugh's Opera House in Washington for the epoch-making international conference which opened on Sunday, March 25, 1888, with religious services conducted entirely by women, as if to prove to the world that women in the pulpit were appropriate and adequate. Fifty-three national organizations sent representatives, and delegates came from England, France, Norway, Denmark, Finland, India, and Canada.

Presiding over all sixteen sessions, Susan rejoiced over a record attendance. Her thoughts went back to the winter of 1854 when she and Ernestine Rose had held their first woman's rights meetings in Washington, finding only a handful ready to listen. The intervening thirty-four years had worked wonders. Now women were willing to travel not only across the continent but from Europe and Asia to discuss and demand equal educational advantages, equal opportunities for training in the professions and in business, equal pay for equal work, equal suffrage, and the same standard of morals for all. Aware of their responsibility to their countries, they asked for the tools, education and the franchise, to help solve the world's problems. They were listened to with interest and respect, and were received at the White House by President and Mrs. Cleveland.

Through it all, a dynamic, gray-haired woman in a black silk dress with a red shawl about her shoulders was without question the heroine of the occasion. "This lady," observed the Baltimore Sun, "daily grows upon all present; the woman suffragists love her for her good works, the audience for her brightness and wit, and the multitude of press representatives for her frank, plain, open, business-like way of doing everything connected with the council.... Her word is the parliamentary law of the meeting. Whatever she says is done without murmur or dissent."[363]

A permanent International Council of Women to meet once every five years was organized with Millicent Garrett Fawcett of England as president, and a National Council to meet every three years was formed as an affiliate with Frances Willard as president and Susan as vice-president at large. Emphasizing education and social and moral reform, the International Council did not rank suffrage first as Susan had hoped. Nevertheless, she was happy that an international movement of enterprising women was well on its way. They would learn by experience.

Of all the favorable results of the International Council of Women, two were of special importance to Susan, meeting Anna Howard Shaw and overtures from Lucy Stone for a union of the National and American Woman Suffrage Associations.

Prejudiced against Anna Howard Shaw, who had aligned herself with Mary Livermore and Lucy Stone, and who she assumed, was a narrow Methodist minister, Susan was unprepared to find that the pleasing young woman in the pulpit on the first day of the conference, holding her audience spellbound with her oratory, was Anna Howard Shaw. Here was a warm personality, a crusader eager to right human wrongs, and above all a matchless public speaker. Anna too had heard much criticism of Susan and had formed a distorted opinion of her which was quickly dispelled as she watched her preside. They liked each other the moment they met.

Anna Howard Shaw had grown up on the Michigan frontier, her indomitable spirit and her eagerness for learning conquering the hardships and the limitations of her surroundings. Encouraged by Mary Livermore, who by chance lectured in her little town, she worked her way through Albion College and Boston University Theological School, from which she graduated in 1878. She then served as the pastor of two Cape Cod churches, but was refused ordination by the Methodist Episcopal church because of her sex. Eventually she was ordained by the Methodist Protestant church. During her pastorate, she studied medicine at Boston University, and because of her ability as a speaker was in demand as a lecturer for temperance and woman suffrage groups. Through the Massachusetts Woman Suffrage Association, she met an inspiring group of reformers, and their influence and that of Frances Willard, in whose work she was intensely interested, led her to leave the ministry for active work in the temperance and woman suffrage movements. After several years as a lecturer and organizer for the Massachusetts Woman Suffrage Association, she was placed at the head of the franchise department of the W.C.T.U. This was her work when she met Susan B. Anthony.

Anna Howard Shaw

The more Susan talked with Anna, the better she liked her, and the feeling was mutual. This wholesome woman of forty-one, with abundant vitality, unmarried and without pressing family ties to divert her, seemed particularly well fitted to assist Susan in the arduous campaigns which lay ahead. A natural orator, she could in a measure take the place of Mrs. Stanton, who could no longer undertake western tours. Before the International Council adjourned, Susan had Anna's promise that she would lecture for the National Association.

One of Susan's nieces, Lucy E. Anthony, also felt drawn to Anna after meeting her at the International Council. A warm friendship quickly developed and continued throughout their lives. Within a few years they were living together, Lucy serving as Anna's secretary and planning her lecture tours and campaign trips. Educated in Rochester through the help of her aunts, Susan and Mary, living in their home and loving them both, Lucy readily made their interests her own and devoted her life to the suffrage movement. Neither a public speaker nor a campaigner, she put her executive ability to work, and her tasks, though less spectacular, were important and freed both Susan and Anna from many details.

Just as the International Council of Women had broken down Anna Howard Shaw's prejudice regarding Susan B. Anthony and her National Woman Suffrage Association, just so it clarified the opinions of other young women, now aligning themselves with the cause. Admiring the leaders of both factions, these young women saw no reason why the two groups should not work together in one large strong organization, and this seemed increasingly important as they welcomed women from other countries to this first international conference. Unfamiliar with the personal antagonisms and the sincere differences in policy which had caused the separation after the Civil War, they did not understand the difficulties still in the way of union. So strongly, however, did they press for a united front that the leaders of both groups felt themselves swept along toward that goal. Susan herself had long looked forward to the time when all suffragists would again work together, but since the unsuccessful overtures of her group in 1870, she had made no further efforts in that direction. She was completely taken by surprise when in the fall of 1887 the American Association proposed that she and Lucy Stone confer regarding union.

The negotiations revived old arguments in the minds of zealous partisans, and in the Woman's Journal, the Woman's Tribune, and elsewhere, attempts were made to fasten the blame for the twenty-year-old rift upon this one and that one; but so strong ran the tide for union among the younger women that this excursion into the past aroused little interest.

The election of the president of the merged organizations was the most difficult hurdle. Lucy Stone suggested that neither she, Mrs. Stanton, nor Susan allow their names to be proposed, since they had been blamed for the division, but this was easier said than done. The clamor for Susan and Mrs. Stanton was so strong and continuous among the younger members that it soon became apparent that unless one or the other were chosen, there would be no hope of union. The odds were in Susan's favor. Her popularity in the National Association was tremendous. Although Mrs. Stanton was revered as the mother of woman suffrage and admired for her brilliant mind and her poise as presiding officer, she now spent so much time in Europe with her daughter Harriot that many who might otherwise have voted for her felt that the office should go to Susan, who was always on the job.

Harriot Stanton Blatch

Most of the American Association regarded Susan as safer and less radical than Mrs. Stanton, less likely to stray from the straight path of woman suffrage, and Henry Blackwell recommended her election.

Susan did not want the presidency. She wanted it for Mrs. Stanton, who had headed the National Association so ably for so many years. She pleaded earnestly with the delegates of the National Association: "I will say to every woman who is a National and who has any love for the old Association, or for Susan B. Anthony, that I hope you will not vote for her for president.... Don't you vote for any human being but Mrs. Stanton.... When the division was made 22 years ago it was because our platform was too broad, because Mrs. Stanton was too radical.... And now ... if Mrs. Stanton shall be deposed ... you virtually degrade her.... I want our platform to be kept broad enough for the infidel, the atheist, the Mohammedan, or the Christian.... These are the broad principles I want you to stand upon."[364]

When the two organizations met in February 1890 to effect formal union as the National American Woman Suffrage Association, Elizabeth Cady Stanton was elected president by a majority of 41 votes, while Susan was the almost unanimous choice for vice-president at large. With Lucy Stone chosen chairman of the executive committee, Jane Spofford treasurer, and Rachel Foster and Alice Stone Blackwell secretaries,[365] the new organization was well equipped with able leaders for the work ahead. It was dedicated to work for both state and federal woman suffrage amendments and its official organ would be the Woman's Journal.

Susan now faced the future with gratitude that a strong unified organization could be handed down to the younger women who would gradually take over the work she had started, and her confidence in these young women grew day by day. Working closely with Rachel Foster and May Wright Sewall, she knew their caliber. Anna Howard Shaw and Alice Stone Blackwell showed great promise, and Harriot Stanton Blatch was living up to her expectations. In England where Harriot had made her home since her marriage in 1882, she was active in the cause, and on her visits to her mother in New York, she kept in touch with the suffrage movement in the United States. She took part in the union meeting, and in her diary, Susan recorded these words of commendation, "Harriot said but a few words, yet showed herself worthy of her mother and her mother's lifelong friend and co-worker. It was a proud moment for me."[366] To such she could entrust her beloved cause.

Victories In The West

New western states were coming into the Union, North and South Dakota, Montana, Washington, Idaho, and Wyoming, and in Susan's opinion it was highly important that they be admitted as woman suffrage states, for she had not forgotten that disturbing line of the Supreme Court decision in the Virginia Minor case which read, "No new State has ever been admitted to the Union which has conferred the right of suffrage on women, and this has never been considered a valid objection to her admission."[367] Susan wanted to start a new trend.

Opposition to Wyoming's woman suffrage provision was strong in Congress in spite of the fact that it had the unanimous approval of Wyoming's constitutional convention. To Susan in the gallery of the House of Representatives, listening anxiously to the debate on the admission of Wyoming, defeat was unthinkable after women had voted in the Territory of Wyoming for twenty years; but Democrats, wishing to block the admission of a preponderantly Republican state, used woman suffrage as an excuse. With a sinking heart, she heard an amendment offered, limiting suffrage in Wyoming to males. At the crucial moment, however, the tide was turned by a telegram from the Wyoming legislature, the words of which rejoiced Susan, "We will remain out of the Union a hundred years rather than come in without woman suffrage."[368] After this, the House voted to admit Wyoming, 139 to 127, but the Senate delayed, renewing the attack on the woman suffrage provision. Not until July 1890, while she was speaking to a large audience in the opera house at Madison, South Dakota, did the good news of the admission of Wyoming reach her. Jubilant as she commented on this great victory, she spoke as one inspired, for she saw this as the turning point in her forty long years of uphill work.

Neither North Dakota nor South Dakota had wanted to risk their chances of statehood by incorporating woman suffrage in their constitutions.[369] Yet public opinion in both states was friendly, South Dakota directing its first legislature to submit the question to the voters. It was this that brought Susan to South Dakota in 1890. Sentiment for woman suffrage in South Dakota had previously been created almost entirely by the W.C.T.U., and this had linked woman suffrage and prohibition together. Now, the liquor interests made prohibition an issue in this woman suffrage campaign, as they rallied their forces for the repeal of prohibition which had been adopted when South Dakota was admitted to statehood. Through the propaganda of the liquor interests the 30,000 foreign-born voters became formidable opponents, and newly naturalized Russians, Scandinavians, and Poles, given the vote before American women, wore badges carrying the slogan, "Against Woman Suffrage and Susan B. Anthony."[370] Both Republicans and Democrats cultivated these foreign-born voters, turning a cold shoulder to the woman suffrage amendment and refusing to endorse it in their state conventions. Even the Farmers' Alliance and the Knights of Labor, previously friendly to woman suffrage, now joined with the Prohibitionists to form a third political party which also failed to endorse the woman suffrage amendment. On top of all this, anti-suffragists from Massachusetts, calling themselves Remonstrants, flooded South Dakota with their leaflets.

It now seemed to Susan as if every clever politician had lined up against women. During these trying days, Anna Howard Shaw joined her, and together they covered the state, hoping by the truth and sincerity of their statements to quash the propaganda against woman suffrage. Often they traveled in freight cars, as transportation was limited, or drove long distances in wagons over the sun-baked prairie. The heat was intense and the hot winds, blowing incessantly, seared everything they touched. After two years of drouth, the farmers were desperately poor, and Susan, concerned over their plight, wondered why Congress could not have appropriated the money for artesian wells to help these honest earnest people, instead of voting $40,000 for an investigating commission.[371]

Occasionally Susan and Anna spent the night in isolated sod houses where ingenious pioneer women cooked their scant meals over burning chips of buffalo bones gathered on the prairie. Glorying in the valiant spirit of these women, who in loneliness and hardship played an important but unheralded role in the conquest of this new country, Susan was generous with her praise. To them her words of commendation were like a benediction, and few of them ever forgot a visit from Susan B. Anthony.

By this time life on the frontier was an old story to her, for she had campaigned under similar conditions in Kansas and in the far West. Nonetheless, the hardships were trying. Yet this plucky woman of seventy wrote friends in the East, "Tell everybody that I am perfectly well in body and in mind, never better, and never doing more work.... O, the lack of modern comforts and conveniences! But I can put up with it better than any of the young folks.... I shall push ahead and do my level best to carry this State, come weal or woe to me personally.... I never felt so buoyed up with the love and sympathy and confidence of the good people everywhere...."[372]

Young vigorous Anna Howard Shaw proved to be a campaigner after Susan's own heart, tireless, uncomplaining, and good-tempered, an exceptional speaker, witty and quick to say the right word at the right time. It was a joy to find in Anna the same devotion to the cause that she herself felt, the same crusading fervor and reliability. During the long drives over the prairie, she talked to Anna of the work that must be done, of what it would mean to the women of the future, and she fired Anna's soul "with the flame that burned in her own."[373]

Another young western woman, Carrie Chapman Catt, also attracted Susan's attention at this time. She had volunteered for the South Dakota campaign, after attending her first national woman suffrage convention; and Susan, meeting her in Huron, South Dakota, to map out a speaking tour for her, found a tall handsome confident young woman ready to attack the work and see it through, in spite of the hardships which confronted her.

Carrie Lane, a graduate of Iowa State College, had briefly studied law and taught school before her marriage to Lee Chapman. Now, four years after his death, she had married George W. Catt of Seattle, a promising young engineer and a former fellow-student at Iowa State College. What particularly impressed Susan was that Carrie, in spite of her marriage in June, had kept her pledge to come to South Dakota. She was pleased with the way Carrie not only heroically filled every difficult engagement, but sized up the campaign for herself and planned for the future. In Carrie's report of her work there was a ruthless practicality which was rare and which instantly won Susan's approval. Here was a young woman to watch and to keep in the work.

The Anthony home, Rochester, New York - Image: Dmadeo

The visible result of six months of campaigning was defeat, with the vote 22,972 for woman suffrage and 45,632 opposed, and as Susan remembered the maneuvers of the politicians, the trading of votes for the location of the state capital, and the scheming of the liquor interests, she felt she was championing a lonely cause.

From now on Susan hoped to turn over to the younger women much of the lecturing and organizing in the West, and she needed an anchorage, a home of her own from which she could direct the work. Her mother had willed 17 Madison Street to Mary, who had rented the first floor and was living on the second where there was a room for Susan. Now that Susan planned to spend more time at home and Mary had retired from teaching, they decided to take over the whole house, modernize and redecorate it, and enjoy it the rest of their lives. Mary as usual took charge, but Susan had definite ideas about what should be done. Mary, who had learned to be cautious and frugal, was more willing than Susan to make old furnishings do, but their friends came to the rescue, showering them with gifts.

Freshly painted and papered, with new rugs on the floor, lace curtains at the windows, easy chairs and new furniture here and there, the house was all Susan had wished for, and everywhere were familiar touches, such as her mother's spinning wheel by the fireplace in the back parlor.

She spent most of her time in her study on the second floor. Here she hung her pictures of the reformers she admired and loved; and right over her desk, looking down at her, was the comforting picture of her dearest friend, Mrs. Stanton.

Hour after hour, she sat at this desk, writing letters, hurriedly dashing off one after another, writing just as the thoughts came, as if she were talking, bothering little with punctuation, using dashes instead, and vigorously underlining words and phrases for emphasis. Instructions to workers in all parts of the country, letters of friendship and sympathy, answers to the many questions which came in every mail, these were signed and sealed one after another, and slipped into the mail box when she took a brisk walk before going to bed.

She started each day with the morning newspaper, stepping out on the front veranda to pick it up, taking a deep breath of fresh air, and enjoying the green grass and the tall graceful chestnut trees in front of the house. Then sitting down in the back parlor beside the big table covered with magazines and mail, she carefully read her paper before beginning the work at her desk, for she must keep up-to-date on the news.

Rochester was important to her. It was her city, and she was on hand with her colleagues whenever there was an opportunity for women to express interest in its government, progress, or welfare. Not only did she encourage women to make use of their newly won right to vote in school elections, she also urged municipal suffrage for women. Appealing to the governor to appoint a woman to fill a vacancy on the board of trustees of Rochester's State Industrial School, she herself received the appointment which the Democrat and Chronicle called "a fitting recognition of one of the ablest and best women in the commonwealth."[374]

One of her first acts as trustee was a practical one for the girls. "Spent entire day at State Industrial School," she wrote in her diary, "getting the laundry girls—who had always washed for the entire institution by hand and ironed that old way—transferred to the boys' laundry room to use its machinery—am sure it will work well—girls 12 of them delighted."[375] She also taught the boys to patch and darn, and later asked for coeducation.

Susan looked forward to welcoming Mrs. Stanton at 17 Madison Street when she returned to this country in 1891, particularly because she had sold her home in Tenafly after her husband's death, in 1887, and now had no home to go to. Susan hoped that as they again worked together she could persuade Mrs. Stanton to concentrate on more serious writing than the chatty reminiscences she had just published and which Susan felt were "not the greatest" of herself.[376] When she heard that Mrs. Stanton seriously contemplated living in New York with two of her children, she begged her to reconsider, writing, "This is the first time since 1850 that I have anchored myself to any particular spot, and in doing it my constant thought was that you would come here ... and stay for as long, at least, as we must be together to put your writings into systematic shape to go down to posterity. I have no writings to go down, so my ambition is not for myself, but is for the one by the side of whom I have wrought these forty years, and to get whose speeches before audiences ... has been the delight of my life."[377]

Mrs. Stanton decided to make her home in New York, but first she visited Susan who found her as stimulating as ever and brimful of ideas. They plotted and planned as of old and managed to stir up public opinion on the question of admitting women to the University of Rochester. With women enrolled at the University of Michigan since 1870, and at Cornell since 1872, and with Columbia University yielding at last to women's entreaties by establishing Barnard College in 1889, they felt it their duty to awaken Rochester, and although their agitation produced no immediate results, it did start other women thinking and made news for the press. The cartoons on the subject delighted them both.[378]

Susan soon realized that the writing she had planned for Mrs. Stanton would never be done, for Mrs. Stanton had already made up her mind to write for magazines and newspapers on new and controversial subjects, feeling this was the best contribution she could make to the cause. Susan also found it increasingly difficult to hold her old friend to the straight path of woman suffrage, Mrs. Stanton insisting that too much concentration on this one subject was narrowing and left women unprepared for the intelligent use of the ballot. Women, Mrs. Stanton argued, needed to be stirred up to think, and this they would not do as long as their minds were dominated by the church, which, she believed, had for generations hampered their development by emphasizing their inferiority and subordination. She was determined to analyze and rebel, and Susan could in no way divert her. Completely absorbed in trying to prove that the Bible, accurately translated and interpreted, did not teach the inferiority or the subordination of women, she was writing a book which she called The Woman's Bible, chapters of which were already appearing in the Woman's Tribune.

Susan B. Anthony and Elizabeth Cady Stanton

Susan was not unsympathetic to Mrs. Stanton's ideas, but she opposed this excursion into religious controversy because she was sure it would stir up futile wrangles among the suffragists and keep Mrs. Stanton from giving her best to the cause. Her lack of interest then and her frank disapproval as The Woman's Bible progressed were a great disappointment to Mrs. Stanton, and these two old friends began to grow somewhat apart as they took different roads to reach their goal, the one intent on freeing women's minds, the other determined to establish their citizenship. Yet their friendship endured.

In 1892 Susan reluctantly consented to Mrs. Stanton's retirement as president of the National American Woman Suffrage Association. Mrs. Stanton's request that she be followed by Susan won unanimous approval, and Anna Howard Shaw was moved up to second place, vice-president at large. For forty years, Susan had watched Mrs. Stanton preside with a poise, warmth, and skill which few could equal. She knew she would miss her dynamic reassuring presence at the conventions. Yet she was obliged to admit to herself that it was more than fitting that she should at last head the ever-growing organization which she had built up. This was the last convention which Mrs. Stanton attended, and it was the last for Lucy Stone who died the next year. Susan appreciated the eager young women who now took their places, but she did not yet feel completely at home with them. "Only think," she wrote an old-time colleague, "I shall not have a white-haired woman on the platform with me, and I shall be alone there of all the pioneer workers. Always with the 'old guard' I had perfect confidence that the wise and right thing would be said. What a platform ours then was of self-reliant strong women! I felt sure of you all.... I can not feel quite certain that our younger sisters will be equal to the emergency, yet they are each and all valiant, earnest, and talented, and will soon be left to manage the ship without even me."[379]

In 1892, the year of the presidential election, Susan hopefully attended the national political conventions. Again the Republicans made their proverbial excuses, explaining that they not only faced a formidable opponent in Grover Cleveland but also the threat of a new People's party. The familiar ring of their alibis, which they had repeated since Reconstruction days, made Susan wonder when and if ever the Republicans would feel able to bear the strain of woman suffrage. Their platform remembered the poor, the foreign-born, and male Negroes, but it still ignored women. Yet hope for the future stirred in her heart as she saw at the convention two women serving as delegates from Wyoming. Here was the entering wedge.

The Democrats as usual were silent on woman suffrage, but undismayed by them or by the Prohibitionists, who this year failed to endorse votes for women, Susan moved on to Omaha with Anna Howard Shaw for the first national convention of the new People's party. Here she met representatives of the Farmers' Alliance and the Knights of Labor, both friendly to woman suffrage, and men from other groups, critical of the two major political parties for their failure to solve the pressing economic problems confronting the nation. Susan was sympathetic with many of the aims of the People's party, having seen with her own eyes the plight of debt-burdened, hard-working farmers and having crusaded in her own paper, The Revolution, for the rights of labor and for the control of industrial monopoly. However, she still viewed minor, reform parties with a highly critical eye. The People's party gave her no woman suffrage plank and she found them "quite as oblivious to the underlying principle of justice to women as either of the old parties...."[380]

With the election of Grover Cleveland, whose opposition to woman suffrage was well known, and with the Democrats in the saddle for another four years, Congressional action on the woman suffrage amendment was blocked. Nevertheless, the cause moved ahead in the states; Colorado was to vote on the question in 1893 and Kansas in 1894, and New York was revising its constitution. In addition, the World's Fair in Chicago in 1893 offered endless opportunities to bring the subject before the people.

As soon as plans for the World's Fair were under way, Susan began to work indirectly through prominent women in Washington and Chicago for the appointment of women to the board of management. "Lady Managers" were appointed, 115 strong, who proved to be very much alive under the leadership of Mrs. Bertha Honoré Palmer. Susan found Mrs. Palmer almost as determined as she to secure equality of rights for women at the World's Fair, and nothing that she herself might have planned could have been more effective than the series of world congresses in which both men and women took part, or than the World's Congress of Representative Women.

Elizabeth Smith Miller and her daughter, Anne

Two of Susan's "girls," as she liked to call them, Rachel Foster Avery[381] and May Wright Sewall, were appointed by Mrs. Palmer to take charge of the World's Congress of Representative Women, and they arranged a meeting of the International Council of Women as a part of this Congress.

Convening soon after the opening of the World's Fair, the Congress of Representative Women drew record crowds at its eighty-one sessions. Twenty-seven countries and 126 organizations were represented. Here Susan, to her joy, heard Negroes, American Indians, and Mormons tell of their progress and their problems, and saw them treated with as much respect as American millionaires, English nobility, or the most virtuous, conservative housewife. Watching these women assemble, talking with them, and listening to their well-delivered speeches, she felt richly rewarded for the lonely work she had undertaken forty years before, when scarcely a woman could be coaxed to a meeting or be persuaded to express her opinions in public. Although only one session of the congress was devoted to the civil and political rights of women, it was gratifying to her that women's need of the ballot was spontaneously brought up in meeting after meeting, showing that women, whatever their cause or whatever their organization, were recognizing that only by means of the vote could their reforms be achieved.

Speaking on the subject to which she had dedicated her life, Susan gave credit to the pioneering suffragists for the change which had taken place in public opinion regarding the position of women. She urged women's organizations to give suffrage their wholehearted support and pointed out the great power of some of the newer organizations, such as the W.C.T.U. with its membership of half a million and the young General Federation of Women's Clubs of 40,000 members. Confessing that her own National American Woman Suffrage Association in comparison was poor in numbers and limited in funds, she added, "I would philosophize on the reason why. It is because women have been taught always to work for something else than their own personal freedom; and the hardest thing in the world is to organize women for the one purpose of securing their political liberty and political equality."[382] Even so, the vital woman's rights organizations, she concluded, drew the whole world to them in spirit if not in person.

Her very presence among them without her words, in fact her very presence on the fair grounds, advertised her cause, for in the mind of the public she personified woman suffrage. This tall dignified woman with smooth gray hair, abundant in energy and spontaneous friendliness, was the center of attraction at the World's Congress of Representative Women. In her new black dress of Chinese silk, brightened with blue, and her small black bonnet, trimmed with lace and blue forget-me-nots, she was the perfect picture of everyone's grandmother, and the people took her to their hearts.[383] She was the one woman all wanted to see. Curious crowds jammed the hall and corridors when she was scheduled to speak, and often a policeman had to clear the way for her. At whatever meeting she appeared, the audience at once burst into applause and started calling for her, interrupting the speakers, and were not satisfied until she had mounted the platform so that all could see her and she had said a few words. Then they cheered her. After years of ridicule and unpopularity, she hardly knew what to make of all this, but she accepted it with happiness as a tribute to her beloved cause. Many who had been critical and wary of her newfangled notions began to reverse their opinions after they saw her and heard her words of good common sense. Even those who still opposed woman suffrage left the World's Fair with a new respect for Susan B. Anthony.

She stayed on in Chicago for much of the summer and fall, for she was in demand as a speaker at several of the world congresses and had five speeches to read for Mrs. Stanton, who felt unable to brave the heat and the crowds. She felt at home in this bustling, rapidly growing city which for so many years had been the halfway station on her lecture and campaign trips through the West. Here she had always found a warm welcome, first from her cousins, the Dickinsons, then from the ever-widening circle of friends she won for her cause. Now she was literally swamped with hospitality.[384] She rejoiced that such great numbers of everyday people were able to enjoy the beauty of the fair grounds and the many interesting exhibits, and when a group of clergymen urged Sunday closing, she took issue with them, declaring that Sunday was the only day on which many were free to attend. Asked by a disapproving clergyman if she would like to have a son of hers attend Buffalo Bill's Wild West Show on Sunday, she promptly and bluntly replied, "Of course I would, and I think he would learn far more there than from the sermons in some churches!"[385] Hearing of this, Buffalo Bill offered her a box at his popular Wild West Show, and she appeared the next day with twelve of her "girls." Dashing into the arena on his spirited horse while the band played and the spotlight flashed on him, Buffalo Bill rode directly up to Susan's box, reined his horse, and swept off his big western hat to salute her. Quick to respond, she rose and bowed, and beaming with pleasure, waved her handkerchief at him while the immense audience applauded and cheered.

She returned home early in November 1893, with happy memories of the World's Fair and to good news from Colorado. "Telegram ... from Denver—said woman suffrage carried by 5000 majority," she recorded in her diary.[386] This laconic comment in no way expressed the joy in her heart.

Her diaries, written hurriedly in small fine script, year after year, in black-covered notebooks about three inches by six, were a brief terse record of her work and her travels. Only occasionally a line of philosophizing shone out from the mass of routine detail, or an illuminating comment on a friend or a difficult situation, but she never failed to record a family anniversary, a birthday, or a death.

The Colorado victory, referred to so casually in her diary, was actually of great importance to her and her cause, for it carried forward the trend initiated by the admission of Wyoming as a woman suffrage state in 1890. Colorado also proved to her that her "girls" could take over her work. So busy had she been winning good will for the cause at the World's Fair that she had left Colorado in the capable hands of the women of the state and of young efficient Carrie Chapman Catt, to whom she now turned over the supervision of all state campaigns.

Encouragement also came from another part of the world, from New Zealand, where the vote was extended to women. This confirmed her growing conviction that equal citizenship was best understood on the frontier and that in her own country victory would come from the West.

Liquor Interests Alert Foreign-Born Voters Against Woman Suffrage

"I am in the midst of as severe a treadmill as I ever experienced, traveling from fifty to one hundred miles every day and speaking five or six nights a week,"[387] Susan wrote a friend in 1894, during the campaign to wrest woman suffrage from the New York constitutional convention. She was now seventy-four years old. Political machines and financial interests were deeply intrenched in New York, and although two governors had recommended that women be represented in the constitutional convention and a bill had been passed making women eligible as delegates, neither Republicans nor Democrats had the slightest intention of allowing women to slip into men's stronghold. It was obvious to Susan that without representation at the convention and without power to enforce their demands, women's only hope was an intensive educational campaign which she now directed with vigor. Whenever she could, she conferred with Mrs. Stanton, whose judgment she valued, and there was zest in working together as they had during the previous constitutional convention in 1867.

The women of New York were aroused as never before. Young able speakers went through the state, piling up signatures on their petitions, but they had few influential friends among the delegates. Anti-suffragists were active, encouraged by Bishop Doane of the Protestant Episcopal church and Mrs. Lyman Abbott, whose name carried the prestige and influence of her husband's popular magazine, The Outlook.

With the election of Joseph Choate of New York as president of the convention, Susan knew that woman suffrage was doomed, for Choate had political aspirations and was not likely to let his sympathies for an unpopular cause jeopardize his chances of becoming governor. While he gave women every opportunity to be heard, at the same time he arranged for the defeat of woman suffrage by appointing men to consider the subject who were definitely opposed, and they submitted an adverse report. Here was a situation similar to that in 1867, when her one-time friend, Horace Greeley, had deserted women for political expediency.

"I am used to defeat every time and know how to pick up and push on for another attack," she wrote as she now turned her attention to Kansas.[388]

The Republicans in Kansas had sponsored school and municipal suffrage for women and had passed a woman suffrage amendment to be referred to the people in 1894. Yet they proved to be as great a disappointment to Susan as they were in 1867, when as a last resort she had been obliged to campaign with the Democrats and George Francis Train. The population of Kansas had changed with the years, as immigrants from Europe had come into the state, and Susan was again confronted with the powerful opposition of foreign-born voters for whose support the political parties bargained. The liquor interests were also active, and the Republicans, who had brought prohibition to Kansas, now left the question discreetly alone, even making a deal with German Democrats for their votes by promising to ignore in their platform both prohibition and woman suffrage. Prohibition and woman suffrage were synonymous in the minds of voters, because women had generally voted for enforcement in municipal elections, and no matter how hard Susan tried, she found it impossible to have woman suffrage considered on its own merits.

Watching the straws in the wind, she saw Republican supremacy seriously threatened by the new Populist party. Convinced that she could no longer count on help from Kansas Republicans, she turned to the Populist party, ignoring the pleas of Republican women who warned her she would hurt the cause by association with such a radical group. The Populists were generally regarded as the party of social unrest, of a regulated economy, and unsound money, and they were looked upon with suspicion. To many they represented a threat to the American free-enterprise system, and they were blamed for the labor troubles which had flared up in the bloody Homestead strike in the steel mills of Pennsylvania and in the Pullman strike, defying the powerful railroads. Susan was never afraid to side with the underdog, and she could well understand why western farmers, in the hope of relief, were eagerly flocking into the Populist party when their corn sold for ten cents a bushel and the products they bought were high-priced and their mortgage interest was never lower than 10 per cent.

To the Populist convention, she declared, "I have labored for women's enfranchisement for forty years and I have always said that for the party that endorsed it, whether Republican, Democratic, or Populist, I would wave my handkerchief."[389]

"We want more than the waving of your handkerchief, Miss Anthony," interrupted a delegate, who then asked her, "If the People's party put a woman suffrage plank in its platform, will you go before the voters of this state and tell them that because the People's party has espoused the cause of woman suffrage, it deserves the vote of every one who is a supporter of that cause?"

"I most certainly will," she replied, adding as the audience cheered her wildly, "for I would surely choose to ask votes for the party which stood for the principle of justice to women, though wrong on financial theories, rather than for the party which was sound on questions of money and tariff, and silent on the pending amendment to secure political equality to half of the people."

"I most certainly will" was the phrase which was remembered and was flashed through the country, and as a result, the Republican press and Susan's Republican friends harshly criticized her for taking her stand with the radicals.

Like all political parties, the Populists found it hard to comprehend justice for women, but after a four-hour debate, the convention endorsed the woman suffrage amendment, absolving, however, members who refused to support it. The rank and file rejoiced as if each and every one of them were heart and soul for the cause. They cheered, they waved their canes, they threw their hats high in the air, and then swarmed around Susan and Anna Shaw to shake their hands and welcome them into the Populist party.

With woman suffrage at last a political issue in Kansas, Susan left the field to her "girls." Her homecoming brought reporters to 17 Madison Street for the details about her alignment with the Populist party. "I didn't go over to the Populists," she told them. "I have been like a drowning man for a long time, waiting for someone to throw a plank in my direction. I didn't step on the whole platform, but just on the woman suffrage plank.... Here is a party in power which is likely to remain in power, and if it will give its endorsement to our movement, we want it."[390]

This explanation, however, did not satisfy her critics, and as the Republican press circulated false stories about her enthusiasm for the Populist party, letters of protest poured in, among them one from Henry Blackwell. To him, she replied, "I shall not praise the Republicans of Kansas, or wish or work for their success, when I know by their own confessions to me that the rights of the women of their state have been traded by them in cold blood for the votes of the lager beer foreigners and whisky Democrats.... I never, in my whole forty years work, so utterly repudiated any set of politicians as I do those Republicans of Kansas.... I never was surer of my position that no self-respecting woman should wish or work for the success of a party that ignores her political rights."[391]

The contest in Kansas was close and bitter. Kansas women carried on an able campaign with the help of Anna Howard Shaw and Carrie Chapman Catt. When Susan returned to the state in October, she not only found that the Democrats had entered the fight with an anti-suffrage plank but the Populists had noticeably lost ground since the Pullman strike riots, the court injunction against the strikers, and the arrest of Eugene V. Debs. Again this prairie state, from which she had hoped so much, refused to extend suffrage to women. Impulsively she recommended a little "Patrick Henryism" to the women of Kansas, suggesting that they fold their hands and refuse to help men run the churches, the charities, and the reform movements.[392]

California was the next state to demand Susan's attention. A Republican legislature had submitted a woman suffrage amendment to be voted on by the people in 1896, and the women of California asked for her help. She toured the state in the spring of 1895 with Anna Howard Shaw, and everywhere she won friends. The continuous travel and speaking, however, taxed her far more than she realized, and soon after her return to the East, she collapsed. As this news flashed over the wires, letters poured in from her friends, begging her to spare herself. Two of these letters were especially precious. One in bold vigorous script was from her good comrade, Parker Pillsbury, now eighty-six, who had been an unfailing help during the most difficult years of her career and whom she probably trusted more completely than any other man. The other from her dearest friend, Elizabeth Stanton, read, "I never realized how desolate the world would be to me without you until I heard of your sudden illness. Let me urge you with all the strength I have, and all the love I bear you, to stay at home and rest and save your precious self."[393]

She now realized that rest was imperative for a time, but it troubled her that people thought of her as old and ill, and she wrote Clara Colby never to mention anyone's illness in her Woman's Tribune, adding, "It is so dreadful to get public thought centered on one as ill—as I have had it the last two months."[394]

She had no intention of retiring from the field. She knew her own strength and that her life must be one of action. "I am able to endure the strain of daily traveling and lecturing at over three-score and ten," she observed, "mainly because I have always worked and loved work.... As machinery in motion lasts longer than when lying idle, so a body and soul in active exercise escapes the corroding rust of physical and mental laziness, which prematurely cuts off the life of so many women."[395]

Yet she did slow up a little, refusing an offer from the Slayton Lecture Bureau for a series of lectures at $100 a night, and she engaged a capable secretary, Emma B. Sweet, to help her with her tremendous correspondence. "Dear Rachel" had given her a typewriter, and now instead of dashing off letters at her desk late at night, she learned to dictate them to Mrs. Sweet at regular hours. As requests came in from newspapers and magazines for her comments on a wide variety of subjects, she answered those that made possible a word on the advancement of women.

Bicycling had come into vogue and women as well as men were taking it up, some women even riding their bicycles in short skirts or bloomers. What did she think of this? "If women ride the bicycle or climb mountains," she replied, "they should don a costume which will permit them the use of their legs." Of bicycling she said, "I think it has done more to emancipate woman than any one thing in the world. I rejoice every time I see a woman ride by on a wheel. It gives her a feeling of self-reliance and independence the moment she takes her seat; and away she goes, the picture of untrammeled womanhood."[396]

Ida Husted Harper

Susan returned to California in February 1896. Through the generosity and interest of two young Rochester friends, her Unitarian minister, William C. Gannett, and his wife, Mary Gannett, she was able to take her secretary with her. Making her home in San Francisco with her devoted friend, Ellen Sargent, she at once began to plan speaking tours for herself and her "girls," many of whom, including her niece Lucy, had come West to help her. She appealed successfully to Frances Willard to transfer the national W.C.T.U. convention to another state, for she was determined to keep the issue of prohibition out of the California campaign.

With the press more than friendly and several San Francisco dailies running woman suffrage departments, she realized the importance of keeping newspapers fed with readable factual material and enlisted the aid of a young journalist, Ida Husted Harper, whom she had met in 1878 while lecturing in Terre Haute, Indiana, and who was in California that winter. When the San Francisco Examiner, William Randolph Hearst's powerful Democratic paper, offered Susan a column on the editorial page if she would write it and sign it, she dictated her thoughts to Mrs. Harper, who smoothed them out for the column, helping her as Mrs. Stanton had in the past, for writing was still a great hardship. Grateful to Mrs. Harper, she sang her praises: "The moment I give the idea—the point—she formulates it into a good sentence—while I should have to haggle over it half an hour."[397]

California women had won suffrage planks from Republicans, Populists, and Prohibitionists, and the prospects looked bright. Rich women came to their aid, Mrs. Leland Stanford, with her railroad fortune, furnishing passes for all the speakers and organizers, and Mrs. Phoebe Hearst contributing $1,000 to their campaign. What warmed Susan's heart, however, was the spirit of the rank and file, the seamstresses and washerwomen, paying their two-dollar pledges in twenty-five-cent installments, the poorly clad women bringing in fifty cents or a dollar which they had saved by going without tea, and the women who had worked all day at their jobs, stopping at headquarters for a package of circulars to fold and address at night. The working women of California made it plain that they wanted to vote.

Susan insisted upon carrying out what she called her "wild goose chase" over the state.[398] People crowded to hear her at farmers' picnics in the mountains, in schoolhouses in small towns, and in poolrooms where chalked up on the blackboard she often found "Welcome Susan B. Anthony." She was at home everywhere and ready for anything. The men liked her short matter-of-fact speeches and her flashes of wit. Her hopes were high that the friendly people she met would not fail to vote justice to women.

She grew apprehensive, however, when the newspapers, pressured by their advertisers, one by one began to ignore woman suffrage. The Liquor Dealers' League had been sending letters to hotel owners, grocers, and druggists, as well as to saloons, warning that votes for women would mean prohibition and would threaten their livelihood. Word was spread that if women voted not one glass of beer would be sold in San Francisco. As in Kansas, liquor interests had persuaded naturalized Irish, Germans, and Swedes to oppose woman suffrage, so now in California, they appealed to the Chinese.

On election day Susan was in San Francisco with Anna Howard Shaw and Ellen Sargent, watching and anxiously waiting for the returns. Telling the story of those last tense hours when women's fate hung in the balance, Anna Howard Shaw reported, "I shall always remember the picture of Miss Anthony and the wife of Senator Sargent wandering around the polls arm in arm at eleven o'clock at night, their tired faces taking on lines of deeper depression with every minute, for the count was against us.... When the final counts came in, we found that we had won the state from the north down to Oakland and from the south up to San Francisco; but there was not sufficient majority to overcome the adverse votes of San Francisco and Oakland. In San Francisco the saloon element and the most aristocratic section ... made an equal showing against us.... Every Chinese vote was against us."[399]

In spite of defeat in California, Susan had the joy of marking up two more states for woman suffrage in 1896. Utah was granted statehood with a woman suffrage provision in its constitution and Idaho's favorable vote, though contested in the courts, was upheld by the State Supreme Court. Now women in Wyoming, Colorado, Idaho, and Utah were voters.

Aunt Susan And Her Girls

The future of the National American Woman Suffrage Association was much on Susan's mind. This organization which she had conceived and nursed through its struggling infancy had grown in numbers and prestige, and she understood, as no one else could, the importance of leaving it in the right hands so that it could function successfully without her.

The young women now in the work, many of them just out of college, were intelligent, efficient, and confident, and yet as she compared them with the vivid consecrated women active in the early days of the movement, she observed in her diary, "[Clarina] Nichols—Paulina Davis—Lucy Stone—Frances D. Gage—Lucretia Mott & E. C. Stanton—each without peer among any of our college graduates—young women of today."[400]

Even so, she appreciated the "young women of today" whom she affectionately called her girls or her adopted nieces, but she still held the reins tightly, although they often champed at the bit. Recognizing, however, that she must choose between personal power and progress for her cause, she characteristically chose progress. Quick to appreciate ability and zeal when she saw it, she seldom failed to make use of it. When Carrie Chapman Catt presented a detailed plan for a thorough overhauling of the mechanics of the organization, she gave her approval, remarking drily, "There never yet was a young woman who did not feel that if she had had the management of the work from the beginning, the cause would have been carried long ago. I felt just that way when I was young."[401]

On four of her adopted nieces, Rachel Foster Avery, Anna Howard Shaw, Harriet Taylor Upton, and Carrie Chapman Catt, Susan felt that the greater part of her work would fall and be "worthily done."[402] Yet she feared that in their enthusiasm for efficient organization they might lose the higher concepts of freedom and justice which had been the driving force behind her work. Not having learned the lessons of leadership when the cause was unpopular, they lacked the discipline of adversity, which bred in the consecrated reformer the wisdom, tolerance, and vision so necessary for the success of her task. What they did understand far better than the highly individualistic pioneers was the value of teamwork, which grew in importance as the National American Association expanded far beyond the ability of one person to cope with it.

Susan B. Anthony and Rachel Foster Avery

Probably first in her affections was Rachel Foster Avery, who had been like a daughter to her since their trip to Europe together in 1883. The confidence she felt in their friendship was always a comfort. Rachel's intelligent approach to problems made her an asset at every meeting, and Susan relied much on her judgment.

In Anna Howard Shaw, ten years older than Rachel, Susan had found the hardy campaigner and orator for whom she had longed. Anna expressed a warmth and understanding that most of the younger women lacked, and best of all she loved the cause as Susan herself loved it. Because of her close friendship with Susan's niece Lucy, she was regarded as one of the family, and whenever possible between lectures she stopped over in Rochester for a good talk with "Aunt Susan."

Harriet Taylor Upton of Warren, Ohio, had enlisted in the ranks in the 1880s when her father was a member of Congress. Because of her influence in Washington and Ohio, Harriet was invaluable, and Susan speedily brought her into the official circle of the National American Association as treasurer, even thinking of her as a possible president.[403] Harriet's jovial irrepressible personality readily won friends, and Susan found her a refreshing and comfortable companion, able to see a bit of humor in almost every situation. When differences of opinion at meetings threatened to get out of hand, Harriet could always be relied on to break the tension with a few witty remarks.

Harriet Taylor Upton

Carrie Chapman Catt gave every indication of developing into an outstanding executive. Not another one of Susan's "girls" could so quickly or so intelligently size up a situation as Carrie, nor could they so effectively put into action well-thought-out plans. Not as popular a speaker as the more emotional Anna Howard Shaw, she held her audiences by her appeal to their intelligence. Tall, handsome, and well dressed, she never failed to leave a favorable impression. Only her name irked Susan, and as Susan wrote Clara Colby, "If Catt it must be then I insist, she should keep her own father's name—Lane—and not her first husband's name—Chapman,"[404] but the three Cs intrigued Carrie and she continued to be known as Carrie Chapman Catt. Now living in the East because her husband's expanding business had brought him to New York, she was easily accessible, and from her beautiful new home at Bensonhurst, a suburb of Brooklyn, she carried on the rapidly growing work of the organization committee until a New York City office became imperative. In Carrie, Susan recognized qualities demanded of a leader at this stage of the campaign when suffragists must learn to be as keen as politicians and as well organized.

"Spring is not heralded in Washington by the arrival of the robin," commented a Washington newspaper, "but by the appearance of Miss Anthony's red shawl." Susan was still the dominating figure at the annual woman suffrage conventions. Everyone looked eagerly for the tall lithe gray-haired woman with a red shawl on her arm or around her shoulders. Once when Susan appeared on the platform with a new white crepe shawl, the reporters immediately registered their displeasure by putting down their pencils. This did not escape her, and always on good terms with the newsmen and informal with her audiences, she called out, "Boys, what is the matter?"[405]

"Where is the red shawl?" one of them asked. "No red shawl, no report."

Enjoying this little by-play, she sent her niece Lucy back to the hotel for the red shawl, and when Lucy brought it up to the platform and put it about her shoulders, the audience burst into applause, for the red shawl, like Susan herself, had become the well-loved symbol of woman suffrage.

Susan was convinced that the annual national convention should always be held in Washington, where Congress could see and feel the growing strength and influence of the movement. Her "girls," on the other hand, wanted to take their conventions to different parts of the country to widen their influence. Not as certain as Susan that work for a federal amendment must come first, many of them contended that a few more states won for woman suffrage would best help the cause at this time. The southern women, now active, were firm believers in states' rights and supported state work.[406] Susan's experience had taught her the impracticability of direct appeal to the voters in the states, now that foreign-born men in increasing numbers were arrayed against votes for women. In spite of her arguments and her pleas, the National American Association voted in 1894 to hold conventions in different parts of the country in alternate years. Disappointed, but trying her best graciously to follow the will of the majority, she traveled to Atlanta and to Des Moines for the conventions of 1895 and 1897.

Nor did the younger women welcome the messages which Mrs. Stanton, at Susan's insistence, sent to every convention. Susan herself often wished her good friend would stick more closely to woman suffrage instead of introducing extraneous subjects, such as "Educated Suffrage," "The Matriarchate," or "Women and the Church," but nevertheless she proudly read her papers to successive conventions. Insisting that the conventions were too academic, Mrs. Stanton urged Susan to inject more vitality into them by broadening their platform. Susan, however, had come to the conclusion that concentration on woman suffrage was imperative in order to unite all women under one banner and build up numbers which Congressmen were bound to respect. With this her "girls" agreed 100 per cent. While all of them were convinced suffragists, they were divided on other issues, and few of them were wholehearted feminists, as were Susan and Mrs. Stanton.

With the publication of The Woman's Bible in 1895, Mrs. Stanton almost upset the applecart, stirring up heated controversy in the National American Woman Suffrage Association. The Woman's Bible was a keen and sometimes biting commentary on passages in the Bible relating to women. It questioned the traditional interpretation which for centuries has fastened the stigma of inferiority upon women, and pointed out that the female as well as the male was created in the image of God. To those who regarded every word of the Bible as inspired by God, The Woman's Bible was heresy, and both the clergy and the press stirred up a storm of protest against it. Suffragists were condemned for compiling a new Bible and were obliged to explain again and again that The Woman's Bible expressed Mrs. Stanton's personal views and not those of the movement.

Susan regarded The Woman's Bible as a futile, questionable digression from the straight path of woman suffrage. To Clara Colby, who praised it in her Woman's Tribune, she wrote, "Of all her great speeches, I am always proud—but of her Bible commentaries, I am not proud—either of their spirit or letter.... I could cry a heap—every time I read or think—if it would undo them—or do anybody or myself or the cause or Mrs. Stanton any good—they are so entirely unlike her former self—so flippant and superficial. But she thinks I have gone over to the enemy—so counts my judgment worth nothing more than that of any other narrow-souled body.... But I shall love and honor her to the end—whether her Bible please me or not. So I hope she will do for me."[407]

She was, however, wholly unprepared for the rebellion staged by her "girls" at the Washington convention of 1896, when, led by Rachel Foster Avery, they repudiated The Woman's Bible and proposed a resolution declaring that their organization had no connection with it. This was clear proof to Susan that her "girls" lacked tolerance and wisdom.

Listening to the debate, she was heartsick. Anna Howard Shaw and Mrs. Catt as well as Alice Stone Blackwell spoke for the resolution. Only a few raised their voices against it, among them her sister Mary, Clara Colby, Mrs. Blake, and a young woman new to the ranks, Charlotte Perkins Stetson.

Susan was presiding, and leaving the chair to express her opinions, she firmly declared, "To pass such a resolution is to set back the hands on the dial of reform.... We have all sorts of people in the Association and ... a Christian has no more right on our platform than an atheist. When this platform is too narrow for all to stand on, I shall not be on it.... Who is to set up a line? Neither you nor I can tell but Mrs. Stanton will come out triumphant and that this will be the great thing done in woman's cause. Lucretia Mott at first thought Mrs. Stanton had injured the cause of woman's rights by insisting on the demand for woman suffrage, but she had sense enough not to pass a resolution about it....[408]

"Are you going to cater to the whims and prejudices of people?" she asked them. "We draw out from other people our own thought. If, when you go out to organize, you go with a broad spirit, you will create and call out breadth and toleration. You had better organize one woman on a broad platform than 10,000 on a narrow platform of intolerance and bigotry."

Her voice tense with emotion, she concluded, "This resolution adopted will be a vote of censure upon a woman who is without a peer in intellectual and statesmanlike ability; one who has stood for half a century the acknowledged leader of progressive thought and demand in regard to all matters pertaining to the absolute freedom of women."[409]

When the resolution was adopted 53 to 40, she was so disappointed in her "girls" and so hurt by their defiance that she was tempted to resign. Hurrying to New York after the convention to talk with Mrs. Stanton, she found her highly indignant and insistent that they both resign from the ungrateful organization which had repudiated the women to whom it owed its existence. The longer Susan considered taking this step, the less she felt able to make the break. She severely reprimanded Mrs. Catt, Rachel, Harriet Upton, and Anna, telling them they were setting up an inquisition. Finally she wrote Mrs. Stanton, "No, my dear, instead of my resigning and leaving those half-fledged chickens without any mother, I think it my duty and the duty of yourself and all the liberals to be at the next convention and try to reverse this miserable narrow action."[410]

To a reporter who wanted her views on The Woman's Bible, she made it plain that she had no part in writing the book, but added, "I think women have just as good a right to interpret and twist the Bible to their own advantage as men have always twisted it and turned it to theirs. It was written by men, and therefore its reference to women reflects the light in which they were regarded in those days. In the same way the history of our Revolutionary War was written, in which very little is said of the noble deeds of women, though we know how they stood by and helped the great work; it is so with history all through."[411]

For some years, Susan's girls had been urging her to write her reminiscences, spurred on by the fact that Mrs. Stanton, Mary Livermore, and Julia Ward Howe were writing theirs. There were also other good reasons for putting her to work at this task. Writing would keep her safely at home and away from the strenuous work in the field which they feared was sapping her strength. It would keep her well occupied so that they could develop the work and the conventions in their own way.

Susan put off this task from month to month and from year to year, torn between her desire to leave a true record of her work and her longing to be always in the thick of the suffrage fight. Finally she began looking about for a collaborator, convinced that she herself could never write an interesting line. Ida Husted Harper, with her newspaper experience and her interest in the cause, seemed the logical choice, and in the spring of 1897, she came to 17 Madison Street to work on the biography.[412]

The attic had been remodeled for workrooms and here Susan now spent her days with Mrs. Harper, trying to reconstruct the past. She had definite ideas about how the book should be written, holding up as a model the biography of William Lloyd Garrison recently written by his children. Mrs. Harper also had high standards, and influenced by the formalities of the day, edited Susan's vivid brusque letters—hurriedly written and punctuated with dashes—so that they conformed with her own easy but more formal style. To this Susan readily consented, for she always depreciated her own writing ability. On one point, however, she was adamant, that her story be told without dwelling upon the disagreements among the old workers.

The household was geared to the "bog," as they called the biography. Mary, supervising as usual, watched over their meals and the housework with the aid of a young rosy-cheeked Canadian girl, Anna Dann, who had recently come to work for them and whom they at once took to their hearts, making her one of the family. Soon another young girl, Genevieve Hawley from Fort Scott, Kansas, was employed to help with the endless copying, sorting of letters, and pasting of scrapbooks, and with the current correspondence which piled up and diverted Susan from the book.[413]

Through 1897 and 1898, they worked at top speed.

The Life and Work of Susan B. Anthony, A Story of the Evolution of the Status of Women, in two volumes, by Ida Husted Harper, was published by the Bowen Merrill Company of Indianapolis just before Christmas 1898. Happy as a young girl out of school, Susan inscribed copies for her many friends and eagerly watched for reviews, pleased with the favorable comments in newspapers and magazines throughout this country and Europe.[414]

By this time the Cuban rebellion was crowding all other news out of the papers, and Susan followed it closely, for this struggle for freedom instantly won her sympathy. She hoped that Spain under pressure from the United States might be persuaded to give Cuba her independence, but the blowing up of the battleship Maine and the war cries of the press and of a faction in Congress led to armed intervention in April 1898. Always opposed to war as a means of settling disputes, she wrote Rachel, "To think of the mothers of this nation sitting back in silence without even the power of a legal protest—while their sons are taken without a by-your-leave! Well all through—it is barbarous ... and I hope you and all our young women will rouse to work as never before—and get the women of the Republic clothed with the power of control of conditions in peace—or when it shall come again—which Heaven forbid—in war."[415]

Not only did she express these sentiments in letters to her friends, but in a public meeting, where only patriotic fervor and flag-waving were welcome, she dared criticize the unsanitary army camps and the greed and graft which deprived soldiers of wholesome food. "There isn't a mother in the land," she declared, "who wouldn't know that a shipload of typhoid stricken soldiers would need cots to lie on and fuel to cook with, and that a swamp was not a desirable place in which to pitch a camp.... What the government needs at such a time is not alone bacteriologists and army officers but also women who know how to take care of sick boys and have the common sense to surround them with sanitary conditions."[416] At this her audience, at first hostile, burst into applause.

More and more disturbed by the inefficient care of the wounded and the feeding of enlisted men, she wrote Rachel, "Every day's reports and comments about the war only show the need of women at the front—not as employees permitted to be there because they begged to be—but there by right—as managers and dictators in all departments in which women have been trained—those of feeding and caring for in health and nursing the sick."[417]

The war over, the problem of governing the Philippines, Puerto Rico, and Hawaii was of great interest to her, and she at once asked for the enfranchisement of the women of these newly won island possessions. She regarded it as an outrage for the most democratic nation in the world to foist upon them an exclusively masculine government, a "male oligarchy," as she called it. "I really believe I shall explode," she wrote Clara Colby, "if some of you young women don't wake up and raise your voice in protest.... I wonder if when I am under the sod—or cremated and floating in the air—I shall have to stir you and others up. How can you not be all on fire?"[418]

The unwillingness of her "girls" to relate woman suffrage to contemporary public affairs such as this, repeatedly disappointed her. Yet she was well aware that the younger generation would never see the work through her eyes, or exactly follow her pattern.

Disappointed that her National American Woman Suffrage Association did not attract members as did the W.C.T.U. or the General Federation of Women's Clubs, she confessed to Clara Colby, "It is the disheartening part of my life that so very few women will work for the emancipation of their own half of the race."[419] Watching women flock into these other organizations and contributing to all sorts of charities, she was obliged to admit that "very few are capable of seeing that the cause of nine-tenths of all the misfortunes which come to women, and to men also, lies in the subjection of women, and therefore the important thing is to lay the ax at the root."[420]

She also discovered that it was one thing to build up a large organization and another to keep women so busy with pressing work for the cause that they did not find time to expend their energies on the mechanics of organization. Not only did she chafe at the red tape most of them spun, but she often felt that they were too prone to linger in academic by-ways, listening to speeches and holding pleasant conventions. Since the California campaign of 1896, only one state, Washington, had been roused to vote on a woman suffrage amendment, which was defeated and only one more state Delaware had granted women the right to vote for members of school boards.

Again and again she warned her "girls" that some kind of action on woman suffrage by Congress every year was important. A hearing, a committee report, a debate, or even an unfavorable vote would, she was convinced, do more to stir up the whole nation than all the speakers and organizers that could be sent through the country.

Such thoughts as these, relative to the work which was always on her mind, she dashed off to one after another of her young colleagues. "Your letters sound like a trumpet blast," wrote Anna Howard Shaw, grateful for her counsel. "They read like St. Paul's Epistles to the Romans, so strong, so clear, so full of courage."[421]

At seventy-eight, Susan realized that the time was approaching when she must make up her mind to turn over to a younger woman the presidency of the National American Association, and during the summer of 1898 she announced to her executive committee that she would retire on her eightieth birthday in 1900.

Passing On The Torch

The last year of Susan's presidency was particularly precious to her. In a sense it represented her farewell to the work she had carried on most of her life, and at the same time it was also the hopeful beginning of the period leading to victory. Yet she had no illusion of speedy or easy success for her "girls" and she did her best to prepare them for the obstacles they would inevitably meet. She warned them not to expect their cause to triumph merely because it was just. "Governments," she told them, "never do any great good things from mere principle, from mere love of justice.... You expect too much of human nature when you expect that."[422]

The movement had reached an impasse. The temper of Congress, as shown by the admission of Hawaii as a territory without woman suffrage, was both indifferent and hostile. That this attitude did not express the will of the American people, she was firmly convinced. It was due, she believed, to the political influence of powerful groups opposed to woman suffrage—the liquor interests controlling the votes of increasing numbers of immigrants, machine politicians fearful of losing their power, and financial interests whose conservatism resisted any measure which might upset the status quo. How to undermine this opposition was now her main problem, and she saw no other way but persistent agitation through a more active, more effective, ever-growing woman suffrage organization, reaching a wider cross section of the people. She herself had established a press bureau which was feeding interesting factual articles on woman suffrage to newspapers throughout the country, for as she wrote Mrs. Colby, the suffrage cause "needs to picture its demands in the daily papers where the unconverted can see them rather than in special papers where only those already converted can see them."[423]

Of greatest importance to her was winning the support of organized labor. Samuel Gompers, the president of the American Federation of Labor, had already shown his friendliness toward equal pay and votes for women and was putting women organizers in the field to speed the unionization of women. Even so she was surprised at the enthusiasm with which she was received at the American Federation of Labor convention in 1899, when the four hundred delegates by a rising vote adopted a strong resolution urging favorable action on a federal woman suffrage amendment.

So far as possible she had always established friendly relations with labor organizations, first in 1869 with William H. Sylvis's National Labor Union and then with the Knights of Labor and their leader, Terrence V. Powderly.[424] When Eugene V. Debs, president of the American Railway Union, was arrested during the Pullman strike in 1894 for defying a court injunction, she did not rate him, as so many did, a dangerous radical, but as an earnest reformer, crusading for an unpopular cause. They had met years before in Terre Haute, where at his request she had lectured on woman suffrage, and immediately they had won each other's sympathy and respect. She did not see indications of anarchy in the Pullman and Homestead strikes or in the Haymarket riot, but regarded them as an unfortunate phase of an industrial revolution which in time would improve the relations of labor and capital.

That women would be effected by this industrial revolution was obvious to her, and she wanted them to understand it and play their part in it. For this reason she saw the importance of keeping the National American Woman Suffrage Association informed on all developments affecting wage-earning women and to her delight she found three young suffragists wide awake on this subject. One of them, Florence Kelley, had joined forces with that remarkable young woman, Jane Addams, in her valuable social experiment, Hull House, in the slums of Chicago, and was now devoting herself to improving the working conditions of women and children. She represented a new trend in thought and work—social service—which made a great appeal to college women and set in motion labor legislation designed to protect women and children. Another young woman of promise, Gail Laughlin, pioneering as a lawyer, approached the subject from the feminist viewpoint, seeking protection for women not through labor legislation based on sex, but through trade unions, the vote, equal pay, and a wider recognition of women's right to contract for their labor on the same terms as men. Her survey of women's working conditions, presented at a convention of the National American Association was so valuable and attracted so much attention that she was appointed to the United States Labor Commission. Harriot Stanton Blatch also understood the significance of the industrial revolution and woman's part in it, and she too opposed labor legislation based on sex. Coming from England occasionally to visit her mother in New York, she brought her liberal viewpoint into woman suffrage conventions with a flare of oratory matching that of her gifted parents. "The more I see of her," Susan remarked to a friend, "the more I feel the greatness of her character."[425]

Although it was Susan's intention to hew to the line of woman suffrage and not to comment publicly on controversial issues, she could not keep silent when confronted with injustice. Religious intolerance, bigotry, and racial discrimination always forced her to take a stand, regardless of the criticism she might bring on herself.

The treatment of the Negro in both the North and the South was always of great concern to her, and during the 1890s, when a veritable epidemic of lynchings and race riots broke out, she expressed herself freely in Rochester newspapers. She noted the dangerous trend as indicated by new anti-Negro societies and the limitation of membership to white Americans in the Spanish-American War veterans' organization. Whenever the opportunity presented itself, she put into practice her own sincere belief in race equality. During every Washington convention, she arranged to have one of her good speakers occupy the pulpit of a Negro church, and in the South she made it a point to speak herself in Negro churches and schools and before their organizations, even though this might prejudice southerners. In her own home, she gladly welcomed the Negro lecturers and educators who came to Rochester. This seeking out of the Negro in friendliness was a religious duty to her and a pleasure. She demanded of everyone employed in her household, respectful treatment of Negro guests. She rejoiced when she saw Negroes in the audience at woman suffrage conventions in Washington, and it gave her great satisfaction to hear Mary Church Terrell, a beautiful intelligent Negro who had been educated at Oberlin and in Europe, making speeches which equaled and even surpassed those of the most eloquent white suffragists.

Susan did not fail to keep in touch with the international feminist movement, and in the summer of 1899, when she was seventy-nine years old, she headed the United States delegation to the International Council of Women, meeting in London. Visiting Harriot Stanton Blatch at her home in Basingstoke, she first conferred with the leading British feminists, bringing herself up to date on the progress of their cause. In England as in the United States, the burden of the suffrage campaign had shifted from the shoulders of the pioneers to their daughters, and they were carrying on with vigor, pressing for the passage of a franchise bill in the House of Commons.

Moving on to London, she was acclaimed as she had been at the World's Fair in Chicago. "The papers here have been going wild over Miss Anthony, declaring her to be the most unaggressive woman suffragist ever seen," reported a journalist to his newspaper in the United States.

From China, India, New Zealand, and Australia, from South Africa, Palestine, Persia, and the Argentine, as well as from Europe and the United States, women had come to London to discuss their progress and their problems, and Susan, pointing out to them the goal toward which they must head, declared with confidence, "The day will come when man will recognize woman as his peer, not only at the fireside but in the councils of the nation. Then, and not until then, will there be the perfect comradeship ... between the sexes that shall result in the highest development of the race."[426]

She had hoped that Queen Victoria would receive the delegates at Windsor Castle, thus indicating her approval of the International Council. She longed to talk with this woman who had ruled so long and so well. That a queen sat on the throne of England, this in itself was important to her and she wanted to express her gratitude, although she was well aware that the Queen had never used her influence for the improvement of laws relating to women. She had hoped to convince her of the need of votes for women, but Queen Victoria never gave her the opportunity. All that influential Englishwomen were able to arrange was the admission of the delegates to the courtyard of Windsor Castle to watch the Queen start on her drive and to tea in the banquet room without the Queen.

Carrie Chapman Catt

Returning home late in August 1899, Susan began at once to make definite plans to turn over the presidency of the National American Woman Suffrage Association to a younger woman. Although she well knew that the choice of her successor was actually in the hands of the membership, it was her intention to do what she could within the bounds of democratic procedure to insure the best possible leadership. To fill the office, she turned instinctively to Anna Howard Shaw whom she loved more dearly as the years went by and whose selfless devotion to the cause she trusted implicitly. Yet Anna, in spite of her many qualifications, lacked a few which were exceptional in Carrie Chapman Catt—creative executive ability, diplomacy, a talent for working with people, directing them, and winning their devotion. With growing admiration, Susan had been watching Mrs. Catt's indefatigable work in the states where she had been building up active branches. Her flare for raising money was outstanding, and Susan realized, as few others did, the crying need of funds for the campaigns ahead. In addition Mrs. Catt had no personal financial worries, for her husband, successful in business, was sympathetic to her work. Anna, on the other hand, would have to support herself by lecturing and carry as well the burden of the presidency of a rapidly growing organization.

Anna made the decision for Susan. She urged the candidacy of Mrs. Catt, although her highest ambition had always been to succeed her beloved Aunt Susan. As she later confessed to Susan, this was a personal sacrifice which cost her many a heartache, but she "honestly felt that Mrs. Catt was better fitted ... as well as freer to go into an unpaid field."[427] Susan therefore approached Mrs. Catt through Rachel and Harriet Upton, and was relieved when she consented to stand for election.

Rumors of Susan's retirement aroused ambitions in Lillie Devereux Blake, who from the point of seniority and devoted work in New York was regarded as being next in line for the presidency by Mrs. Stanton and Mrs. Colby. Unable to visualize Mrs. Blake as the leader of this large organization with its diverse strong personalities, Susan nevertheless conceded her right to compete for the office. Although she appreciated Mrs. Blake's valuable work for the cause, there never had been understanding or sympathy between them. Temperamentally the blunt stern New Englander with untiring drive had little in common with the southern beauty turned reformer.

A change in the presidency needed wise and patient handling as personal ambitions, prejudices, and misunderstandings reared their heads. When there were murmurings of secession among a small group if Mrs. Catt were elected, Susan wrote Mrs. Colby that such talk was "very immature, very despotic, very undemocratic," and she hoped she was not one of the malcontents.[428]

Another problem was the future of the organization committee which under Mrs. Catt's chairmanship had carried on a large part of the work. Its influence was considerable and could readily develop so as to conflict with that of the officers, thus threatening the unity of the whole organization. To dissolve the committee seemed to Susan and her closest advisors the wisest procedure. Mary Garrett Hay, who had worked closely with Mrs. Catt on the organization committee, opposed this plan, but after earnest discussion the officers, including Mrs. Catt, agreed to dissolve the organization committee.

As Susan appeared on the platform at the opening session of the Washington convention in February 1900, there was thunderous applause from an audience tense with emotion at the thought of losing the leader who had guided them for so many years. The tall gray-haired woman in black satin, with soft rich lace at her throat and the proverbial red shawl about her shoulders, had become the symbol of their cause. Now, as she looked down upon them with a friendly smile and motherly tenderness, tears came to their eyes, and they wanted to remember always just how she looked at that moment. Then she broke the tension with a call to duty, a summons to press for the federal amendment, and one more plea that they always hold their annual conventions in the national capital.

Difficult and sad as this official leave-taking was, she had made up her mind to carry if through with good cheer. Tirelessly she presided at three sessions daily. With the pride of a mother, she listened to the many reports and with particular satisfaction to that of the treasurer which showed all debts paid and pledges amounting to $10,000 to start the new year. Susan herself had made this possible, raising enough to pay past debts and securing pledges so that the new administration could start its work free from financial worries.

"I have fully determined to retire from the active presidency of the Association," she announced when the reports and speeches were over. "I am not retiring now because I feel unable, mentally or physically, to do the necessary work, but because I wish to see the organization in the hands of those who are to have its management in the future. I want to see you all at work, while I am alive, so I can scold if you do not do it well. Give the matter of selecting your officers serious thought. Consider who will do the best work for the political enfranchisement of women, and let no personal feelings enter into the question."[429]

Watching developments with the keen eye of a politician, she was confident that Mrs. Catt would be elected to succeed her, although Mrs. Blake's candidacy was still being assiduously pressed and circulars recommending her, signed by

Mrs. Stanton, Mrs. Russell Sage and Dr. Mary Putnam Jacobi, were being widely distributed. Just before the balloting, however, Mrs. Blake withdrew her name in the interest of harmony. This left the field to Mrs. Catt, who received 254 votes of the 278 cast.

A burst of applause greeted the announcement of Mrs. Catt's election. Then abruptly it stopped, as the realization swept over the delegates that Aunt Susan was no longer their president. Walking to the front of the platform, Susan took Mrs. Catt by the hand, and while the delegates applauded, the two women stood before them, the one showing in her kind face the experience and wisdom of years, the other young, intelligent, and beautiful, her life still before her. There were tears in Susan's eyes and her voice was unsteady as she said, "I am sure you have made a wise choice.... 'New conditions bring new duties.' These new duties, these changed conditions, demand stronger hands, younger heads, and fresher hearts. In Mrs. Catt, you have my ideal leader. I present to you my successor."[430]

Susan's joyous confidence in the new administration was rudely jolted as controversy over the future of the organization committee flared up during the last days of the convention. Under strong pressure from Mary Garrett Hay, Mrs. Catt had counseled with Henry Blackwell, and at one of the last sessions he had slipped in a motion authorizing the continuance of the organization committee.[431]

Stunned by this development and looking upon it as a threat to the harmony of the new administration, Susan, supported by Harriet Upton and Rachel, prepared to take action, and the next morning, at the first post-convention executive committee meeting at which Mrs. Catt presided, Susan proposed that the national officers, headed by Mrs. Catt, take over the duties of the organization committee. This precipitated a heated debate, during which Henry Blackwell and his daughter, Alice, called such procedure unconstitutional, and Mary Hay resigned. As the discussion became too acrimonious, Mrs. Catt put an end to it by calling up unfinished business, and thus managed to steer the remainder of the session into less troubled waters. The next day, however, Susan brought the matter up again, and on her motion the organization committee was voted out of existence with praise for its admirable record of service.

Here were all the makings of a factional feud which, if fanned into flame, could well have split the National American Association. Not only had the old organization interfered with the new, indirectly reprimanding Mrs. Catt, but Susan, by her own personal influence and determination, had reversed the action of the convention. As a result, Mrs. Catt was indignant, hurt, and sorely tempted to resign, but after sending a highly critical letter to every member of the business committee, she took up her work with vigor.

Disappointed and heartsick over the turn of events, Susan searched for a way to re-establish harmony and her own faith in her successor. Realizing that a mother's cool counsel and guiding hand were needed to heal the misunderstandings, and convinced that unity and trust could be restored only by frank discussion of the problem by those involved, she asked for a meeting of the business committee at her home. "What can we do to get back into trust in each other?" she wrote Laura Clay. "That is the thing we must do—somehow—and it cannot be done by letter. We must hold a meeting—and we must have you—and every single one of our members at it."[432]

Impatient at what to her seemed unnecessary delay, she kept prodding Mrs. Catt to call this meeting. Fortunately both Susan and Mrs. Catt were genuinely fond of each other and placed the welfare of the cause above personal differences. Both were tolerant and steady and understood the pressures put on the leader of a great organization. Anxious and troubled as she waited for this meeting, Susan appreciated Anna Shaw's visits as never before, marking them as red-letter days on her calender.

Late in August 1900, all the officers finally gathered at 17 Madison Street, and Susan listened to their discussions with deep concern. She was confident she could rely completely on Harriet Upton, Rachel, and Anna and could count on Laura Clay's "level head and good common sense."[433] She never felt sure of Alice Stone Blackwell and knew there was great sympathy and often a working alliance between her, her father, and Mrs. Catt. Of the latest member of the official family, Catharine Waugh McCulloch, she had little first-hand knowledge. Mrs. Catt, whom she longed to fathom and trust, was still an enigma. During those hot humid August days, misunderstandings were healed, unity was restored, and Susan was reassured that not a single one of her "girls" desired "other than was good for the work."[434]

Susan had always been a champion of coeducation, speaking for it as early as the 1850s at state teachers' meetings and proposing it for Columbia University in her Revolution. In 1891, she and Mrs. Stanton had agitated for the admission of women to the University of Rochester. Seven years later the trustees consented to admit women provided $100,000 could be raised in a year, and Susan served on the fund-raising committee with her friend, Helen Barrett Montgomery. Because the alumni of the University of Rochester opposed coeducation and the city's wealthiest men were indifferent, progress was slow, but the trustees were persuaded to extend the time and to reduce by one half the amount to be raised.

With so much else on her mind in 1900, including the sudden death of her brother Merritt, she had given the fund little thought until the committee appealed to her in desperation when only one day remained in which to raise the last $8,000. Immediately she went into action. Remembering that Mary had talked of willing the University $2,000 if it became coeducational, she persuaded her to pledge that amount now. Then setting out in a carriage on a very hot September morning, she slowly collected pledges for all but $2,000. As the trustees were in session and likely to adjourn any minute, she appealed to Samuel Wilder, one of Rochester's prominent elder citizens who had already contributed, to guarantee that amount until she could raise it. To this he gladly agreed. Reaching the trustees' meeting with Mrs. Montgomery just in time, with pledges assuring the payment of the full $50,000, she was amazed at their reception. Instead of rejoicing with them, the trustees began to quibble over Samuel Wilder's guarantee of the last $2,000 because of the state of his health. When she offered her life insurance as security, they still put her off, telling her to come back in a few days. Even then they continued to quibble, but finally admitted that the women had won. Disillusioned, she wrote in her diary, "Not a trustee has given anything although there are several millionaires among them."[435] Only her life insurance policy and her dogged persistence had saved the day.

This effort to open Rochester University to women, on top of a very full and worrisome year, was so taxing and so disillusioning that she became seriously ill. When she recovered sufficiently for a drive, she asked to be taken to the university campus and afterward wrote in her diary, "As I drove over the campus, I felt 'these are not forbidden grounds to the girls of the city any longer.' It is good to feel that the old doors sway on their hinges—to women! Will the vows be kept to them—will the girls have equal chances with the boys? They promised well—the fulfilment will be seen—whether there shall not be some hitch from the proposed to a separate school."[436]

Still keeping her watchful eye on the National American Association, Susan traveled to Minneapolis in the spring of 1901 for the first annual convention under the new administration. There was talk of an "entire new deal," the retirement of all who had served under Miss Anthony, and the election of a "new cabinet of officers," and Susan was so concerned that there might also be a change in the presidency that she felt she must be on hand to guide and steady the proceedings.[437]

Mrs. Catt was re-elected and Susan returned to Rochester well satisfied and ready to devote herself to completing the fourth volume of the History of Woman Suffrage on which she and Mrs. Harper had been working intermittently for the past year. It was published late in 1902. While working on the History, Susan, although more than satisfied with Mrs. Harper's work, often thought nostalgically of her happy stimulating years of collaboration with Mrs. Stanton. She seldom saw Mrs. Stanton now, but they kept in touch with each other by letter.

In the spring of 1902, she visited Mrs. Stanton twice in New York, and planned to return in November to celebrate Mrs. Stanton's eighty-seventh birthday. In anticipation, she wrote Mrs. Stanton, "It is fifty-one years since we first met and we have been busy through every one of them, stirring up the world to recognize the rights of women.... We little dreamed when we began this contest ... that half a century later we would be compelled to leave the finish of the battle to another generation of women. But our hearts are filled with joy to know that they enter upon this task equipped with a college education, with business experience, with the freely admitted right to speak in public—all of which were denied to women fifty years ago.... These strong, courageous, capable, young women will take our place and complete our work. There is an army of them where we were but a handful...."[438]

Two weeks before Mrs. Stanton's birthday, Susan was stunned by a telegram announcing that her old comrade had passed away in her chair. Bewildered and desolate, she sat alone in her study for several hours, trying bravely to endure her grief. Then came the reporters for copy which only this heartbroken woman could give. "I cannot express myself at all as I feel," she haltingly told them. "I am too crushed to speak. If I had died first, she would have found beautiful phrases to describe our friendship, but I cannot put it into words."[439]

From New York, where she had gone for the funeral, she wrote in anguish to Mrs. Harper, "Oh, the voice is stilled which I have loved to hear for fifty years. Always I have felt that I must have Mrs. Stanton's opinion of things before I knew where I stood myself. I am all at sea—but the Laws of Nature are still going on—with no shadow or turning—what a wonder it is—it goes right on and on—no matter who lives or who dies."[440]

National woman suffrage conventions were still red-letter events to Susan and she attended them no matter how great the physical effort, traveling to New Orleans in 1903. Of particular concern was the 1904 convention because of Mrs. Catt's decision at the very last moment not to stand for re-election on account of her health. Looking over the field, Susan saw no one capable of taking her place but Anna Howard Shaw. Not to be able to turn to Mrs. Stanton's capable daughter, Harriot Stanton Blatch, at this time was disappointing, but Harriot's long absence in England had made her more or less of a stranger to the membership of the National American Association, and for some reason she did not seem to fit in, lacking her mother's warmth and appeal.[441]

1873 Petition in the handwriting of Susan B. Anthony

"I don't see anybody in the whole rank of our suffrage movement to take her [Mrs. Catt's] place but you," Susan now wrote Anna Howard Shaw. "If you will take it with a salary of say, $2,000, I will go ahead and try to see what I can do. We must not let the society down into feeble hands.... Don't say no, for the life of you, for if Mrs. Catt persists in going out, we shall simply have to accept it and we must tide over with the best material that we have, and you are the best, and would you have taken office four years ago, you would have been elected over-whelmingly."[442]

Anna could not refuse Aunt Susan, and when she was elected with Mrs. Catt as vice-president, Susan breathed freely again.

It warmed Susan's heart to enter the convention on her eighty-fourth birthday to a thundering welcome, to banter with Mrs. Upton who called her to the platform, and to stop the applause with a smile and "There now, girls, that's enough."[443] Nothing could have been more appropriate for her birthday than the Colorado jubilee over which she presided and which gave irrefutable evidence of the success of woman suffrage in that state. There was rejoicing too over Australia, where women had been voting since 1902 and over the new hope in Europe, in Denmark, where women had chosen her birthday to stage a demonstration in favor of the pending franchise bill.

For the last time, she spoke to a Senate committee on the woman suffrage amendment. Standing before these indifferent men, a tired warrior at the end of a long hard campaign, she reminded them that she alone remained of those who thirty-five years before, in 1869, had appealed to Congress for justice. "And I," she added, "shall not be able to come much longer.

"We have waited," she told them. "We stood aside for the Negro; we waited for the millions of immigrants; now we must wait till the Hawaiians, the Filipinos, and the Puerto Ricans are enfranchised; then no doubt the Cubans will have their turn. For all these ignorant, alien peoples, educated women have been compelled to stand aside and wait!" Then with mounting impatience, she asked them, "How long will this injustice, this outrage continue?"[444]

Their answer to her was silence. They sent no report to the Senate on the woman suffrage amendment. Yet she was able to say to a reporter of the New York Sun, "I have never lost my faith, not for a moment in fifty years."[445]

Susan B. Anthony Of The World

Susan was on the ocean in May 1904 with her sister Mary and a group of good friends, headed for a meeting of the International Council of Women in Berlin. What drew her to Berlin was the plan initiated by Carrie Chapman Catt to form an International Woman Suffrage Alliance prior to the meetings of the International Council. This had been Susan's dream and Mrs. Stanton's in 1883, when they first conferred with women of other countries regarding an international woman suffrage organization and found only the women of England ready to unite on such a radical program. Now that women had worked together successfully in the International Council for sixteen years on other less controversial matters relating to women, she and Mrs. Catt were confident that a few of them at least were willing to unite to demand the vote.

Chosen as a matter of course to preside over this gathering of suffragists in Berlin, Susan received an enthusiastic welcome. For her it was a momentous occasion, and eager to spread news of the meeting far and wide, she could not understand the objections of many of the delegates to the presence of reporters who they feared might send out sensational copy.

"My friends, what are we here for?" she asked her more timid colleagues. "We have come from many countries, travelled thousands of miles to form an organization for a great international work, and do we want to keep it a secret from the public? No; welcome all reporters who want to come, the more, the better. Let all we say and do here be told far and wide. Let the people everywhere know that in Berlin women from all parts of the world have banded themselves together to demand political freedom. I rejoice in the presence of these reporters, and instead of excluding them from our meetings let us help them to all the information we can and ask them to give it the widest publicity."[446]

This won the battle for the reporters, who gave her rousing applause, and the news flashed over the wires was sympathetic, dignified, and abundant. It told the world of the formation of the International Woman Suffrage Alliance by women from the United States, Great Britain, Germany, The Netherlands, Sweden, Australia, Norway, and Denmark, "to secure the enfranchisement of women of all nations." It praised the honorary president, Susan B. Anthony, and the American women who took over the leadership of this international venture, Carrie Chapman Catt, the president, and Rachel Foster Avery, corresponding secretary.

To celebrate the occasion, German suffragists called a public mass meeting, and Susan, eager to rejoice with them, was surprised to find members of the International Council disgruntled and accusing the International Woman Suffrage Alliance of stealing their thunder and casting the dark shadow of woman suffrage over their conference. To placate them and restore harmony, she stayed away from this public meeting, but she could not control the demand for her presence.

"Where is Susan B. Anthony?" were the first words spoken as the mass meeting opened. Then immediately the audience rose and burst into cheers which continued without a break for ten minutes. Anna Howard Shaw there on the platform and deeply moved by this tribute to Aunt Susan, later described how she felt: "Every second of that time I seemed to see Miss Anthony alone in her hotel room, longing with all her big heart to be with us, as we longed to have her.... Afterwards, when we burst in upon her and told her of the great demonstration, the mere mention of her name had caused, her lips quivered and her brave old eyes filled with tears."[447]

The next morning her "girls" brought her the Berlin newspapers, translating for her the report of the meeting and these heart-warming lines, "The Americans call her 'Aunt Susan.' She is our 'Aunt Susan' too."

This was but a foretaste of her reception throughout her stay in Berlin. To the International Council, she was "Susan B. Anthony of the World," the woman of the hour, whom all wanted to meet. Every time she entered the conference hall, the audience rose and remained standing until she was seated. Every mention of her name brought forth cheers. The many young women, acting as ushers, were devoted to her and eager to serve her. They greeted her by kissing her hand. Embarrassed at first by such homage, she soon responded by kissing them on the cheek.

Susan B. Anthony in 1900 at the age of eighty

The Empress Victoria Augusta, receiving the delegates in the Royal Palace, singled out Susan, and instead of following the custom of kissing the Empress's hand, Susan bowed as she would to any distinguished American, explaining that she was a Quaker and did not understand the etiquette of the court. The Empress praised Susan's great work, and unwilling to let such an opportunity slip by, Susan offered the suggestion that Emperor William who had done so much to build up his country might now wish to raise the status of German women. To this the Empress replied with a smile, "The gentlemen are very slow to comprehend this great movement."[448]

When the talented Negro, Mary Church Terrell, addressing the International Council in both German and French, received an ovation, Susan's cup of joy was filled to the brim, for she glimpsed the bright promise of a world without barriers of sex or race.

The newspapers welcomed her home, and in her own comfortable sitting room she read Rochester's greeting in the Democrat and Chronicle, "There are woman suffragists and anti-suffragists, but all Rochester people, irrespective of opinion ... are Anthony men and women. We admire and esteem one so single-minded, earnest and unselfish, who, with eighty-four years to her credit, is still too busy and useful to think of growing old."[449]

Her happiness over this welcome was clouded, however, by the serious illness of her brother Daniel, and she and Mary hurried to Kansas to see him. Two months later he passed away. Now only she and Mary were left of all the large Anthony family. Without Daniel, the world seemed empty. His strength of character, independence, and sympathy with her work had comforted and encouraged her all through her life. A fearless editor, a successful businessman, a politician with principles, he had played an important role in Kansas, and proud of him, she cherished the many tributes published throughout the country.

Courageously she now picked up the threads of her life. Her precious National American Woman Suffrage Association was out of her hands, but she still had the History of Woman Suffrage to distribute, and it gave her a great sense of accomplishment to hand on to future generations this record of women's struggle for freedom.[450]

Missing the stimulus of work with her "girls," she took more and more pleasure in the company of William and Mary Gannett of the First Unitarian Church, whose liberal views appealed to her strongly. She liked to have young people about her and followed the lives of all her nieces and nephews with the greatest interest, spurring on their ambitions and helping finance their education. The frequent visits of "Niece Lucy" were a great joy during these years, as was the nearness of "Niece Anna O,"[451] who married and settled in Rochester. The young Canadian girl, Anna Dann, had become almost indispensable to her and to Mary, as companion, secretary, and nurse, and her marriage left a void in the household. Anna Dann was married at 17 Madison Street by Anna Howard Shaw with Susan beaming upon her like a proud grandmother.

Longing to see one more state won for suffrage, Susan carefully followed the news from the field, looking hopefully to California and urging her "girls" to keep hammering away there in spite of defeats. Her eyes were also on the Territory of Oklahoma, where a constitution was being drafted preparatory to statehood. "The present bill for the new state," she wrote Anna Howard Shaw, in December 1904, "is an insult to women of Oklahoma, such as has never been perpetrated before. We have always known that women were in reality ranked with idiots and criminals, but it has never been said in words that the state should ... restrict or abridge the suffrage ... on account of illiteracy, minority, sex, conviction of felony, mental condition, etc.... We must fight this bill to the utmost...."[452]

The brightest spot in the West was Oregon, where suffrage had been defeated in 1900 by only 2,000 votes. In June 1905, when the National American Association held its first far western convention in Portland during the Lewis and Clark Exposition, Susan could not keep away, although she had never expected to go over the mountains again. As she traveled to Portland with Mary and a hundred or more delegates in special cars, she recalled her many long tiring trips through the West to carry the message of woman suffrage to the frontier. In comparison, this was a triumphal journey, showing her, as nothing else could, what her work had accomplished. Greeted at railroad stations along the way by enthusiastic crowds, showered with flowers and gifts, she stood on the back platform of the train with her "girls," shaking hands, waving her handkerchief, and making an occasional speech.

Presiding over the opening session of the Portland convention, standing in a veritable garden of flowers which had been presented to her, she remarked with a droll smile, "This is rather different from the receptions I used to get fifty years ago.... I am thankful for this change of spirit which has come over the American people."[453]

On Woman's Day, she was chosen to speak at the unveiling of the statue of Sacajawea, the Indian woman who had led Lewis and Clark through the dangerous mountain passes to the Pacific, winning their gratitude and their praise. In the story of Sacajawea who had been overlooked by the government when every man in the Lewis and Clark expedition had been rewarded with a large tract of land, Susan saw the perfect example of man's thoughtless oversight of the valuable services of women. Looking up at the bronze statue of the Indian woman, her papoose on her back and her arm outstretched to the Pacific, Susan said simply, "This is the first statue erected to a woman because of deeds of daring.... This recognition of the assistance rendered by a woman in the discovery of this great section of the country is but the beginning of what is due." Then, with the sunlight playing on her hair and lighting up her face, she appealed to the men of Oregon for the vote. "Next year," she reminded them, "the men of this proud state, made possible by a woman, will decide whether women shall at last have the rights in it which have been denied them so many years. Let men remember the part women have played in its settlement and progress and vote to give them these rights which belong to every citizen."[454]

Reporters were at Susan's door, when she returned to Rochester, for comments on ex-President Cleveland's tirade against clubwomen and woman suffrage in the popular Ladies' Home Journal. "Pure fol-de-rol," she told them, adding testily, "I would think that Grover Cleveland was about the last person to talk about the sanctity of the home and woman's sphere." This was good copy for Republican newspapers and they made the most of it, as women throughout the country added their protests to Susan's. A popular jingle of the day ran, "Susan B. Anthony, she took quite a fall out of Grover C."[455]

Susan, however, had something far more important on her mind than fencing with Grover Cleveland—an interview with President Theodore Roosevelt. Here was a man eager to right wrongs, to break monopolies, to see justice done to the Negro, a man who talked of a "square deal" for all, and yet woman suffrage aroused no response in him.

In November 1905, she undertook a trip to Washington for the express purpose of talking with him. The year before, at a White House reception, he had singled her out to stand at his side in the receiving line. She looked for the same friendliness now. Memorandum in hand, she plied him with questions which he carefully evaded, but she would not give up.

"Mr. Roosevelt," she earnestly pleaded, "this is my principle request. It is almost the last request I shall ever make of anybody. Before you leave the Presidential chair recommend to Congress to submit to the Legislatures a Constitutional Amendment which will enfranchise women, and thus take your place in history with Lincoln, the great emancipator. I beg of you not to close your term of office without doing this."[456]

To this he made no response, and trying once more to wring from him some slight indication of sympathy for her cause, she added, "Mr. President, your influence is so great that just one word from you in favor of woman suffrage would give our cause a tremendous impetus."

"The public knows my attitude," he tersely replied. "I recommended it when Governor of New York."

"True," she acknowledged, "but that was a long time ago. Our enemies say that was the opinion of your younger years and that since you have been President you have never uttered one word that could be construed as an endorsement."

"They have no cause to think I have changed my mind," he suavely replied as he bade her good-bye. In the months that followed he gave her no sign that her interview had made the slightest impression.

One of the most satisfying honors bestowed on Susan during these last years was the invitation to be present at Bryn Mawr College in 1902 for the unveiling of a bronze portrait medallion of herself. Bryn Mawr, under its brilliant young president, M. Carey Thomas, herself a pioneer in establishing the highest standards for women's education, showed no such timidity as Vassar where neither Susan nor Elizabeth Cady Stanton had been welcome as speakers. At Bryn Mawr, Susan talked freely and frankly with the students, and best of all, became better acquainted with M. Carey Thomas and her enterprising friend, Mary Garrett of Baltimore, who was using her great wealth for the advancement of women. She longed to channel their abilities to woman suffrage and a few years later arranged for a national convention in their home city, Baltimore, appealing to them to make it an outstanding success.[457]

Arriving in Baltimore in January 1906 for this convention, Susan was the honored guest in Mary Garrett's luxurious home. Frail and ill, she was unable to attend all the sessions, as in the past, but she was present at the highlight of this very successful convention, the College Evening arranged by M. Carey Thomas. With women's colleges still resisting the discussion of woman suffrage and the Association of Collegiate Alumnae refusing to support it, the College Evening marked the first public endorsement of this controversial subject by college women. Up to this time the only encouraging sign had been the formation in 1900 of the College Equal Suffrage League by two young Radcliffe alumnae, Maud Wood Park and Inez Haynes Irwin. Now here, in conservative Baltimore, college presidents and college faculty gave woman suffrage their blessing, and Susan listened happily as distinguished women, one after another, allied themselves to the cause: Dr. Mary E. Woolley, who as president of Mt. Holyoke was developing Mary Lyons' pioneer seminary into a high ranking college; Lucy Salmon, Mary A. Jordan, and Mary W. Calkins of the faculties of Vassar, Smith, and Wellesley; Eva Perry Moore, a trustee of Vassar and president of the Association of Collegiate Alumnae, with whom she dared differ on this subject; Maud Wood Park, representing the younger generation in the College Equal Suffrage League; and last of all, the president of Bryn Mawr, M. Carey Thomas. After expressing her gratitude to the pioneers of this great movement, Miss Thomas turned to Susan and said, "To you, Miss Anthony, belongs by right, as to no other woman in the world's history, the love and gratitude of all women in every country of the civilized globe. We your daughters in spirit, rise up today and call you blessed.... Of such as you were the lines of the poet Yeats written:

'They shall be remembered forever,
They shall be alive forever,
They shall be speaking forever,
The people shall hear them forever.'"[458]

During the thundering applause, Susan came forward to respond, her face alight, and the audience rose. "If any proof were needed of the progress of the cause for which I have worked, it is here tonight," she said simply. "The presence on the stage of these college women, and in the audience of all those college girls who will someday be the nation's greatest strength, tell their story to the world. They give the highest joy and encouragement to me...."[459]

During her visit at the home of Mary Garrett, Susan spoke freely with her and with M. Carey Thomas of the needs of the National American Association, particularly of the Standing Fund of $100,000 of which she had dreamed and which she had started to raise. Now, like an answer to prayer, Mary Garrett and President Thomas, fresh from their successful money-raising campaigns for Johns Hopkins and Bryn Mawr, offered to undertake a similar project for woman suffrage, proposing to raise $60,000—$12,000 a year for the next five years.

"As we sat at her feet day after day between sessions of the convention, listening to what she wanted us to do to help women and asking her questions," recalled M. Carey Thomas in later years, "I realized that she was the greatest person I had ever met. She seemed to me everything that a human being could be—a leader to die for or to live for and follow wherever she led."[460]

Immediately after the convention, Susan went to Washington with the women who were scheduled to speak at the Congressional hearing on woman suffrage. In her room at the Shoreham Hotel, a room with a view of the Washington Monument which the manager always saved for her, she stood at the window looking out over the city as if saying farewell. Then turning to Anna Shaw, she said with emotion, "I think it is the most beautiful monument in the whole world."[461]

That evening she sat quietly through the many tributes offered to her on her eighty-sixth birthday, longing to tell all her friends the gratitude and hope that welled up in her heart. Finally she rose, and standing by Anna Howard Shaw who was presiding, she impulsively put her hand on her shoulder and praised her for her loyal support. Then turning to the other officers, she thanked them for all they had done. "There are others also," she added, "just as true and devoted to the cause—I wish I could name everyone—but with such women consecrating their lives—" She hesitated a moment, and then in her clear rich voice, added with emphasis, "Failure is impossible."[462]

In Rochester, in the home she so dearly loved, she spent her last weeks, thinking of the cause and the women who would carry it on. Longing to talk with Anna Shaw, she sent for her, but Anna, feeling she was needed, came even before a letter could reach her. With Anna at her bedside, Susan was content.

"I want you to give me a promise," she pleaded, reaching for Anna's hand. "Promise me you will keep the presidency of the association as long as you are well enough to do the work."[463]

Deeply moved, Anna replied, "But how can I promise that? I can keep it only as long as others wish me to keep it."

"Promise to make them wish you to keep it," Susan urged. "Just as I wish you to keep it...."

After a moment, she continued, "I do not know anything about what comes to us after this life ends, but ... if I have any conscious knowledge of this world and of what you are doing, I shall not be far away from you; and in times of need I will help you all I can. Who knows? Perhaps I may be able to do more for the Cause after I am gone than while I am here."

A few days later, on March 13, 1906, she passed away, her hand in Anna's.

Susan B. Anthony, 1905

Asked, a few years before, if she believed that all women in the United States would ever be given the vote, she had replied with assurance, "It will come, but I shall not see it.... It is inevitable. We can no more deny forever the right of self-government to one-half our people than we could keep the Negro forever in bondage. It will not be wrought by the same disrupting forces that freed the slave, but come it will, and I believe within a generation."[464]

She had so longed to see women voting throughout the United States, to see them elected to legislatures and Congress, but for her there had only been the promise of fulfillment in Wyoming, Utah, Colorado, and Idaho, and far away in New Zealand and Australia.

"Failure is impossible" was the rallying cry she left with her "girls" to spur them on in the long discouraging struggle ahead, fourteen more years of campaigning until on August 26, 1920, women were enfranchised throughout the United States by the Nineteenth Amendment.

Even then their work was not finished, for she had looked farther ahead to the time when men and women everywhere, regardless of race, religion, or sex, would enjoy equal rights. Her challenging words, "Failure is impossible," still echo and re-echo through the years, as the crusade for human rights goes forward and men and women together strive to build and preserve a free world.

Notes

CHAPTER I — QUAKER HERITAGE

[1] Report of the International Council of Women, 1888 (Washington, 1888), p. 163.

[2] Charles B. Waite, "Who Were the Voters in the Early History of This Country?" Chicago Law Times, Oct., 1888.

[3] Janet Whitney, Abigail Adams (Boston, 1947), p. 129. In 1776, Abigail Adams wrote her husband, John Adams, at the Continental Congress in Philadelphia, "In the new code of laws which I suppose it will be necessary for you to make, I desire you would remember the ladies and be more generous and favorable to them than your ancestors! Do not put such unlimited powers into the hands of husbands. Remember all men would be tyrants if they could. If particular care and attention is not paid to the ladies, we are determined to foment a rebellion, and will not hold ourselves bound by any laws in which we have no voice or representation." Ethel Armes, Stratford Hall (Richmond, Va., 1936), pp. 206-209.

[4] Under the Missouri Compromise, Maine was admitted as a free state, Missouri as a slave state, and slavery was excluded from all of the Louisiana Purchase, north of latitude 36°31'.

[5] The meeting house, built in 1783, is still standing. It is owned by the town of Adams, and cared for by the Adams Society of Friends Descendants. Susan traced her ancestry to William Anthony of Cologne who migrated to England and during the reign of Edward VI, was made Chief Graver of the Royal Mint and Master of the Scales, holding this office also during the reign of Queen Mary and part of Queen Elizabeth's reign. In 1634, one of his descendants, John Anthony, settled in Rhode Island, and just before the Revolution, his great grandson, David, Susan's great grandfather, bought land near Adams, Massachusetts, then regarded as the far West.

[6] Ida Husted Harper, The Life and Work of Susan B. Anthony (Indianapolis, 1898), I, p. 10.

[7] Daniel and Susannah Richardson Read gave Lucy and Daniel Anthony land for their home, midway between the Anthony and Read farms. Here Susan was born in a substantial two-story, frame house, built by her father.

[8] Ms., Diary, 1837.

[9] Harper, Anthony, I, p. 25.

[10] Ms., Diary, Jan. 21, Feb. 10, 1838

[11] Harper, Anthony, I, p. 31.

[12] Ms., Diary, Feb. 26, 1838.

[13] Ibid., Feb. 6, 1838.

[14] Ibid., May 7, 1838.

[15] Harper, Anthony, I, p. 36.

[16] Ibid., p. 37.

[17] Ibid., p. 40.

[18] Ibid., p. 39.

[19] Ibid.

[20] Ibid., pp. 43-44.

CHAPTER II — WIDENING HORIZONS

[21] Anthony Collection, Museum of Arts and Sciences, Rochester, New York.

[22] Hannah Anthony married Eugene Mosher, a merchant of Easton, New York, on September 4, 1845.

[23] Ms., Susan B. Anthony Memorial Collection, Rochester, New York.

[24] Harper, Anthony, I, p. 48.

[25] Ibid., p. 50.

[26] May 28, 1848, Lucy E. Anthony Collection.

[27] Harper, Anthony, I, p. 53.

[28] Ms., Susan B. Anthony Papers, Library of Congress.

[29] Report of the International Council of Women, 1888, p. 327.

[30] To Nora Blatch, n.d., Elizabeth Cady Stanton Papers, Vassar College Library, Poughkeepsie, New York.

[31] Harper, Anthony, I. p. 52.

[32] Amy H. Croughton, Antislavery Days in Rochester (Rochester, N.Y., 1936). Anyone implicated in the escape of a slave was liable to $1000 fine, to the payment of $1000 to the owner of the fugitive, and to a possible jail sentence of six months.

CHAPTER III — FREEDOM TO SPEAK

[33] Harper, Anthony, I, p. 65.
[34] The Lily, May, 1852.
[35] Elizabeth Cady Stanton, Susan B. Anthony, and Matilda Joslyn Gage, History of Woman Suffrage (New York, 1881), I, p. 489.
[36] Harper, Anthony, I, p. 77.
[37] Ibid., p. 78.
[38] Ibid., p. 90.
[39] Theodore Stanton and Harriot Stanton Blatch, Eds., Elizabeth Cady Stanton, As Revealed in Her Letters, Diary, and Reminiscences (New York, 1922), II, p. 52.
[40] Aug., 1853, Harper, Anthony, I, pp. 98-99; History of Woman Suffrage, I, pp. 513-515.
[41] Susan B. Anthony Scrapbook, Library of Congress.
[42] Ms., Diary, 1853.

CHAPTER IV — A PURSE OF HER OWN

[43] Judge William Hay of Saratoga Springs, New York.
[44] Feb. 19, 1854, Elizabeth Cady Stanton Papers, Library of Congress.
[45] Harper, Anthony, I, p. 116. Among those who wore the bloomer costume were Angelina and Sarah Grimké, many women in sanitoriums and some of the Lowell, Mass. mill workers. In Ohio, the bloomer was so popular that 60 women in Akron wore it at a ball, and in Battle Creek, Michigan, 31 attended a Fourth of July celebration in the bloomer. Amelia Bloomer, moving to the West wore it for eight years. Garrison, Phillips, and William Henry Channing disapproved of the bloomer costume, but Gerrit Smith continued to champion it and his daughter wore it at fashionable receptions in Washington during his term in Congress.
[46] History of Woman Suffrage, I, p. 608.
[47] 1854 (copy), Blackwell Papers, Edna M. Stantial Collection.
[48] Harper, Anthony, I, pp. 111-112.
[49] March 3, 1854 (copy), Blackwell Papers, Edna M. Stantial Collection.
[50] Ms., Diary, March 24, 28, 1854.
[51] Ibid., March 29, 1854.
[52] Ibid., March 30, 1854.
[53] The New England Emigrant Aid Company, headed by Eli Thayer of Worcester, was formed to send free-soil settlers to Kansas, offering reduced fare and farm equipment. Their first settlers reached Kansas in August, 1854, founding the town of Lawrence in honor of one of their chief patrons, the wealthy Amos Lawrence of Massachusetts.
[54] Harper, Anthony, I, p. 121.
[55] Diary, April 28, 1854.
[56] Leonard C. Ehrlich, God's Angry Man (New York, 1941), p. 57.
[57] Harper, Anthony, I, p. 122.
[58] Caroline Cowles Richards, Village Life in America (New York, 1913), p. 49.
[59] 1858, Blackwell Papers, Edna M. Stantial Collection.
[60] Harper, Anthony, I, p. 133.
[61] Ibid.
[62] Eliza J. Eddy's husband, James Eddy, took their two young daughters away from their mother and to Europe, causing her great anguish. This led her father, Francis Jackson, to give liberally to the woman's rights cause. Mrs. Eddy, herself, left a bequest of $56,000 to be divided between Susan B. Anthony and Lucy Stone.
[63] Harper, Anthony, I, pp. 131-133.
[64] Ibid., p. 138.
[65] Ibid., p. 139.

[66] Jan. 18, 1856, Garrison Papers, Sophia Smith Collection, Smith College.
[67] Harper, Anthony, I, pp. 140-141.
[68] May 25, 1856, Blackwell Papers, Edna M. Stantial Collection.

CHAPTER V — NO UNION WITH SLAVEHOLDERS

[69] Harper, Anthony, I, pp. 144-145. As John Brown visited Frederick Douglass in Rochester, it is possible that Susan B. Anthony had met him.
[70] Oct. 19, 1856, Blackwell Papers, Edna M. Stantial Collection.
[71] Harper, Anthony, I, p. 148.
[72] Ibid., p. 151; also quotation following.
[73] Alice Stone Blackwell, Lucy Stone (Boston, 1930), pp. 197-198.
[74] Ms., Susan B. Anthony Papers, Library of Congress.
[75] Harper, Anthony, I, p. 152.
[76] April 20, 1857, Abby Kelley Foster Papers, American Antiquarian Society, Worcester, Massachusetts.
[77] Parker Pillsbury, The Acts of the Antislavery Apostles (Concord, N.H., 1883).
[78] Harper, Anthony, I. p. 160.
[79] March 22, 1858, Blackwell Papers, Edna M. Stantial Collection.
[80] N.d., Alma Lutz Collection.
[81] Charles A. and Mary B. Beard, The Rise of American Civilization (New York, 1930), II, p. 9.
[82] A. M. Schlesinger and H. C. Hockett, Land of the Free (New York, 1944), p. 297.
[83] March 19, 1859, Antislavery Papers, Boston Public Library.
[84] Francis Jackson, William Lloyd II, and Wendell Phillips Garrison, William Lloyd Garrison, 1805-1879 (New York, 1889), III, p. 486.
[85] Ibid., p. 490.
[86] Harper, Anthony, I, p. 181.
[87] Ibid., p. 180.
[88] Henrietta Buckmaster, Let My People Go (New York, 1941), p. 269; Ehrlich, God's Angry Man, pp. 344-345, 350.
[89] Susan B. Anthony Scrapbook, Library of Congress. In 1890, after visiting the John Brown Memorial at North Elbe, New York, Susan B. Anthony wrote: "John Brown was crucified for doing what he believed God commanded him to do, 'to break the yoke and let the oppressed go free,' precisely as were the saints of old for following what they believed to be God's commands. The barbarism of our government was by so much the greater as our light and knowledge are greater than those of two thousand years ago." Harper, Anthony, II, p. 708.

CHAPTER VI — THE TRUE WOMAN

[90] Harper, Anthony, I, pp. 173-174, 198.
[91] Ibid., p. 160.
[92] May 26, 1856, Elizabeth Cady Stanton Papers, Vassar College Library.
[93] Ibid., June 5, 1856. Antoinette Brown Blackwell was often called Nette.
[94] Ms., Susan B. Anthony Papers, Library of Congress.
[95] 1856, Elizabeth Cady Stanton Papers, Library of Congress.
[96] Ms., Susan B. Anthony Papers, Library of Congress. A notation on this ms. reads, "Written by Elizabeth Cady Stanton—Delivered by Susan B. Anthony."
[97] Harper, Anthony, I, p. 143.
[98] Stanton and Blatch, Stanton, II, p. 71.
[99] Harper, Anthony, I, p. 162.
[100] June 10, 1856, Elizabeth Cady Stanton Papers, Library of Congress.
[101] Harper, Anthony, I, p. 171.
[102] Sept. 27, 1857, Elizabeth Cady Stanton Papers, Library of Congress.
[103] Harper, Anthony, I, p. 175.
[104] Ms., Diary, 1855.
[105] Sept. 27, 1857, Elizabeth Cady Stanton Papers, Library of Congress.

[106] Elizabeth Barrett Browning, Aurora Leigh (New York, 1857), p. 316; quotations following, pp. 53-54, pp. 364-365.

[107] Harper, Anthony, I, p. 170.

[108] Ibid., p. 177. Mary Hallowell, a liberal Rochester Quaker, always interested in Susan B. Anthony and her work.

CHAPTER VII — THE ZEALOT

[109] History of Woman Suffrage, I. p. 689. Henry Ward Beecher's speech, The Public Function of Women, delivered at Cooper Union, Feb. 2, 1860, was widely distributed as a tract.

[110] April 16, 1860, Elizabeth Cady Stanton Papers, Library of Congress.

[111] June 16, 1857, Blackwell Papers, Edna M. Stantial Collection.

[112] History of Woman Suffrage, I, p. 717.

[113] Ibid., p. 725.

[114] Ibid., p. 732.

[115] Ibid., p. 735.

[116] Harper, Anthony, I, p. 196.

[117] Elizabeth Cady Stanton, Eighty Years and More (New York, 1898), p. 219. Samuel Longfellow whispered to Mrs. Stanton in the midst of the debate, "Nevertheless you are right and the convention will sustain you."

[118] Harper, Anthony, I. p. 195.

[119] Ibid., p. 197.

[120] Aug. 25, 1860, Elizabeth Cady Stanton Papers, Vassar College Library.

[121] Charles Sumner was the First prominent statesman to speak for emancipation, Oct., 1861, at the Massachusetts Republican Convention.

[122] Harper, Anthony, I, p. 198.

[123] Ms., Susan B. Anthony Papers, Library of Congress.

[124] Harper, Anthony, I, p. 198.

[125] Garrisons, Garrison, III, p. 504; Beards, The Rise of American Civilization, II, p. 63.

[126] Garrisons, Garrison, III, p. 508.

[127] Jan. 18, 1861, Antislavery Papers, Boston Public Library.

[128] Harper, Anthony, I, p. 210.

[129] Susan B. Anthony Scrapbook, 1861, Library of Congress.

[130] Carl Sandburg, Abraham Lincoln, The War Years (New York, 1939), I, p. 125.

[131] Harper, Anthony, I, p. 202. Mrs. Phelps later found a more permanent home with the author, Elizabeth Ellet.

[132] Ibid., pp. 203-204.

[133] Ibid., p. 198.

CHAPTER VIII — A WAR FOR FREEDOM

[134] Garrisons, Garrison, IV, pp. 30-31.

[135] Lydia Mott to W. L. Garrison, May 8, 1861, Boston Public Library; Stanton and Blatch, Stanton, II, p. 89.

[136] Harper, Anthony, I, p. 215.

[137] Ibid., p. 216. Harriet Tubman, a fugitive slave, was often called the Moses of her people because she led so many of them into the promised land of freedom.

[138] Ibid.

[139] Ibid., p. 198.

[140] Anna E. Dickinson was born in Philadelphia in 1842. The death of her father, two years later, left the family in straightened circumstances, and Anna, after attending a Friends school, began very early to support herself by copying in lawyers' offices and by working at the U.S. Mint. Speaking extemporaneously at Friends and antislavery meetings, she discovered she had a gift for oratory and was soon in demand as a speaker.

[141] Harper, Anthony, I, p. 219.

[142] April, 1862. History of Woman Suffrage, I, p. 748.

[143] Harper, Anthony, I, pp. 218, 222.

[144] Emancipation, the Duty of Government, Ms., Lucy E. Anthony Collection. Reading that General Grant had returned 13 slaves to their masters, an indignant Susan B. Anthony wrote Mrs. Stanton, "Such gratuitous outrage should be met with instant death—without judge or jury—if any offense may." Feb. 27, 1862, Elizabeth Cady Stanton Papers, Library of Congress.

[145] Harper, Anthony, I, p. 221.

[146] Jan. 24, 1904, Anna Dann Mason Collection.

[147] Harper, Anthony, p. 226.

[148] The first woman in the United States to obtain a medical degree, 1849.

[149] History of Woman Suffrage, II, pp. 57-58.

[150] Harper, Anthony, I, p. 230. Members of the Women's National Loyal League wore a silver pin showing a slave breaking his last chains and bearing the inscription, "In emancipation is national unity." Susan B. Anthony to Mrs. Drake, Sept. 18, 1863, Alma Lutz Collection.

[151] Harper, Anthony, I, p. 234.

[152] Ibid., To Samuel May, Jr., Sept. 21, 1863, Alma Lutz Collection.

[153] April 14, 1864, Anna E. Dickinson Papers, Library of Congress.

[154] Harper, Anthony, I, p. 230.

[155] June 12, 1864, Elizabeth Cady Stanton Papers, July 1, 1864, Anna E. Dickinson Papers, Library of Congress. About this time, a friend of Susan B. Anthony's youth, now a widower living in Ohio in comfortable circumstances, unsuccessfully urged her to marry him.

[156] Sept. 23, 1864, Elizabeth Cady Stanton Papers, Library of Congress.

[157] Stanton and Blatch, Stanton, II, pp. 103-104.

[158] March 14, 1864, Anna E. Dickinson Papers, Library of Congress.

CHAPTER IX — THE NEGRO'S HOUR

[159] Daniel R. Anthony married Anna Osborne of Edgartown, Martha's Vineyard, in 1864.

[160] Before buying the house on Madison Street, then numbered 7, Mrs. Anthony and Mary lived for a time at 69 North Street, Rochester. Hannah and Eugene Mosher bought the adjoining house on Madison Street in 1866. Aaron McLean took over his father-in-law's profitable insurance business.

[161] Harper, Anthony, I, p. 241.

[162] Feb. 14, 1865, Elizabeth Cady Stanton Papers, Library of Congress.

[163] Ms., Diary, April 27, 1862.

[164] Feb. 14, 1862, Elizabeth Cady Stanton Papers, Library of Congress.

[165] Ibid.

[166] Ibid., April 19, 1862.

[167] Ms., Diary, April 26, 27, 1865.

[168] Harper, Anthony, I, p. 245.

[169] The Liberator ceased publication, Dec. 29, 1865.

[170] Ms., Diary, June 30, July 3, 1865.

[171] Harper, Anthony, II, pp. 960-967.

[172] Stanton and Blatch, Stanton, II, p. 105.

[173] Ibid.; Harper, Anthony, I, p. 244.

[174] Ms., Diary, Aug. 7, Sept. 5, 20, 1865.

[175] Ibid., Nov. 26-27, 1865.

[176] Harper, Anthony, I, p. 251.

[177] History of Woman Suffrage, II, pp. 96-97.

[178] Harper, Anthony, I, p. 260.

[179] Ibid., pp. 261, 323.

[180] History of Woman Suffrage, II, pp. 322-324. One of Thaddeus Stevens' drafts read: "If any State shall disfranchise any of its citizens on account of color, all that class shall be counted out of the basis of representation." Then the question arose whether or not disfranchising Negro women would carry this penalty and the result was a rewording which struck out "color" and added "male."

[181] Beards, The Rise of American Civilization, II, pp. 111-112; Joseph B. James, The Framing of the Fourteenth Amendment (Urbana, Ill., 1956), pp. 59, 166, 196-200.
[182] History of Woman Suffrage, II, p. 103. Senator Henry B. Anthony of Rhode Island, Susan B. Anthony's cousin, spoke and voted for woman suffrage.
[183] Ibid., p. 101. The New York Post, which had been friendly to woman suffrage under the editorship of William Cullen Bryant, now came out against it.
[184] John Albree, Editor, Whittier Correspondence from Oakknoll (Salem, Mass., 1911), p. 158. Frances D. Gage of Ohio, Caroline H. Dall of Massachusetts, and Clarina Nichols of Kansas also supported woman suffrage at this time.

CHAPTER X — TIMES THAT TRIED WOMEN'S SOULS

[185] Ms., Petition, Jan. 9, 1867, Alma Lutz Collection
[186] Ms., note, 1893, Elizabeth Cady Stanton Papers, Library of Congress.
[187] Harper, Anthony, I, p. 278; History of Woman Suffrage, II, p. 284.
[188] Harper, Anthony, I, p. 279.
[189] History of Woman Suffrage, II, p. 287. Petitions with 20,000 signatures were presented.
[190] Ibid., p. 285.
[191] Aug. 25, 1867, Alma Lutz Collection.
[192] History of Woman Suffrage, II, p. 287.
[193] Ibid., pp. 234-235, 239.
[194] Ibid., p. 252.
[195] A famous family of singers who enlivened woman's rights, antislavery, and temperance meetings with their songs.
[196] July 9, 1867, Anthony Papers, Kansas State Historical Society, Topeka, Kansas.
[197] Harper, Anthony, I, p. 284.
[198] History of Woman Suffrage, II, p. 242.
[199] Harper, Anthony, I, p. 287. George Francis Train on his own initiative spoke for woman suffrage before the New York Constitutional Convention.
[200] George Francis Train, The Great Epigram Campaign of Kansas (Leavenworth, Kansas, 1867), p. 68.
[201] History of Woman Suffrage, II, pp. 248-249.
[202] Train, The Great Epigram Campaign of Kansas, p. 40.
[203] Harper, Anthony, I, p. 290.
[204] Inscription by Susan B. Anthony on copy of Train's The Great Epigram Campaign of Kansas, Library of Congress.
[205] Harper, Anthony, I, p. 293.
[206] Ibid., p. 295.

CHAPTER XI — HE ONE WORD OF THE HOUR

[207] July 6, 1866, Anna E. Dickinson Papers, Library of Congress.
[208] The Revolution, I, Jan. 8, 1868, pp. 1-12.
[209] Ibid.
[210] Ibid., April 23, June 25, 1868, pp. 49, 392.
[211] Harper, Anthony, I, pp. 296-297, 302-303; The Revolution, I, Jan. 22, 1868, p. 34.
[212] The Revolution, I, Jan. 29, 1868, p. 243.
[213] Harper, Anthony, I, p. 301.
[214] March 18, May 4, 1868, Anna E. Dickinson Papers, Library of Congress. Susan had a room at the Stantons until they prepared to move to their new home in Tenafly, New Jersey.
[215] Aug. 20, 1868, Higginson Papers, Boston Public Library.
[216] The Revolution, II, July 9, 1868, p. 1.
[217] Ibid., July 16, 1868, p. 17.
[218] Ibid., Aug. 6, 1868, p. 72.
[219] July 10, 1868, Anna E. Dickinson Papers, Library of Congress.

CHAPTER XII — WORK, WAGES, AND THE BALLOT

[220] Feb. 18, 1868, Anna E. Dickinson Papers, Library of Congress.

[221] The Revolution, II, Sept. 24, 1868, p. 198. L. A. Hines of Cincinnati, publisher of Hine's Quarterly, assisted Miss Anthony in organizing women in the sewing trades.

[222] Ibid., p. 204.

[223] Harper, Anthony, II, pp. 999-1000.

[224] The Revolution, II, Oct. 1, 1868, p. 204.

[225] Ibid., p. 200.

[226] Ibid., Oct. 8, 1868, p. 214. A Woman's Exchange was also initiated by the Workingwomen's Association.

[227] Ibid., June 24, 1869, p. 394.

[228] Ibid., March 18, 1869, p. 173.

[229] Ibid., Feb. 4, 1869, p. 73.

[230] Ibid., Sept. 9, 1869, p. 154.

[231] Ibid., Aug. 26, 1869, p. 120.

CHAPTER XIII — THE INADEQUATE FIFTEENTH AMENDMENT

[232] The Revolution, II, Dec. 24, 1868, p. 385.

[233] George W. Julian, Political Recollections, 1840-1872 (Chicago, 1884), pp. 324-325.

[234] The Revolution, III, March 11, 1869, p. 148.

[235] The very proper Sorosis would not meet at the Women's Bureau while it housed the radical Revolution, and as women showed so little interest in her project, Mrs. Phelps gave it up after a year's trial.

[236] The Revolution, III, May 20, 1869, pp. 305-307.

[237] History of Woman Suffrage, II, p. 392.

[238] Harper, Anthony, I, pp. 327-328.

[239] Ibid., p. 332.

CHAPTER XIV — A HOUSE DIVIDED

[240] Lucy Stone to Frank Sanborn, Aug. 18, 1869, Alma Lutz Collection.

[241] Lucy Stone to Esther Pugh, Aug. 30, 1869, Ida Husted Harper Collection, Henry E. Huntington Library, San Marino, California.

[242] Mary Livermore to W. L. Garrison, Oct. 4, 1869, Boston Public Library. Wendell Phillips did not sign the call or attend the convention for "reasons that are good to him," wrote Lucy Stone to Garrison, Sept. 27, 1869, Boston Public Library.

[243] The Revolution, IV, Oct. 21, 1869, p. 265.

[244] Ibid., p. 266.

[245] The Empire Sewing Machine Co., Benedict's Watches, Madame Demorest's dress patterns, Sapolio, insurance companies, savings banks, the Union Pacific, offering first mortgage bonds.

[246] Harper, Anthony, I, pp. 354-355. In 1873, Anson Lapham cancelled notes, amounting to $4000, and praised Susan for her continued courageous work for women.

[247] The Revolution, IV, Dec. 2, 1869, p. 343.

[248] Harriet Beecher Stowe to Susan B. Anthony, Dec., 1869, Alma Lutz Collection.

[249] The Revolution, IV, Dec. 23, 1869, p. 385.

[250] Woman's Journal, Jan. 8, 1870.

[251] Ms., Diary, Jan. 18, 1870.

[252] Stanton and Blatch, Stanton, II, pp. 124-125.

[253] The Revolution, V, Feb. 24, 1870, pp. 117-118. Susan attributed the Tribune editorial to Whitelaw Reid. Susan B. Anthony Scrapbook, Library of Congress.

[254] Feb. 21, 1870, Anna E. Dickinson Papers, Library of Congress. Anna E. Dickinson sent Miss Anthony generous checks to help finance The Revolution. Although she lectured at Cooper Union for the National Woman Suffrage

Association shortly after it was organized, she never became a member of the organization or attended its conventions. This was a great disappointment to Miss Anthony.

[255] Finally, Miss Anthony and Mrs. Stanton against their best judgment were persuaded by younger members of the National Woman Suffrage Association to drop the name National and replace it with Union and then to try to negotiate further with the American Association. Theodore Tilton was elected president of the Union Woman Suffrage Society. This proved to be an organization in name only, and in a short time these same younger members clamored for the return to office of Miss Anthony and Mrs. Stanton and reestablished the National Woman Suffrage Association.

[256] The Revolution, V, March 10, 1870, p. 153. Mrs. Stanton's Lyceum lectures were undertaken to finance the education of her 7 children.

[257] Harper, Anthony, I, p. 362.

[258] The Revolution, V, May 26, 1870, p. 328.

[259] Sept. 19, 1870, Anna E. Dickinson Papers, Library of Congress.

[260] To E. A. Studwell, Sept. 15, 1870, Radcliffe Women's Archives, Cambridge, Massachusetts.

[261] To Elizabeth Cady Stanton, Oct. 15, 1871, Lucy E. Anthony Collection

CHAPTER XV — A NEW SLANT ON THE FOURTEENTH AMENDMENT

[262] A former Congressman from Ohio, a personal friend of Senator Benjamin Wade who was a loyal friend of woman suffrage.

[263] The Revolution, V, March 19, 1870, pp. 154-155, 159.

[264] Clipping from Woodhull & Claflin's Weekly, Susan B. Anthony Scrapbook, Library of Congress.

[265] Emanie, Sachs, The Terrible Siren (New York, 1928), p. 87. After hearing Victoria Woodhull speak at a woman suffrage meeting in Philadelphia, Lucretia Mott wrote her daughters, March 21, 1871, "I wish you could have heard Mrs. Woodhull ... so earnest yet modest and dignified, and so full of faith that she is divinely inspired for her work. The 30 or 40 persons present were much impressed with her work and beautiful utterances." Garrison Papers, Sophia Smith Collection, Smith College.

[266] May 20, 1871, Ida Husted Harper Collection, Henry E. Huntington Library.

[267] The Golden Age, Dec., 1871.

[268] Harper, Anthony, I, p. 388.

[269] Ibid., pp. 389-390.

[270] Ibid., pp. 391-394. Laura Fair, who reportedly had been the mistress of Alexander P. Crittenden for six years, was acquitted of his murder on the grounds that his death was not due to her pistol shot but to a disease from which he was suffering. Julia Cooley Altrocchi, The Spectacular San Franciscans (New York, 1949).

[271] Ms., Diary, July 13-23, 1871.

[272] Harper, Anthony, I, p. 396.

[273] Ibid.

[274] Ms., Diary, Oct. 13, 1871.

[275] Harper, Anthony, I, p. 403.

[276] Ms., Diary, Dec. 15, 1871.

[277] Harper, Anthony, I, p. 396.

[278] Ms., Diary, Jan. 2, 1872.

[279] Woodhull & Claflin's Weekly, Jan. 23, 1873.

[280] Harper, Anthony, I, pp. 410-411.

[281] Ibid., p. 413.

[282] Ms., Diary, May 8, 10, 12, 1872.

[283] Harper, Anthony, I, pp. 416-417.

[284] Ms., Diary, Sept. 21, 1872. Lucy Stone wrote in the Woman's Journal, July 27, 1872, "We are glad that the wing of the movement to which these ladies belong have decided to cast in their lot with the Republican party. If they had done so sooner, it would have been better for all concerned...."

[285] History of Woman Suffrage, II, p. 519. The Republicans financed a paper, Woman's Campaign, edited by Helen Barnard, which published some of Susan's speeches and which Susan for a time hoped to convert into a woman suffrage paper.

[286] Harper, Anthony, I, p. 422.

[287] Ibid.

CHAPTER XVI — TESTING THE FOURTEENTH AMENDMENT

[288] Ray Strachey, Struggle (New York, 1930), pp. 113-116.
[289] The U.S. Supreme Court upheld the decision of a lower court that without specific legislation by Congress, the 14th Amendment could not overrule the law of the District of Columbia which limited suffrage to male citizens over 21. History of Woman Suffrage, II, pp. 587-601.
[290] Harper, Anthony, I, p. 423.
[291] Nov. 5, 1872, Ida Husted Harper Collection, Henry E. Huntington Library. Miss Anthony had assured the election inspectors that she would pay the cost of any suit which might be brought against them for accepting women's votes.
[292] Harper, Anthony, I, p. 426. The Anthony home was then numbered 7 Madison Street.
[293] An Account of the Proceedings of the Trial of Susan B. Anthony on the Charge of Illegal Voting (Rochester, New York, 1874), p. 16.
[294] Harper, Anthony, I, p. 428.
[295] Ibid., p. 433.
[296] Trial, pp. 2-3.
[297] N.d., Susan B. Anthony Papers, New York Public Library.
[298] Trial, pp. 151, 153. Judge Story, Commentaries on the Constitution of the United States, Sec. 456: "The importance of examining the preamble for the purpose of expounding the language of a statute has long been felt and universally conceded in all juridical discussion." History of Woman Suffrage, II, p. 477.
[299] Harper, Anthony, II, pp. 978, 986-987.
[300] Ms., Diary, May 10, June 7, 1873.
[301] Suffrage clubs in New York, Buffalo, Chicago, and Milwaukee sent $50 and $100 contributions. Susan's cousin, Anson Lapham, cancelled notes for $4000 which she had signed while struggling to finance The Revolution. The women of Rochester rallied behind her, forming a Taxpayers' Association to protest taxation without representation.
[302] Harper, Anthony, II, pp. 994-995.
[303] Ibid., I, p. 429.

CHAPTER XVII — "IS IT A CRIME FOR A CITIZEN ... TO VOTE?"

[304] Ms., Diary, April 26, 1873.
[305] Trial, p. 17.
[306] Ibid., pp. 62-68.
[307] Ms., Diary, June 18, 1873.
[308] Susan B. Anthony Scrapbook, 1873, Library of Congress.
[309] Trial, pp. 81-85.
[310] This booklet also included the speeches of Susan B. Anthony and Matilda Joslyn Gage, delivered prior to the trial, and a short appraisal of the trial, Judge Hunt and the Right of Trial by Jury, by John Hooker, the husband of Isabella Beecher Hooker. The Rochester Democrat and Chronicle called the booklet "the most important contribution yet made to the discussion of woman suffrage from a legal standpoint." The Woman's Suffrage Journal, IV, Aug. 1, 1873, p. 121, published in England by Lydia Becker, said: "The American law which makes it a criminal offense for a person to vote who is not legally qualified appears harsh to our ideas."
[311] Harper, Anthony, I, pp. 455-456.
[312] History of Woman Suffrage, II, pp. 737-739, 741-742.
[313] Trial, p. 191.

CHAPTER XVIII — SOCIAL PURITY

[314] Ms., Diary, Nov. 4, 1874.
[315] Harper, Anthony, I, p. 457. Frances Willard took her stand for woman suffrage in the W.C.T.U. in 1876.
[316] Ms., Diary, Sept., 1877.
[317] To James Redpath, Dec. 23, 1870, Alma Lutz Collection.

[318] New York Graphic, Sept. 12, 1874. Mrs. Hooker believed her half-brother guilty and repeatedly urged him to confess, assuring him she would join him in announcing "a new social freedom." Kenneth R. Andrews, Nook Farm (Cambridge, Mass., 1950), pp. 36-39. Rumors that Mrs. Hooker was insane were deliberately circulated.

[319] Harper, Anthony, I, p. 463.

[320] Ibid. Only a few entries relating to the Beecher-Tilton case remain in the Susan B. Anthony diaries, now in the Library of Congress, and the diary for 1875 is not there.

[321] Ibid., p. 462.

[322] Ibid., II, pp. 1007-1009.

[323] Ibid., I, p. 468.

[324] Ibid., p. 470. Miss Anthony interrupted her lecturing for nine weeks to nurse her brother Daniel after he had been shot by a rival editor in Leavenworth.

[325] Ibid., p. 472.

[326] Ibid., p. 473.

CHAPTER XIX — A FEDERAL WOMAN SUFFRAGE AMENDMENT

[327] Ms., Diary, June 18, 1876.

[328] Katherine D. Blake and Margaret Wallace, Champion of Women, The Life of Lillie Devereux Blake (New York, 1943), pp. 124-126.

[329] History of Woman Suffrage, III, pp. 31, 34. The Woman's Journal surprised Susan with a friendly editorial, "Good Use of the Fourth of July," written by Lucy Stone, July 15, 1876.

[330] History of Woman Suffrage, III, p. 43. The Philadelphia Press praised the Declaration of Rights and the women in the suffrage movement. The report of the New York Post was patronizingly favorable, pointing out the indifference of the public to the subject.

[331] Harper, Anthony, I, pp. 485-486.

[332] Ms., Susan B. Anthony Papers, Library of Congress.

[333] This amendment was re-introduced in the same form in every succeeding Congress until it was finally passed in 1919 as the Nineteenth Amendment. It was ratified by the states in 1920, 14 years after Susan B. Anthony's death. When occasionally during her lifetime it was called the Susan B. Anthony Amendment by those who wished to honor her devotion to the cause, she protested, meticulously giving Elizabeth Cady Stanton credit for making the first public demand for woman suffrage in 1848. She also made it clear that although she worked for the amendment long and hard, she did not draft it. After her death, during the climax of the woman suffrage campaign, these facts were overlooked by the younger workers who made a point of featuring the Susan B. Anthony Amendment, both because they wished to immortalize her and because they realized the publicity value of her name.

[334] Harper, Anthony, I, p. 484.

[335] History of Woman Suffrage, III, p. 66.

[336] Harper, Anthony, II, p. 544.

[337] History of Woman Suffrage, III, p. 153; II, pp. 3-12, 863-868; Sarah Ellen Blackwell, A Military Genius, Life of Anna Ella Carroll of Maryland (Washington, D.C., 1891), I, pp. 153-154.

[338] "Woman Suffrage as a Means of Moral Improvement and the Prevention of Crime" by Alexander Dumas, History of Woman Suffrage, III, p. 190. Theodore Stanton, foreign correspondent for the New York Tribune, now lived in Paris.

CHAPTER XX — RECORDING WOMEN'S HISTORY

[339] The only such history available was the History of the National Woman's Rights Movement for Twenty Years (New York, 1871), written by Paulina Wright Davis to commemorate the first national woman's rights convention in Worcester, Massachusetts, in 1850. This brief record, ending with Victoria Woodhull's Memorial to Congress, was inadequate and placed too much emphasis on Victoria Woodhull who had flashed through the movement like a meteor, leaving behind her a trail of discord and little that was constructive.

[340] Aaron McLean, Eugene Mosher, his daughter Louise, Merritt's daughter, Lucy E. Anthony from Fort Scott, Kansas, and later Lucy's sister "Anna O."

[341] Mrs. Stanton moved to the new home she had built in Tenafly, New Jersey, in 1868.

[342] Fowler & Wells furnished the paper, press work, and advertising and paid the authors 12½% commission on sales. They did not look askance at such a controversial subject, having published the Fowler family's phrenological books. In addition the women of the family were suffragists.

[343] In 1855, at the instigation of her father. Miss Anthony began to preserve her press clippings. She now found them a valuable record, and she hired a young girl to paste them in six large account books. Thirty-two of her scrapbooks are now in the Library of Congress.

[344] Aug. 30, 1876, Ida Husted Harper Collection, Henry E. Huntington Library. The history of the American Woman Suffrage Association was compiled for Volume II from the Woman's Journal and Mary Livermore's The Agitator by Harriot Stanton.

[345] Nov. 30, 1880, Amelia Bloomer Papers, Seneca Falls Historical Society, Seneca Falls, N. Y.

[346] Harper, Anthony, II, p. 531. The History received friendly and complimentary reviews, the New York Tribune and Sun giving it two columns.

[347] June 28, 1881, Amelia Bloomer Papers, Seneca Falls Historical Society, Seneca Falls, N. Y. The cost of a cloth copy of the History was $3.

[348] Dec. 19, 1880, Susan B. Anthony Papers, Library of Congress. Rachel Foster's mother was a life-long friend of Elizabeth Cady Stanton and sympathetic to her work for women. The widow of a wealthy Pittsburgh newspaperman, she was now active in Pennsylvania suffrage organizations. Her daughters, Rachel and Julia, early became interested in the cause.

[349] E. C. Stanton to Laura Collier, Jan. 21, 1886, Elizabeth Cady Stanton Papers, Vassar College Library. Mary Livermore criticized the History as poorly edited.

[350] After her marriage in 1882, to William Henry Blatch of Basingstoke, Harriot made her home in England for the next 20 years.

[351] Harper, Anthony, II, p. 549.

[352] Ibid., pp. 553, 558, 562. Miss Anthony spent a week with her old friends, Ellen and Aaron Sargent in Berlin where Aaron was serving as American Minister to Germany. In Paris she visited Theodore Stanton and his French wife.

[353] Lydia Becker, Mrs. Jacob Bright, Helen Taylor, Priscilla Bright McLaren, Margaret Bright Lucas, Alice Scatcherd, and Elizabeth Pease Nichol. A bill to enfranchise widows and spinsters was pending in Parliament. Only a few women were courageous enough to demand votes for married women as well.

[354] Harper, Anthony, II, p. 582.

[355] Ibid., pp. 591, 583.

CHAPTER XXI — IMPETUS FROM THE WEST

[356] Harper, Anthony, II, p. 592.

[357] Ibid., p. 658.

[358] Miss Anthony first met Frances Willard in 1875 when she lectured in Rochester. Invited to sit on the platform, by her side, she thoughtfully refused, adding "You have a heavy enough load to carry without me." Harper, Anthony, I, p. 472. When Frances Willard took her stand for woman suffrage in the W.C.T.U. in 1876, Miss Anthony wrote her, "Now you are to go forward. I wish I could see you and make you feel my gladness." Mary Earhart, Frances Willard (Chicago, 1944), p. 153.

[359] During the debate, Frances Willard rendered valuable aid with a petition for woman suffrage, signed by 200,000 women. This counteracted in a measure the protests against woman suffrage by President Eliot of Harvard and 200 New England clergymen.

[360] Harper, Anthony, II, pp. 622-623.

[361] Ibid., p. 612.

[362] So successful was Mrs. Colby's Washington venture that she continued to publish her Woman's Tribune there for the next 16 years

[363] Harper, Anthony, II, p. 637.

[364] Woman's Tribune, Feb. 22, 1890.

[365] The credit for achieving union after two years of patient negotiation goes to Rachel Foster Avery, secretary of the National Association, and to Lucy Stone's daughter, Alice Stone Blackwell, secretary of the American Association.

[366] Harper, Anthony, II, p. 675.

CHAPTER XXII — VICTORIES IN THE WEST

[367] Minor vs. Happersett, History of Woman Suffrage, II, pp. 741-742. North and South Dakota, Washington and Montana were admitted in 1889, Wyoming and Idaho in 1890.

[368] Ibid., IV, pp. 999-1000.

[369] North Dakota's constitution provided that the legislature might in the future enfranchise women.

[370] History of Woman Suffrage, IV, p. 556.

[371] Harper, Anthony, II, p. 690.

[372] Ibid., p. 688.

[373] Anna Howard Shaw, The Story of a Pioneer (New York, 1915), p. 202.

[374] Harper, Anthony, II, p. 731.

[375] Ms., Diary, Feb. 28, April 18, 1893.

[376] Published first in the Woman's Tribune, then as a book in 1898 under the title, Eighty Years and More.

[377] Harper, Anthony, II, p. 712.

[378] During this visit the young sculptor, Adelaide Johnson, modeled busts of Miss Anthony and Mrs. Stanton which later were chiseled in marble and were exhibited with the bust of Lucretia Mott at the World's Fair in Chicago in 1893. They are now in the Capitol in Washington.

[379] To Clarina Nichols. Harper, Anthony, II, p. 544. Miss Anthony wrote in her diary, Oct. 18, 1893, "Lucy Stone died this evening at her home—Dorchester, Mass. aged 75—I can but wonder if the spirit now sees things as it did 25 years ago!" The wound inflicted by Lucy's misunderstanding of her motives had never healed.

[380] Ibid., p. 727.

[381] Rachel Foster was married in 1888 to Cyrus Miller Avery.

[382] May Wright Sewall, Editor, The World's Congress of Representative Women (Chicago, 1894), p. 464.

[383] Statement by Lucy E. Anthony, Una R. Winter Collection.

[384] Miss Anthony's diary, 1893, mentions visiting "dear Mrs. Coonley" (Lydia Avery Coonley) in her beautiful, friendly home. May Wright Sewall, and devoted Emily Gross. Her sister Mary, Daniel, Merritt, and their families joined her at the Fair for a few weeks.

[385] Shaw, The Story of a Pioneer, pp. 205-207.

[386] Ms., Diary, Nov. 8, 1893.

CHAPTER XXIII — LIQUOR INTERESTS ALERT FOREIGN-BORN VOTERS AGAINST WOMAN SUFFRAGE

[387] Harper, Anthony, II, p. 763.

[388] To Elizabeth Smith Miller, July 25, 1894, Elizabeth Smith Miller Papers, New York Public Library.

[389] Harper, Anthony, II, p. 788.

[390] Ibid., p. 791.

[391] Ibid., p. 794.

[392] To Clara Colby, July 22, 1895, Anthony Collection, Henry E. Huntington Library.

[393] Harper, Anthony, II, p. 842.

[394] N.d., Anthony Collection, Henry E. Huntington Library.

[395] Harper, Anthony, II, p. 843.

[396] Ibid., pp. 844, 859.

[397] Ms., Diary, July 10, 1896.

[398] Sept. 8, 1896, Anthony Collection, Henry E. Huntington Library.

[399] Shaw, The Story of a Pioneer, pp. 274-275.

CHAPTER XIV — AUNT SUSAN AND HER GIRLS

[400] Ms., Diary, Nov. 7, 1895

[401] Mary Gray Peck, Carrie Chapman Catt (New York, 1944), p. 84.

[402] Ms., Diary, Nov. 27, 1895.

[403] To Mrs. Upton, Sept. 5, 1890, University of Rochester Library, Rochester, New York.

[404] Feb. 10, 1894, Anthony Collection, Henry E. Huntington Library.

[405] Harper, Anthony, III, p. 1113.

[406] Miss Anthony's first attempt to win Southern women to suffrage was at the time of the New Orleans Exposition in 1885. Because of her reputation as an abolitionist, she had much resistance to overcome in the South.

[407] Dec. 18, 1895, Anthony Collection, Henry E. Huntington Library.

[408] Woman's Tribune, Feb. 1, 1896.

[409] History of Woman Suffrage, IV, p. 264.

[410] Harper, Anthony, II, p. 855. The action of the National American Woman Suffrage Association on the Woman's Bible was never reversed.

[411] Ibid., p. 856.

[412] Susan thought seriously of Clara Colby as a collaborator but concluded she was too involved with the Woman's Tribune. Susan agreed to share royalties with Mrs. Harper on the biography and any other work on which they might collaborate. On her 75th birthday Susan's girls had presented her with an annuity of $800 a year. This made it possible for her to give up lecturing and concentrate on her book.

[413] Genevieve Hawley left an interesting record of these years in letters to her aunt, many of which are preserved in the Susan B. Anthony Memorial Collection in Rochester, New York.

[414] Both the New York Herald and Chicago Inter-Ocean gave the book full-page reviews. A third volume was published in 1908.

[415] Aug. 10, 1898, Susan B. Anthony Papers, Library of Congress.

[416] Harper, Anthony, III, p. 1121.

[417] Aug. 10, 1898, Susan B. Anthony Papers, Library of Congress.

[418] Dec. 17, 1898, Anthony Collection, Henry E. Huntington Library. Clara Colby, making her headquarters in Washington, kept Susan informed on developments and they carried on an animated, voluminous correspondence during these years.

[419] March 12, 1894, Anthony Collection, Henry E. Huntington Library.

[420] Harper, Anthony, II, p. 920.

[421] Harper, Anthony, II, p. 924.

CHAPTER XXV — PASSING ON THE TORCH

[422] Rachel Foster Avery, Ed., National Council of Women, 1891 (Philadelphia, 1891), p. 229.

[423] Dec. 1, 1898, Anthony Collection, Henry E. Huntington Library. Mrs. Elnora Babcock of New York was in charge of the press bureau.

[424] Miss Anthony was enrolled as a member of the Knights of Labor and invited this organization to send delegates to the International Council of Women in 1888.

[425] To Ellen Wright Garrison, 1900, Sophia Smith Collection, Smith College.

[426] Harper, Anthony, III, p. 1137. A few years later, militant suffragists, led by Emmeline Pankhurst, were active in London. Mrs. Pankhurst heard Miss Anthony speak in Manchester in 1904.

[427] Ida Husted Harper Ms., Catharine Waugh McCulloch Papers, Radcliffe Women's Archives.

[428] Nov. 20, 1899, Anthony Collection, Henry E. Huntington Library.

[429] History of Woman Suffrage, IV, p. 385. Miss Anthony was "moved up," as she expressed it, to Honorary President.

[430] Peck, Catt, p. 107, Washington Post quotation.

[431] To Laura Clay, April 15, 1900, University of Kentucky Library, Lexington, Kentucky.

[432] Ibid., March 15, 1900.

[433] Ibid.

[434] Ibid., Sept. 7, 1900.

[435] Ms., Diary, Nov. 10, 1900.

[436] Ibid., Sept. 26, 1900. A separate woman's college was established at the University of Rochester and not until 1952 were the men's and women's colleges merged.

[437] May 20, 1901, Note, Susan B. Anthony Memorial Collection, Rochester, New York.

[438] History of Woman Suffrage, V, pp. 741-742.

[439] Harper, Anthony, III, p. 1263.

[440] Oct. 28, 1902, Anthony Collection, Henry E. Huntington Library.

[441] Oct. 27, 1904, Elizabeth Smith Miller Collection, New York Public Library. A few years later, Mrs. Blatch made a vital contribution to the cause through the Women's Political Union which she organized and which brought more militant methods and new life into the woman suffrage campaign in New York State.

 [442] Jan. 27, 1904, Lucy E. Anthony Collection. Mrs. Blake who had been a candidate in 1900 had by this time formed her own organization, the National Legislative League.

[443] History of Woman Suffrage, V, p. 99.

[444] Harper, Anthony, III, p. 1308.

[445] Ibid.

CHAPTER XVI — SUSAN B. ANTHONY OF THE WORLD

[446] Harper, Anthony, III, p. 1325.

[447] Shaw, The Story of a Pioneer, p. 210.

[448] Harper, Anthony, III, p. 1319.

[449] Ibid., p. 1336.

[450] Miss Anthony also carefully prepared her scrapbooks, her books, and bound volumes of The Revolution, woman's rights and antislavery magazines for presentation to the Library of Congress, inscribing each with a note of explanation.

[451] Ann Anthony Bacon.

[452] New York Suffrage Newsletter, Jan., 1905.

[453] History of Woman Suffrage, V, p. 122.

[454] Harper, Anthony, III, p. 1365. The statue of Sacajawea, presented to the Exposition by the clubwomen of America, was the work of Alice Cooper of Denver. Woman suffrage was again defeated in Oregon in 1906.

[455] Harper, Anthony, III, pp. 1357, 1359.

[456] Ibid., pp. 1376-1377.

[457] The medallion, the work of Leila Usher of Boston, was commissioned by Mary Garrett.

[458] Harper, Anthony, III, p. 1395.

[459] Ibid., pp. 1395-1396.

[460] Sept., 1935, Statement, Una R. Winter Collection.

[461] Harper, Anthony, III, p. 1409.

[462] Ibid.

[463] Shaw, The Story of a Pioneer, pp. 230-232.

[464] Harper, Anthony, III, p. 1259.

Bibliography

Manuscript Collections

American Antiquarian Society, Worcester, Massachusetts:
Abby Kelley Foster Papers.
Lucy E. Anthony and Ann Anthony Bacon Papers:
Susan B. Anthony Diaries, Letters, and Speeches.
Boston Public Library, Manuscript Division:
Antislavery, Garrison, and Higginson Papers.
Matilda Joslyn Gage Collection.
Henry E. Huntington Library and Art Gallery, San Marino, California, Manuscript Division:
Ida Husted Harper Collection.
Anthony Collection.
Kansas State Historical Society, Topeka, Kansas:
Anthony Papers.
Library of Congress, Washington, D.C., Manuscript Division:
Susan B. Anthony Papers, including Diaries.
Anna E. Dickinson Papers.
Elizabeth Cady Stanton Papers.
Library of Congress, Washington, D.C., Rare Book Room:
Susan B. Anthony Scrapbooks.
Alma Lutz Collection.
Anna Dann Mason Collection.
Museum of Arts and Sciences, Rochester, New York:
Anthony Collection.
New York Public Library, Manuscript Division:
Susan B. Anthony Papers.
Elizabeth Cady Stanton Papers.
Elizabeth Smith Miller Papers.
Ohio State Library, Columbus, Ohio:
Ohioana Library Collection.
Seneca Falls Historical Society, Seneca Falls, New York:
Amelia Bloomer Papers.
Smith College, Northampton, Massachusetts:
Sophia Smith Collection.
Edna M. Stantial Collection:
Blackwell Papers.
Susan B. Anthony Memorial Collection, 17 Madison Street, Rochester, New York.
Radcliffe Women's Archives, Radcliffe College, Cambridge, Massachusetts.
University of California, Bancroft Library, Berkeley, California:
Susan B. Anthony Papers.
Keith Papers.
University of Kentucky Library, Lexington, Kentucky:
Laura Clay Papers.
University of Rochester Library, Rochester, New York:
Susan B. Anthony Papers.
Vassar College Library, Poughkeepsie, New York:
Elizabeth Cady Stanton Papers.
Margaret Stanton Lawrence Papers.
Una R. Winter Collection.

Published Material

Abbott, Mrs. Lyman. Mrs. Lyman Abbott on Woman Suffrage. Pamphlet. New York, n.d.

Albree, John (ed.). Whittier Correspondence from Oakknoll. Salem, Mass., 1911.

Altrocchi, Julia Cooley. The Spectacular San Franciscans. New York, 1949.

An Account of the Proceedings of the Trial of Susan B. Anthony on the Charge of Illegal Voting. Rochester, N.Y., 1874.

Ames, Mary Clemmer. A Memorial of Alice and Phoebe Cary. New York, 1873.

Andrews, Kenneth. Nook Farm. Cambridge, Mass., 1950.

Anthony, Charles L. Genealogy of the Anthony Family from 1495 to 1904. Sterling, Ill., 1904.

Anthony, Katharine. Susan B. Anthony, Her Personal History and Her Era. New York, 1954.

Anthony, Susan B. "Woman's Half Century of Evolution," North American Review, December 1902.

———. "Educating Husbands for the Twentieth Century," McClure's Syndicate, 1901.

———. "The Status of Women Past, Present and Future," The Arena, May 1897.

———. "Why Some Marriages Are Failures," McClure's Syndicate, 1901.

———. "The Wrongs of Man," McClure's Syndicate, 1901.

———. "What I Would Have Done with a Bad Husband," McClure's Syndicate, 1901.

Armes, Ethel. Stratford Hall. Richmond, Va., 1936.

Avery, Rachel Foster (ed.). National Council of Women, 1891. Philadelphia, 1891.

Barnes, Gilbert H. The Antislavery Impulse. New York, 1933.

Beard, Charles A. and Mary R. The American Spirit. New York, 1927.

———. The Rise of American Civilization. New York, 1930.

Beard, Charles A. and William. The American Leviathan. New York, 1930.

Beecher, Henry Ward. Woman's Influence in Politics. Pamphlet. Boston, 1870.

Birney, Catherine H. The Grimké Sisters. Boston, 1885.

Blackwell, Alice Stone. Lucy Stone. Boston, 1930.

Blackwell, Sarah Ellen. A Military Genius, Life of Anna Ella Carroll of Maryland. Washington, D.C., 1891.

Blake, Katherine D., and Wallace, Margaret. Champion of Women, The Life of Lillie Devereux Blake. New York, 1943.

Blatch, Harriot Stanton, and Lutz, Alma. Challenging Years. New York, 1940.

Bloomer, D. C. Life and Writings of Amelia Bloomer. Boston, 1895.

Boas, Louise S. Elizabeth Barrett Browning. New York, 1930.

Bowditch, William I. Woman Suffrage a Right, Not a Privilege. Pamphlet. Cambridge, Mass., 1879.

Brink, Carol. Harps in the Wind, The Story of the Singing Hutchinsons. New York, 1947.

Brockett, Dr. L. F. Woman: Her Rights, Wrongs, Privileges, and Responsibilities. Hartford, Conn., 1869.

Brown, Olympia (ed.). Democratic Ideals, A Memorial Sketch of Clara B. Colby. Portland, Ore., 1917.

Browne, Junius Henri. The Great Metropolis, A Mirror of New York. Hartford, Conn., 1869.

Browne, William B. "Laphams Were Among the First Quakers to Settle Within the Town of Adams." Transcript (North Adams, Mass.), September 6, 1924.

Browning, Elizabeth Barrett. Aurora Leigh. New York, 1857.

Buckmaster, Henrietta. Let My People Go. New York, 1941.

Burnham, Carrie S. Woman Suffrage, The Argument of Carrie S. Burnham before the Supreme Court of Pennsylvania. Pamphlet. Philadelphia, 1873.

Calhoun, Lucia Gilbert. "Modern Women and What Is Said of Them." Pamphlet reprinted from The Saturday Review. New York, 1868.

Catt, Carrie Chapman, and Shuler, Nettie Rogers. Woman Suffrage and Politics. New York, 1923.

Channing, William Henry. Review of the History of Woman Suffrage. Pamphlet reprinted in 1881 from the Inquirer (London), November 5, 1881.

Chester, Giraud. Embattled Maiden, The Life of Anna Dickinson. New York, 1951.

Claflin, Tennessee. Constitutional Equality, A Right of Woman. New York, 1871.

Cole, Arthur Charles. The Irrepressible Conflict, 1850-1865. New York, 1934.

Colman, Lucy M. Reminiscences. Buffalo, N.Y., 1891.

Croughton, Amy H. Antislavery Days in Rochester. Rochester, N.Y., 1936.

Curtis, George William. Equal Rights for Women. Pamphlet. Boston, 1869.

Dahlgren, Madeline Vinton. Thoughts on Female Suffrage and in Vindication of Woman's True Rights. Pamphlet. Washington, 1871.

Davis, Paulina Wright. History of the National Woman's Rights Movement for Twenty Years. New York, 1871.

Debs, Eugene V. "Susan B. Anthony, Pioneer of Freedom," Pearsons Magazine, July 1917.

Dictionary of American Biography.

Dorr, Rheta Childe. Susan B. Anthony, The Woman Who Changed the Mind of a Nation. New York, 1928.

Douglass, Frederick. The Life and Times of Frederick Douglass. Hartford, Conn., 1881.

Duniway, Abigail Scott. Path Breaking. Portland, Ore., 1914.

Earhart, Mary. Frances Willard. Chicago, 1944.

Ehrlich, Leonard C. God's Angry Man. New York, 1941.

Eminent Women of the Age. Hartford, Conn., 1869.

Finch, Edith. Carey Thomas of Bryn Mawr. New York, 1947.

Garrison, Francis J., William Lloyd II, and Wendell P. William Lloyd Garrison, 1805-1879. New York, 1885-1889.

Ginger, Ray. The Bending Cross, A Biography of Eugene Victor Debs. New Brunswick, N.J., 1949.

Goodman, Clavia. Bitter Harvest, Laura Clay's Suffrage Work. Lexington, Ky., 1946.

Gray, Wood. The Hidden Civil War. New York, 1942.

Greeley, Horace. Recollections of a Busy Life. New York, 1868.

Greenbie, Marjorie B. Lincoln's Daughters of Mercy. New York, 1944.

———. My Dear Lady, The Story of Anna Ella Carroll. New York, 1940.

Greenbie, Marjorie B., and Sydney. Anna Ella Carroll and Abraham Lincoln. Tampa, Fla., 1952.

Hallowell, Anna Davis. James and Lucretia Mott. Boston, 1884.

Hamilton, Gail. "A Call to My Country-Women," Atlantic Monthly, March 1863.

Hare, Lloyd C. M. Lucretia Mott, The Greatest American Woman. New York, 1937.

Harlow, Ralph V. Gerrit Smith. New York, 1939.

Harper, Ida Husted. The Life and Work of Susan B. Anthony. Indianapolis, 1898, 1908.

———. History of Woman Suffrage, Vols. V and VI. New York, 1922.

Harper, Ida Husted, and Anthony, Susan B. History of Woman Suffrage, Vol. IV. Rochester, N.Y., 1902.

Hayek, F. A. John Stuart Mill and Harriet Taylor. Chicago, 1951.

Hebard, Grace Raymond. How Woman Suffrage Came to Wyoming. Pamphlet. New York, 1940.

Henry, Alice. The Trade Union Woman. New York, 1923.

Hibben, Paxton. Henry Ward Beecher. New York, 1927.

Higginson, Mary Thatcher (ed.). Letters and Journals of Thomas Wentworth Higginson. Boston, 1921.

Higginson, Thomas Wentworth. Women and the Alphabet. Boston, 1881.

Hooker, Isabella Beecher. The Constitutional Rights of Women of the United States. Washington, 1888.

Howe, Julia Ward. Reminiscences, 1819-1899. Boston, 1900.

Hutchinson, John Wallace. The Story of the Hutchinsons. Boston, 1896.

International Woman Suffrage Conference. Washington, D.C., 1902.

Isely, J. A. Horace Greeley and the Republican Party, 1853-1861. Princeton, N.J., 1947.

James, Joseph B. The Framing of the Fourteenth Amendment. Urbana, Ill., 1956.

Johns, Helen. "This Is a Day Full of Meaning to Friends of Woman Suffrage," Public Ledger (Philadelphia), Feb. 14, 1920.

Johnson, Oliver. William Lloyd Garrison and His Times. Boston, 1879.

Julian, George W. Political Recollections, 1840-1872. Chicago, 1884.

Kerr, Laura. Lady in the Pulpit. New York, 1951.

Korngold, Ralph. Two Friends of Man. Boston, 1950.

Livermore, Mary A. The Story of My Life. Hartford, Conn., 1897.

———. My Story of the War. Hartford, Conn., 1889.

Lutz, Alma. Created Equal, A Biography of Elizabeth Cady Stanton. New York, 1940.

———. Emma Willard, Daughter of Democracy. Boston, 1929.

Macy, Jesse. The Antislavery Crusade. New Haven, 1920.

Malin, James C. John Brown and the Legend of Fifty-Six. Philadelphia, 1942.

Mason, Anna Dann. "The Most Unforgettable Character I've Met," Genessee Country Scrapbook, Vol. IV (Rochester, N. Y., 1953).

May, Samuel J. Some Recollections of the Antislavery Conflict. Boston, 1869.

Mill, Elizabeth Taylor. Enfranchisement of Women, reprinted from the Westminster and Quarterly Review, New York, 1868.

Mill, John Stuart. Autobiography. London, 1873.

———. The Social and Political Dependence of Women. Boston, 1868.

———. The Subjection of Women. London, 1869.

———. Suffrage for Women (Speech in British Parliament, May 20, 1867). Pamphlet. Boston, 1869.

Mormon Women's Protest, An Appeal for Freedom, Justice, and Equal Rights. Pamphlet. Salt Lake City, Utah, 1886.

McKelvey, Blake. Rochester, the Flower City, 1855-1890. Cambridge, Mass., 1949.

———. "Susan B. Anthony," Rochester History, April, 1945, Rochester, N. Y.

Nichols, Mrs. C. I. H. The Responsibilities of Woman. Pamphlet. 1851.

Nordholf, Charles. "A Tilt at the Woman Question," Harper's Magazine, February 1863.

Norton, Frank H. Frank Leslie's Historical Register of the U. S. Centennial Exposition, 1876. New York, 1877.

Our Famous Women. Hartford, Conn., 1883.

Pankhurst, Emmeline. My Own Story. New York, 1914.

Parker, P. J. M. Rochester, A Story Historical. Rochester, N.Y., 1884.

Parker, Theodore. A Sermon on the Public Function of Women. Pamphlet. Boston, 1853.

Peck, Mary Gray. Carrie Chapman Catt. New York, 1944.

Phillips, Wendell. Freedom for Woman. Pamphlet. New York, 1868.

Pillsbury, Parker. The Acts of the Antislavery Apostles. Concord, N.H., 1883.

———. The Mortality of Nations. Pamphlet. New York, 1867.

The Place of Women in the Society of Friends. Pamphlet. Oxford, England, 1910.

Powderly, Terrence V. The Path I Trod. New York, 1940.

Proceedings of the Woman's Rights Convention Held at Syracuse, September 8th, 9th, and 10th, 1852. Pamphlet.

Quarles, Benjamin. Frederick Douglass. Washington, D.C., 1948.

Report of the International Council of Women, 1888. Washington, D.C., 1888.

Richards, Caroline Cowles. Village Life in America. New York, 1913.

Richardson, Albert D. Beyond the Mississippi. Hartford, Conn., 1867.

Robinson, Sara T. D. Kansas, Its Interior and Exterior. Lawrence, Kansas, 1899.

Rosenberger, Jesse Leonard. Rochester, The Making of a University. Rochester, N.Y., 1927.

Ross, Ishbel. Angel of the Battlefield. New York, 1956.

———. Ladies of the Press. New York, 1936.

Rourke, Constance. Trumpets of Jubilee. New York, 1927.

Sachs, Emanie. The Terrible Siren. New York, 1928.

Sanborn, F. B. Life and Letters of John Brown. Boston, 1891.

Sandburg, Carl. Abraham Lincoln, The War Years. New York, 1939.

Sanford, Harold W. A Century of Unitarianism in Rochester. Rochester, N.Y., 1939.

Schlesinger, Arthur M. The American As Reformer. Cambridge, Mass., 1950.

———. The Political and Social Growth of the United States, 1852-1933. New York, 1936.

———. The Rise of Modern America, 1865-1951. New York, 1951.

Schlesinger, Arthur M., and Hockett, H. C. Land of the Free. New York, 1944.

Sears, Lorenzo. Wendell Phillips. New York, 1909.

Selden, Clara Sayre. Family Sketches. Rochester, N.Y., 1939.

Sewall, May Wright (ed.). The World's Congress of Representative Women. Chicago, 1894.

Shaw, Anna Howard. The Story of a Pioneer. New York, 1915.

Smith, Gerrit. Letter to Elizabeth Cady Stanton on Woman's Rights and Dress Reform. Pamphlet. Peterboro, N.H., 1855.

Smith, Julia. Abby Smith and Her Cows, With a Report of the Law Case Decided Contrary to Law. Pamphlet. Hartford, Conn., 1877.

Smith, Matthew Hale. Sunshine and Shadow in New York. Hartford, Conn., 1869.

Sprague, William F. Women and the West. Boston, 1940.

Stanton, Elizabeth Cady. Address to the Legislature of New York, February, 1854. Pamphlet. Albany, 1854.

———. Bible and Church Degrade Women. Pamphlet. Chicago, 1884.

———. The Christian Church and Women. Pamphlet reprinted from The Index (Boston), n.d.

———. "The Degradation of Disfranchisement," National Bulletin, March 1891. Pamphlet.

———. Eighty Years and More. New York, 1898.

———. The Slave's Appeal. Pamphlet. Albany, 1860.

———. Significance and History of the Ballot. Pamphlet. Washington, D.C., 1898.

———. The Solitude of Self. Pamphlet. Washington, D.C., 1892.

———. Suffrage, a Natural Right. Pamphlet. Chicago, 1894.

———. The Woman's Bible. New York, 1898.

Stanton, Elizabeth Cady, Anthony, Susan B., and Gage, Matilda Joslyn. History of Woman Suffrage, Vols. I, II, III. New York and Rochester, 1881, 1882, 1886.

Stanton, Theodore. The Woman Question in Europe. New York, 1884.

Stanton, Theodore, and Blatch, Harriot Stanton (Ed.). Elizabeth Cady Stanton, As Revealed in Her Letters, Diary, and Reminiscences, New York, 1922.

Stevens, G. A., New York Typographical Union No. 6. Albany, 1913.

Strachey, Ray. Struggle. New York, 1930.

Ten Broek, Jacobus. The Antislavery Origins of the Fourteenth Amendment. Berkeley, Calif., 1951.

Terrell, Mary Church. A Colored Woman in a White World. Washington, D.C., 1940.

Thornton, Willis. The Nine Lives of Citizen Train. New York, 1948.

Tilton, Theodore. Biography of Victoria C. Woodhull. (Golden Age Tract No. 3.) Pamphlet. New York, 1871.

Tracy, George A. History of the Typographical Union. Indianapolis, 1913.

Train, George Francis. The Great Epigram Campaign of Kansas. Pamphlet. Leavenworth, Kansas, 1867.

————. My Life in Many States and Foreign Lands. New York, 1902.

————. Train's Union Speeches. Pamphlet. Philadelphia, 1862.

Trowbridge, Lydia Jones. Frances Willard of Evanston. Chicago, 1938.

True, Charles H. Ten Years of Woman Suffrage in Wyoming. Pamphlet. Rochester, N.Y., 1879.

Waite, Charles B. "Who Were the Voters in the Early History of this Country?" Chicago Law Times, October 1888.

Willard, Frances. Glimpses of Fifty Years. Chicago, 1889.

Willard, Frances E., and Livermore, Mary A. A Woman of the Century. New York, 1893.

Williams, Blanche Colton. Clara Barton. New York, 1941.

Whitney, Janet. Abigail Adams. Boston, 1947.

Woodhull, Victoria C. The Argument for Women's Electoral Rights under Amendments XIV and XV of the Constitution of the United States. London, 1887.

Woody, Thomas. A History of Women's Education in the United States. New York, 1929.

Newspapers And Periodicals

Adams (Mass.) Freeman
The Agitator
Antislavery Standard
Chicago Daily Tribune
Chicago Inter-Ocean
The Golden Age
Harper's Weekly
The Independent
Ladies' Home Journal
The Liberator
The Lily
New York Daily Graphic
New York Herald
New York Post
New York Suffrage News Letter
New York Sun
New York Times
New York Tribune
New York World
Philadelphia Press
The Revolution
Rochester History
San Francisco Examiner
The Una
Woman's Campaign
Woman's Journal
Woman's Tribune
Woman's Suffrage Journal (London, England)
Woodhull & Claflin's Weekly